CLASSICAL MUSIC AND POSTMODERN KNOWLEDGE

CLASSICAL MUSIC AND POSTMODERN KNOWLEDGE

LAWRENCE KRAMER

UNIVERSITY OF CALIFORNIA PRESS
BERKELEY   LOS ANGELES   LONDON

The music in the appendix is reproduced by permission of the
Music Division, New York Public Library for the Performing
Arts, Astor, Lenox, and Tilden Foundations.

University of California Press
Berkeley and Los Angeles, California

University of California Press, Ltd.
London, England

Library of Congress Cataloging-in-Publication Data

Kramer, Lawrence, 1946–
    Classical music and postmodern knowledge / Lawrence
Kramer.
        p.   cm.
    Includes bibliographical references and index.
    ISBN 0-520-08820-4 (alk. paper)
    1. Music—Philosophy and aesthetics.   2. Postmodernism.
I. Title.
ML3845.K813   1995
781.6'8'01—dc20   94-14391
                                              CIP
                                              MN

Printed in the United States of America
9 8 7 6 5 4 3 2 1

For Nancy and Claire

Contents

Musical Examples and Figures

Musical Examples

Figure

Preface

The purpose of this book is to explore the new possibilities that post-modernist modes of thinking offer to the understanding of Western "classical" music and, by implication, of music in general. Just what the elusive term *postmodernism* means will occupy a substantial part of the first chapter. Suffice it to say here that recent decades have witnessed something like a Nietzschean transvaluation of all values in the human sciences. This development has certainly not gone uncon-tested, and its outcome is far from clear, but its impact is undeniable. A complexly interdisciplinary body of theory, intertwining concerns with language, culture, and subjectivity, has been rethinking, and making it mandatory to rethink, the traditional foundations of thought. Conceptual paradigms have been proliferating which problematize the great ordering principles of rationality, unity, universality, and truth, recasting them as special cases of contingency, plurality, historicity, and ideology. Both knowledge and its objects are increasingly being recognized as decentered, heteronomous, and prismatic. As Donna Haraway puts it, they are being "constructed deconstructively."[1]

A turn to postmodernism in this sense would be bound to have a dramatic, even traumatic, effect on the ways we think about music, which have long been unusually dependent on the concepts under stress. Music has figured familiarly in modern Western culture as the vehicle for everything that cannot be represented or denoted. It em-bodies the feeling or intuition or pure mode of apprehension to which we attain after all the resources of signification have been exhausted.

By one reckoning, music serves this function in Apollonian terms, re-
viving ancient figures of cosmic harmony in the modern form of aesthetic order—the tangible embodiment of rationality, unity, universality, and truth. In music, the forms of thought become manifest as
pleasure by withdrawing themselves from the contents of thought.
The Dionysian complement of this process, in which the withdrawal
appears as a rupture and music taps emotions and desires at depths
beyond the reach of any order, is equally pervasive as a cultural trope.
The opposites, as opposites do, interact and depend on each other.
Music in the modern era can transcend signification both Platonically
and daemonically. Either way, it stands apart from the suasions and
coercions of the real. It figures as a self-enclosed plenitude, an acoustic image of pure interiority.

By undercutting the foundations of this conceptual and representational order, postmodernism has made it necessary to rethink music
from every possible perspective. The force of this necessity stems
from the perception that the resistance to signification once embodied
by music now seems to be an inextricable part of signification itself.
Nothing can signify without resisting, and nothing can resist without
signifying. Nothing that signifies, therefore, can escape a constitutive
tension between an aesthetic and a political impetus, the one denying
or sublimating the force of the real, the other disclosing or exerting it.
When "classical" music is caught up in this dynamic, as it must inevitably be, its whole mode of being comes into question. How can this
music be understood as part of a general signifying process, a network
of cultural practices, and still retain its charismatic quality, its exalted
capacity to wield power and give pleasure? How, to shift the venue of
the question, can we reflect on musical works or traditions—indeed
on any artistic works or traditions—without either overidealizing
(sanctifying, fetishizing) or demonizing them, without either mystify-
ing or crassly disenchanting them?

I hope to suggest some answers to these questions in what follows.
Admittedly, it may be hard to do without the comforting thought that
music, and not only untexted music, is something numinous and,
more important, accessibly, possessibly numinous. If holding that
thought requires us to speak of musical meaning only in the most re-
stricted of terms, be they self-consciously hesitant "emotive" descrip-

tions or the tokens of a formalized semiotics, some who love music will not mind. I once didn't mind, myself. But the thought can be hard to hold, as Wallace Stevens suggests in a remarkable but little-known poem, "Anglais Mort à Florence":

He used his reason, exercised his will,
Turning in time to Brahms as alternate

In speech. He was that music and himself.
They were particles of an order, a single majesty:
But he remembered the time when he stood alone.

He stood at last by God's help and the police;
But he remembered the time when he stood alone.
He yielded himself to that single majesty;

But he remembered the time when he stood alone,
When to be and delight seemed to be one,
Before the colors deepened and grew small.[2]

Stevens's insight is that music acts as a substitute for a blissful sense of full presence felt to have been lost. But the substitution has its limits; a prop itself, music needs props of its own, eventually even the watchdogs of the law. The only thing this exemplary modernist text misses is the further insight that the lost presence, the time when one stood alone, is itself a musical fiction, even the exemplary musical fiction. That presence arises only as an echo thrown in retrospect by the music that supposedly recalls it.

Music so construed is more fantasized than heard. The truth (*sic*) is that we listen, and with feeling, only as we read and act, as speaking subjects in a world of contingencies. In a sense, the project of what is called postmodernism is simply an effort to show that this truth is rather a good thing than otherwise. And the thesis of this book is simply that it is a good thing for music.

The design of what follows is simple. The first two chapters theorize the interrelations of music, musicology, and postmodernist thought. (*Musicology* here should be understood broadly to cover history, theory, criticism, and aesthetics.) The next three chapters explore the consequences, many of them political, of taking up problems in musical aesthetics (representation, narrative, expressivity) from a postmodernist standpoint. Three more chapters explore the consequences, many of them aesthetic, of taking up problems in the cultural politics of music (subject formation, social space, commodity) from the same standpoint. An epilogue brings together many of the leitmotifs of the volume and also brings the conceptual "polyphony" dear to postmodernism into the explicit procedures of the musicological text itself. This envoi forms a candid effort—justified, I trust, by what precedes it—to begin widening further the possibilities of acceptable discourse on music.

A related effort guides the approach taken throughout to questions of musical form and structure. *Classical Music and Postmodern Knowledge* seeks to reach nonspecialist as well as specialist readers. Specialists are addressed as often by subtext as by text; except in a few scattered paragraphs, discussions of musical technique are framed in terms that ought to be widely accessible. Not that technical issues are scanted or begrudged. But they arise strictly in relationship to the cultural, social, and psychical issues that they subtend and are talked about with that relationship in mind. As I suggest below, the lack of a viable public discourse about "classical" music is one reason why the music, cherishable though it is, is losing cultural ground at an alarming rate. I am not sure how much musicology can do to remedy this situation. But I would like to see it try.

My concern on this point necessitates a few closing words on one other. Much of what has been dubbed "the new musicology" has evolved through postmodernist critiques of the formerly (and, if truth be told, still currently) dominant models of musicological knowledge, which for want of better names can be called formalism and positivism. Postmodernism itself has evolved through critiques of modernism. Recently, writers on music seeking either to resist or assimilate postmodernist approaches have decried what they take to be the polemical use of these "-ism" labels as mere pejoratives.[3] Up to a point, this is a caution worth heeding. Without modernism, postmodernism is unthinkable, and not only because of the prefix; postmodernism does more than merely extend modernism's critique of itself, but that is where it starts. And the musical "-isms"—need it be said?—do not represent demonic forces but reasonable ways of specifying a disciplinary commitment to the scrutiny of style and structure on the one hand and the amassing of verifiable knowledge about musical texts and contexts on the other. It makes no sense to wish away the substantial achievements of these approaches, or of the modernism that houses them. But it makes no sense to wish away their limitations, either, or to conflate a critique of those limitations with mere name calling. Without critique, knowledge stagnates; no questions, no advances.

Acknowledgments

Earlier versions of chapters 3 through 5 have been published before; the versions printed here all include significant revisions and/or additions. I am grateful to the following publishers for permission to reprint earlier material: Cambridge University Press (for chapter 3, formerly "Music and Representation: The Instance of Haydn's *Creation*" in *Music and Text: Critical Inquiries,* ed. Steven Paul Scher, 1992, and for chapter 5, formerly *"Felix Culpa:* Goethe and the Image of Mendelssohn" in *Mendelssohn Studies,* ed. R. Larry Todd, 1993), and *Indiana Theory Review* (for chapter 4, Spring and Fall 1992). A small portion of chapter 1, also in an earlier version, appeared in my article "The Musicology of the Future" in *Repercussions* (Spring 1992).

Previous publication aside, a good deal of the work presented here originated in lectures given at various colleges, universities, conferences, and meetings of professional societies. I owe a great debt to the audiences at these events, whose comments and criticisms are reflected beyond my capacity to enumerate them. My particular thanks, however, go to my colleagues Karol Berger, Robert Fink, Walter Frisch, Richard Littlefield, Susan McClary, Steven Paul Scher, Richard Taruskin, and R. Larry Todd, and to Doris Kretschmer, humanities editor at the University of California Press. Thanks, also, to my editors Erika Büky and David Severtson for their scrupulous work.

Personal acknowledgments, while customary in this space, are never truly adequate. In this volume I hope the dedication will speak for itself.

One

Prospects

Postmodernism and Musicology

Early in 1992, *The New Republic* published an omnibus review of four recent books by American musicologists under the headline "The Strange New Direction of Music Criticism." The books in question, by Carolyn Abbate, Susan McClary, Rose Subotnik, and myself, are really too diverse to be lumped together so casually, but they are like-minded enough in taking "classical" music out of its cloister to have sent a common signal. Or, rather, to have touched an uncommon nerve: as the headline indicates, the review was no Schumannesque praise of new paths but a warning against being seduced by these books, even those the reviewer rather liked, into straying from the straight path to the strange.[1]

But was this new direction really so strange? Was it even really new, or more like a renewal of something lost or forgotten? From one standpoint, nothing could be more ordinary than what these books have in common. The new direction in musicology as I understand and support it is simply a demand for human interest. It chafes at the scholastic isolation of music, equally impatient whether heaps of facts or arcane technical anatomies furnish the scholar's frigid cell. "Talk about music," the demand might run, "should bear the impress of what music means to human subjects as thinking, feeling, struggling parts of a world."

But not just any impress will do. The demand for human interest should lead to a revaluation of impressionistic, figurative ways of de-

1

scribing music, but that will not be enough to satisfy it. The object
sought is meaning: concrete, complex, and historically situated. The
search runs counter to the widely held principle—half truism, half aesthetic ideal—that music has no such thing: that, as Theodor Adorno
put it, "Time and again [music] points to the fact that it signifies something, something definite. Only the intention is always veiled."[2] The
best way to satisfy the demand for human interest is not to prove this
powerful statement false but to reveal it as a *historical* truth. If the
intention is always veiled, that is because we accept a conceptual regime that allows us to experience the human interest of music but
forbids us to talk about it. It is because we accept—perhaps even
while rejecting it elsewhere—a hard epistemology that admonishes us
not to impose our merely subjective interpretations on the semantic
indefiniteness of music. When it comes to musical meaning, the famous dictum of the early Wittgenstein has long been exempt from
critique: "Where one cannot speak, there one must be silent."[3]

This admonition cannot, I think, simply be discarded as a once-
estimable but now naive error. Its underlying intention, to make sure
that claims to knowledge are open to genuine collegial debate, would
be difficult to abandon responsibly. But hard epistemology is oppres-
sively and even phobically narrow in its notion of contestable knowledge. Seeking to protect truth from human fallibility, it defines subjectivity as the negative of objectivity and denies the legitimacy of
any claims to knowledge in which traces of the subject—the historical
claimant—have a constructive role. In its zealous will to truth, it
promotes the rhetoric of impersonality into an epistemological first
principle. (The resulting oddities merit separate study. The hard epistemology of eighteenth-century science, for example, took experimenters' reports on their own bodies to be untainted by subjectivity
if the experimenters were genteel males.)[4] A more flexible approach
might accordingly begin by separating the concept of knowledge from
the rhetorical opposition of personal and impersonal expression and
resituating it in the historicity of human subjects and their discourses.
What if our subjective interpretations of music do not falsify its semantic indefiniteness but recognize its semantic capacities as a cultural practice? What if these interpretations are, not substitutes for a
lack of knowledge, but contestable, historically conditioned forms of
knowledge?

Hard epistemology depends on oppositions of fact and value, the intrinsic and the extrinsic, that may seem commonsensical but do so only because the routines of their enforcement have long since dulled our ability to see them otherwise. In order to empower new musicologies, to move from the negativity of critique to the positivity of human interest, we need to defamiliarize and deconstruct those oppositions as they apply to music. We need to reconsider what the disjunctive "and" means when we speak of music and language, or the musical and the extramusical, or subjective musical response and objective musical knowledge. There is no problem about acknowledging that each of these contraries has real historical import. The idea is not to make them disappear, which they are unlikely to do. The idea, rather, is to relativize them: to reduce them from first principles to contingent moments, temporary limits, in an ongoing conceptual dynamic.

The best means to do this, I would suggest, lie in the conceptual and rhetorical world of postmodernism. The aim of the present chapter is to characterize that world and to show its specific pertinence to understanding music. The characterization will proceed along broad lines. It will seek to establish an orientation, not to work up capsule summaries of the various modes of deconstruction, feminist theory, archaeology and genealogy of knowledge, psychoanalysis, ideology critique, neopragmatism, history of sexualities, popular culture studies, and so on that make up the crowded field of postmodernist discourses. The characterization will also be somewhat idealized. It will try to encourage, by envisioning, a generalized climate of postmodernist thought that is at best still nascent. At the same time, it will fight shy of promoting that contradiction in terms, an official or normative or definitive postmodernism. The specifically musical half of the chapter will address the disciplinary oppositions mentioned earlier and connect their postmodernist undoing to past and possible future ways of thinking about music.

For those who care about "classical" music, the possibility of tapping new sources of cultural and intellectual energy may come not a moment too soon. It is no secret that, in the United States anyway, this music is in trouble. It barely registers in our schools, it has neither the prestige nor the popularity of literature and visual art, and it squanders its capacities for self-renewal by clinging to an exceptionally static core repertoire. Its audience is shrinking, graying, and overly palefaced, and the suspicion has been voiced abroad that its claim to occupy a sphere of autonomous artistic greatness is largely a means of veiling, and thus perpetuating, a narrow set of social interests.

In its present constitution as an object of knowledge and pleasure, classical music holds at best an honorific place on the margins of high culture. No one today could write a book such as *The Song of the Lark*, Willa Cather's novel of 1915: a book that translates the traditional narrative of quest romance into a young woman's career as a diva, a book that climaxes at the Metropolitan Opera as the heroine sings Sieglinde in Act 1 of Wagner's *Die Walküre:*

Into one lovely attitude after another the music swept her, love impelled her. And the voice gave out all that was best in it. Like the spring indeed, it blossomed into memories and prophecies, it recounted and foretold, as she sang the story of her friendless life, and of how the thing which was truly herself, "bright as the day, rose to the surface," when in the hostile world she for the first time beheld her Friend. Fervently she rose into the hardier feeling of action and daring. . . . Her impatience for the sword swelled with her anticipation of [Siegmund's] act, and throwing her arms above her head, she fairly tore a sword out of the empty air for him, before *Nothung* had left the tree.[5]

The rhetorical and symbolic action of this passage cries out for comment, as does its Wagnermania, but I must focus here on something else. Unlike Sieglinde, Cather's heroine has friends, all of whom are in the audience to witness her triumph, which forges them into a kind of spiritual community. And perhaps the key figure in this community (saved, as best, for last mention) is an uneducated mariachi artist named Spanish Johnny, "a grey-haired little Mexican, withered and bright as a string of peppers beside an adobe door," from whom the heroine in her girlhood learned to associate music with wildness, freedom, and the sharp savor of cultural identity.[6]

One reason for our remoteness from Cather's image repertoire is the lack, or rather the loss, of a viable public discourse about classical music. During the nineteenth century, esoteric conceptions of music based on its apparent transcendence of signification coexisted and contended with semantic conceptions that imbued music with poetic, narrative, or philosophical meaning and with sociocultural agency.[7]

Traces of both conceptions appear in *The Song of the Lark*. But the twentieth century would witness a decisive victory for the esoteric side, at least as far as Western music is concerned. There were many causes for this: the erosion, in the world of sound recording and mass entertainment media, of musical amateurism and the culture of home performance; the complementary failings, literal-mindedness and fancifulness, of the available semantic approaches; the appalling misappropriation of the great Germanic tradition by the Nazis; and the increasing professionalization of musicology, music analysis, and music theory. The net effect was that by the mid-twentieth century, classical music had passed out of the public sphere.

In trying to reverse this development, the so-called new musicology, like most intellectual movements, is in part a revival. But it is not just a reproduction, like a new piece of period furniture. Its purpose is to recapture, not the content of an earlier discourse, but the role of that discourse in society and culture. If it succeeds, it can help revivify classical music by demystifying and de-idealizing it: by canceling the Faustian bargain that lofts the music beyond the contingencies, uncertainties, and malfeasances of life at the cost of utter irrelevance.

. . . . .

To start on a note of candor: the term *postmodernism* is something of a catchall and susceptible to mere modishness. But it is also, for better or worse, at the center of a momentous intellectual debate. As I use it, loosely following Jean-François Lyotard, the term designates a conceptual order in which grand, synthesizing schemes of explanation have lost their place and in which the traditional bases of rational understanding—unity, coherence, generality, totality, structure—have lost their authority if not their pertinence.[8] An order so hostile to grand syntheses cannot, of course, willingly admit of one itself. Postmodernist strategies of understanding are incorrigibly interdisciplinary and irreducibly plural. Like the theories that ground them, they make up not a system but an ethos.

These strategies are localized, heterogeneous, contestatory, and contested. Rejecting traditional concepts of both subjectivity and objectivity, they focus on diverse, culturally constructed subjectivities and objectivities at diverse levels of entitlement. They are critical, both cognitively and politically, of the ideal of impartial reason, and even more so of claims to embody it; they seek to enhance rather than reduce the mobility of meaning. They insist on the relativity of all knowledge, including self-knowledge, to the disciplines—not just the conceptual presuppositions but the material, discursive, and social practices—that produce and circulate knowledge. They situate human agency, however problematically, within the dynamic processes, the so-called economies, of such production and circulation rather than in the conscious self-possession of a centered and autonomous human subject. And, though they run the risk of fostering fragmentation and intellectual razzle-dazzle for their own sakes, postmodernist strategies of understanding offer, as I hope to show, new and badly needed means for the criticism and historiography of the arts to meet, not only their aesthetic, but also their social and conceptual responsibilities.

We can get a prismatic, partial, but credible image of the postmodernist ethos by focusing on new turns in the conceptualization of four important topics of modernist thought: rationality, generality, subjectivity, and communication.

Rationality. For present purposes, the term *modernism* refers to the conceptual order inaugurated by the European Enlightenment. Taking certain Renaissance (or "early modern") tendencies to their logical, if unforeseen, conclusion, the Enlightenment called on impartial reason to know the world and guide its progress, independent of religious and social authority and unintimidated by them. "All things," wrote Diderot in the *Encyclopedia,* "must be examined, all must be winnowed and sifted without exception and without sparing anyone's sensibilities."[9] As this statement testifies, however, the use of reason requires the suspension of other, less severe faculties such as sympathy and imagination. Reason, a function of the subject, operates as objectivity by assuming a sovereign detachment from its objects.

Familiar critiques of modern reason, such as Theodor Adorno and Max Horkheimer's *Dialectic of Enlightenment,* hone in on this detachment.[10] Although the social aim of Enlightenment is emancipatory, the mandate of detachment produces a fatal slippage toward instrumentality and domination. The effect traverses, not only the disciplines of knowledge, but also the social class, the bourgeoisie, whose interests the Enlightenment chiefly served. A major effort of modernist thought has been to humanize reason without entirely sacrificing its detachment from its objects, which serves as the measure of truth.

Postmodernist thought abandons the second part of this effort. It repeals the mandate of detachment, resituating reason in the midst of the dense, multiform world that reason seeks to know. It treats claims to knowledge as always also political claims, inescapably affected by and affecting the knower's position in a cultural, social, or psychical matrix. Postmodernist reason always serves interests other than truth and *by that means enables itself to serve truth,* however imperfectly. Partial perspective is, not a constraint on knowledge, but its very condition, and not coincidentally the condition of sympathy and imagination, too. As Donna Haraway has argued,

The knowing self is partial in all its guises, never finished, whole, simply there and original; it is always constituted and stitched together imperfectly, and *therefore* able to join with another, to see together without claiming to be another. . . . We do not seek partiality for its own sake, but for the sake of the connections and unexpected openings [its] situated knowledges make possible. The only way to find a larger vision is to be somewhere in particular.[11]

Put in Kantian terms: in the postmodernist ethos, all reason is practical reason.

A few versions of postmodernism, notably those of Jean Baudrillard and Richard Rorty, frankly subordinate the claims of reason to an extreme skeptical relativism. This position has drawn sharp criticism, especially from thinkers on the political left who see it as a hapless surrender to the mystifications of the status quo. Without some appeal to standards of truth and falsehood, reality and illusion, reason and unreason, neither social institutions nor consensus beliefs can competently be criticized.[12]

The majority of postmodernist discourses, however, take the effort to surmount such skepticism as part of their calling. As Haraway, again, puts it, the challenge is

to have *simultaneously* an account of radical historical contingency for all knowledge claims and knowing subjects, a critical practice for recognizing our own "semiotic technologies" for making meanings, *and* a no-nonsense commitment to faithful accounts of the "real" world, one that can be partially shared and friendly to earth-wide projects of finite freedom, adequate material abundance, modest meaning in suffering, and limited happiness.[13]

Admittedly, this conceptual order is a tall one, even given the tough-minded modesty of its social and moral ambitions. At the very least the simultaneity Haraway calls for needs to be reconceived as a fluctuation or negotiation among different standpoints. Yet an order such as this should be feasible if we can get beyond the modernist frame of mind and recognize that contingency and rhetoricity are, not antithetical to reason, but interdependent with it. Each of these terms can illuminate or obscure, adjoin or displace, enable or disable the others. The effect of this interdependence on critical judgment is, not to disarm it, but to expand both its resources and its responsibilities. Truth, in Christopher Norris's words, does not "simply drop out of the picture (or become just a piece of redundant conceptual baggage) as soon as one concedes the fact of its involvement" with contingency and rhetoricity.[14] At the same time, contingency and rhetoricity do profoundly alter and ramify the truths involved with them, some of which *do* drop out of the picture.

Generality. As Diderot suggests with his "all things must be examined," the pursuit of totality is basic to modernist thought. Both conceptual and social reasons can be given for this. Modernist master narratives break with the contents and procedures of dogmatic schemes of explanation but not with their intent to frame a comprehensive system of general truths. The critical force of modern reason could not question this intent because the constructive force of modern reason depended on it. As Jacques Derrida has argued, epistemic modernity depends on the relocation of universals such as form and essence from an "objective" ideality to a human subject "conscious and certain of itself." The result for the subject, the agent of reason, is "a sort of infinite assurance."[15] This assurance, meanwhile, proved indispensable to the social and moral aims of modernism, which quickly evolved from breaking through to modernity from some sort of ancien regime to overcoming the alienating effects of modernity itself. Modernism is shot through with nostalgia for the unity of the world it shatters. It seeks to remedy the dissociative modern conditions of secularity, market economics, psychical fragmentation, and social heterogeneity by advancing the march of science, the ideal of the organic society, or the ideology of the aesthetic.

One way to understand postmodernism is as a critique of this modernist nostalgia, an attempt to enfranchise the forces of decentralization that modernism sought (and seeks) to contain. Given the dangers of a social (de)formation in which mutually indifferent, incomprehending, or hostile groups blindly jostle together, it seems fair to say that this agenda currently makes more sense conceptually than it does practically, a point not lost on critics of postmodernism such as Jürgen Habermas.[16] The practical issue is not directly at stake here. Nonetheless, it may be possible to steal a leaf from Habermas's book and regard the heteroglossic discourses of conceptual postmodernism as models for a viable polyphony of social and communicative actions.

These discourses can be said to seek a *localized generality.* In the place of the comprehensive truths of the master narratives, they install what Lyotard calls the "infinity of heterogeneous finalities" and Haraway the "politics and epistemologies of location, positioning, and situating."[17] They operate by assuming that any formulation of or within a master narrative can be read as responsive to a set of more local interests—local, that is, with respect to the general terms of the master narrative but still general with respect to the phenomena that the narrative seeks to cover. (It can be argued, for instance, that the new science of eighteenth-century microscopy conceived of protozoa in terms meant to protect the image of the *human* body as smooth and self-contained, an image especially important at that point in the history of manners.)[18] One way to write postmodernist criticism, history, or theory is to trace the interplay of the locally general with the local, the general, or both. Only the direct subsumption of the local under the general, which produces what Haraway calls the "god-trick" and the "view from nowhere," drops out of the picture.

Subjectivity. The normative characteristics of the modern subject include identity, boundedness, autonomy, interiority, depth, and centrality. Even acting only as ideals, these supply the subject with much of the "infinite assurance" proper to it. Probably the most familiar of postmodernist claims is that, like it or not, this vaunted subject is an exploded fiction. The true human subject is fragmentary, incoherent, overdetermined, forever under construction in the process of signification. But talk of the decentered subject can be cheap; the concept quickly becomes specious if it is used to deny rather than problematize the force and responsibilities of human agency. The rhetoric of denial was much bandied about during the heyday of structuralism. The conclusion of Michel Foucault's *The Order of Things* provided a watchword, with its questions about the disappearance of "man": "is not . . . [man] in the process of perishing as the being of language continues to shine ever brighter on our horizon? . . . Ought we not give up thinking of man, or, to be more strict, think this disappearance of man—and the ground of possibility of all the sciences of man—as closely as possible in correlation with our concern for language?" Often forgotten was the cautionary statement that followed: "Of course, these are not affirmations; they are at most questions to which it is not possible to reply; they must be left in suspense, where they pose themselves, only with the knowledge that the possibility of posing them may well open the way to a future thought." [19] A subject decentered is a subject still.

Decentered subjectivity typically figures in modernist discourse as alienated, deviant, or comic. And it figures often: by one account, decentering itself is a phenomenon of the modern era, born of the Enlightenment principle that "symbolic tradition" can "no longer contain the subject, no longer bind him to its . . . mandate." [20] Postmodernism is in one sense the project of undoing modernist efforts to distance and regulate decentering. Its own mandate is to establish the means of conceiving, valuing, and practicing a subjectivity that is *unexceptionally* mobile and contingent. In the postmodernist ethos, decentering is not a departure from rational, communicative subjectivity but the very condition of its possibility. Human agency arises, not as a radiation from a central core of being, but as a circulation among positions to be taken in discourse and society.

Communication. Modernism favors models of communication based on the capacity of a single medium, language, to classify, refer to, and make truth claims about the real. It does not matter whether these functions are meant to be cherished or begrudged, cultivated or transcended; what matters is their status as foundational. Whatever their social or aesthetic value, they are epistemologically primary. Put in terms suggested by J. L. Austin, modernism privileges the *consta-*

tive, that which is judged true or false, over the *performative,* that which is judged successful or unsuccessful.[21]

Postmodernism takes much of its impetus from the deconstruction of this hierarchy. It privileges neither the constative nor the performative as such, but the recognition that while all constative acts are also performative, not all performative acts are constative. The performative is the "originary" category within which the constative is produced, enfranchised, recast, subverted, and ramified. In this context, communication appears as a process in which socially and discursively situated subjects act by meaning. Communicative acts arise in signification and at the same time constitutively exceed it.[22]

The effects of this paradigm shift are far-reaching. The constative declines from a first principle to a distinguishing feature of language as a medium, in the process losing some (but by no means all) of its epistemic authority. In its performative or "illocutionary" aspect, language combines with all other media to form a continuous manifold—call it a field, a dynamic, a current, a network, an economy—of communicative acts. Whatever signifies affects, in so doing, the situation(s) recognized or misrecognized, believed or imagined to envelop it.

Both this process itself and the meanings it generates are protean. Particular communicative acts can nearly always be realized in a variety of media and must in principle be capable of varied repetition in an indefinite number of situations. Each must be freshly interpreted rather than merely received, and even the plainest resonates with alternative uses and realizations, with displacements, substitutions, and revaluations, with unexpected alliances and antipathies. This *general transposability* is a hallmark of the communicative economy. One effect of it is to break down the customary divisions between different spheres of action and the motives and meanings proper to each sphere. In the dynamics of acting by meaning, psychical, social, and cultural agencies can intersect and mutually implicate each other at any point. Meanings and values characteristic of each undergo transferences onto the others and invest the communicative economy as a whole.[23]

This economy, in sum, is the locus of what Derrida calls *dissemination:* a process of sowing meaning without hopes of reaping a harvest thereby, a broadcasting of seed/semen/semiosis without claims to possession/paternity/mastery of what grows therefrom. "Lapidarily: dissemination figures that which *cannot become* the father('s)." It can return to no origin, and, unlike polysemia, subtends no ultimate unity, however remote. Dissemination opens out the play of surplus and lack within signification with no prospect of stabilizing or closing it. The result is to unsettle symbolic traditions in both their general and locally general forms, and to do so *affirmatively,* "undoing the eider quilt of the 'symbolic' . . . [with] all the [attendant] risks, but without the metaphysical or romantic pathos of negativity." Dissemination is "an infraction *marking* the 'symbolic'": denoting it, characterizing it, defacing it, branding it, inscribing it with countersigns.[24]

Derrida's uses for the concept of dissemination include a critique of Jacques Lacan's psychoanalytic concept of a symbolic order. Nonetheless, Lacan's work has been mined effectively and often for the means to think about the communicative economy.[25] The focus of this work is not the "self" of individual psychology but the subject as constituted within a multiform process of signification. Particularly in historicizing adaptations, Lacanian psychoanalysis is not a psychology at all. It is, rather, a theory of how certain articulations of identification and alienation, desire and law, continually "mark" the field of communicative action: investing the field as a whole, traversing it (disseminally), and breaking down (but without merely obliterating) the boundaries of its psychical, social, and cultural subfields.

Lacan constructs two "orders" or "registers" of signification which he calls the imaginary and the symbolic. These constitute the terms of a developmental allegory, roughly along Oedipal lines, but they are also, and more importantly, coextensive. The subject must negotiate with and within both registers continually. The imaginary involves proximity to nurture and gratification of the kind first sought from the mother; the formation and disruption of identifications (with self-images, imagoes, idealized others); and the privileging of nonlinguistic representation. The symbolic involves acceptance of distance and privation, consequences of the antithesis between law and desire imposed by the father, or rather in the judicial name-of-the-Father; the collapse of identificatory schemes; and the privileging of language. The imaginary values fantasy over discourse while the symbolic does the reverse; the imaginary misrecognizes its own signifying character while the symbolic signifies avowedly.

Despite all these contrasts, however, the two registers do not form a traditional binary opposition. Both address the same fundamental issue—the subject's constitutive lack of unity and self-presence; they are both more ambivalent than I have been able to indicate here; and they are deeply implicated in each other's workings. Both are also set over against a register outside signification that Lacan designates as the real. But it can nonetheless be said that the imaginary continually revives the hope of plenitude despite continual disturbances and that the symbolic continually disturbs the hope of plenitude despite continual revivals. The musical pertinence of these processes will begin to appear shortly.[26]

· · · · ·

Musical pertinence, indeed, has now resurfaced as my topic. As the preface intimated and the next chapter will show, modernist conceptions of music are profoundly at odds with the postmodernist ethos. No wonder, then, that Harold Powers, delivering the plenary address at the 1990 meeting of the American Musicological Society, should warn his colleagues against rushing incautiously to embrace alien disciplines and perspectives, "casually abandon[ing] traditional modes in favor of ones taken over from easier fields."[27] In the process, Powers joked that the belated arrival of newfangled thinking in musicological circles could hardly be explained by the innate dull-wittedness of musicologists. And he was right.

Modernist forms of musical understanding ascribe a unique self-referentiality to music that renders it largely opaque from "extra-musical" standpoints. Music must somehow be understood from the inside out. This construal is so basic that failures to observe it, let alone efforts to question it, may plausibly count as deviations from reason and common sense. Traditional musicology warded off such deviations by marginalizing the historico-critical interpretation of music, a disciplinary action (in every sense) whose history is written in Joseph Kerman's watershed text *Contemplating Music*.[28] Such interpretation, to be sure, has since gained a musicological room of its own, but devaluing it is still a healthy practice. One need only say, with

Powers in his address, that "musical data are more resistant to verbal explication than the data in other humanistic fields. Indeed, musicology is only partly one of the humanities, which otherwise deal with the visible and above all the verbal arts." [29]

The heart of the matter, indeed, is the relationship of music and language. Preceded by both opera, with its perpetual war of music and words, and philosophical aesthetics, with its parallel opposition between music and definite concepts, musicology has presumed that music and language lie on different sides of an epistemological divide. On this point, the dominant esoteric and marginal semantic traditions agree. And consistent with one strain of nineteenth-century valuation (the other will concern us in the next chapter), as well as with traditional figures of cosmic harmony (which will concern us in the chapter after that), the superior position belongs to music.

This polarity comes in both dualistic and dialectical versions, predominantly the former. The latter can be represented by Theodor Adorno, whose little-known essay on the subject actually insists on music's likeness to language, but only the better to insist that this likeness must be transcended. Both music and language ideally seek to integrate concrete "intentions" into a comprehensive whole. Their efforts, however, have very different ends: "Signifying language would say the absolute in a mediated way, yet the absolute escapes it in each of its intentions, which, in the end, are left behind, as finite. Music reaches the absolute immediately, but in the same instant it darkens, as when a strong light blinds the eye, which can no longer see things that are quite visible." [30] For present purposes, what is most striking about this statement is not its claim—questionable but familiar—that both language and music seek the absolute, but the buried metaphor by which music completes the sacred quest at which language fails, reaching the quasi-divine light even if only for a fleeting glimpse. Language is defined by the aftermath of what it fails to do, music by the aftermath of what it succeeds in doing. Still, even music does not attain to Dante's privilege of actually gazing into the light, and Adorno's conclusions are accordingly sober, even stoical: "Music suffers from its similarity to language and cannot escape from it. . . . Only music that has once been language transcends its similarity to language." [31]

The dualistic version of the music-language polarity can be represented by Charles Seeger. In his well-known formulation, "the core of the [musicological] undertaking is the integration of speech knowledge in general and the speech knowledge of music in particular (which are extrinsic to music and its compositional process) with the music knowledge of music (which is intrinsic to music and its compositional process)."[32] Language on the outside, music on the inside: sounded out deconstructively, the passage is a variation on a classic theme. The inside is a figure of music as a full, immediate presence, music in the metaphysical position of form or essence. The phrase "music knowledge of music" is a circle that fuses the terms for reflection and immediacy. The first "music," designating a means of knowledge, folds over on the second "music," designating the object of knowledge. Knowledge itself, both conceptually and rhetorically, is enveloped by the identity of, fills the (non-)interval between, the one music and the other.

In contrast, the outside is a figure of language as rupture. The phrase "speech knowledge of music" is a series of isolated terms, monads alienated from each other, lumpy substantives. Knowledge is abraded by the nonidentity between speech as the means and music as the object of knowledge. Like "music knowledge of music," "speech knowledge of music" places music in the metaphysical position, but this time as precisely that form or essence which speech cannot capture. In a neat departure from traditional usage, speech, usually a metaphysical term, the privileged figure of presence, is *displaced* by music.

Seeger's opposition between language and music is exemplary and quite helpful in the lucidity of its underlying logic. Beyond a certain point, all too quickly reached, language and music cannot (or is it *must not?*) mix. The fact that language has, and music lacks, a constative dimension becomes foundational and determinative. Language is denied access to music, it cannot represent musical reality; music, indeed, becomes the very means by which the epistemological limits of language, that would-be omnivore, are set. (Here Seeger's dualism and Adorno's dialectic converge.) But if this is so, it leaves musicologists with only two disciplinary choices. Either they can use language to present positive knowledge about the contexts of music—its notation, provenance, performance venues and practices, material and mechanical reproduction, etc.—or they can develop a technical vocabulary that asymptotically draws language so close to the axis of "music knowledge" that musical style and structure can be studied with a minimum of misrepresentation. Any effort to speak *about* or *like* or in some sense *with* music rather than merely *around* it exceeds the acceptable mandate of language. Such efforts must be treated as rhetorical rather than descriptive, as subjective rather than scientific: treated, that is, as criticism.[33]

This rather dry procedural bifurcation tends to work in combination with, and perhaps to rationalize, something more impassioned. Since the early nineteenth century, the difference between music and language has been taken as a sign that the experience of music, or more exactly of musical "masterpieces," is a venue of transcendence. Originally, this attitude involved a naively literal replacement of religion by music. As Carl Dahlhaus puts it, commenting on an exemplary text by W. H. Wackenroder, "whereas music, in the form of church music, used to partake of religion as revealed in the 'Word,' it now, as autonomous music capable of conveying the 'inexpressible,' has become religion itself." Gradually, however, the religious truth signified by autonomous music is effaced by the very autonomy that is, or had once been, its signifier. Where "strict concentration on the work as self-contained musical process"[34] once meant the apprehension of the work in its unworldliness, the same concentration now means the apprehension of the innate character, the complex unity-in-diversity, of the musical process itself. To delineate that character would eventually become the goal of musical analysis, which would thus assume the role, at least ideally, of directing the aesthetic cognition of music.

Whether inflected dryly, to create the necessity of positivist and formalist musicology, or fervently, to invest music with the glamour of what Derrida calls the metaphysics of presence, the opposition of music and language is untenable from a postmodernist perspective. Neither linguistic constatation nor musical immediacy can empower that opposition, constatation because it is no longer foundational for language use, and immediacy because it is no longer either extralinguistic or unworldly. Once music and language are understood, not as antitheses divided by the lack or possession of constative power, but as common elements in the communicative economy, their differences become practical, not radical. Their common resort to certain patterns of inflection, expression, and material and structural rhythm becomes more palpable, the cultural work they do as modes of discourse more accessible. Similarly, once the communicative economy is understood to operate as a continual interanimation of psychical, social, and cultural agencies, immediacy takes on a whole new character. It no longer dwells in a special place or medium, can no longer be opposed to reflection, and, in particular, can no longer be opposed to language. *Immediacy becomes a performative effect.*

It follows from this that musical immediacy, however distinctive and significant we may acknowledge it to be, cannot ground the putative unworldliness of music, either in the strong form that treats music as a numinous presence or in the weak form that acknowledges music to be contextually situated but still affirms a "relative autonomy" that allows some works or styles to transcend the limits of their contexts. Neither music nor anything else can be other than worldly through and through. From a postmodernist perspective, music as musicology has conceived it simply does not exist.

What's more, musical immediacy cannot be taken uncritically as the authorizing locus for the study of music. As a performative effect, such immediacy functions to empower the persons, institutions, and social groups in control of its production. In mystified or idealized form, the same immediacy can become a powerful means of ideological seduction or coercion, not least for those who find it most empowering or liberating.

This is not to say, emphatically not, that immediacy, musical or otherwise, is something spurious and pernicious that must be deconstructed on sight. The last thing a postmodernist musicology wants to be is a neo-Puritanism that offers to show its love for music by ceasing to enjoy it. But it is to say that what we call musical experience needs to be systematically rethought, that the horizons of our musical pleasure need to be redrawn more broadly, and that the embeddedness of music in networks of nonmusical forces is something to be welcomed rather than regretted. Those projects can only be achieved through modes of hermeneutic and historical writing that are always also critical, in the dual sense of performing both criticism and critique: modes of writing that, while conceding and indeed affirming their own "rhetorical" and "subjective" character, rigorously seek to position musical experience within the densely compacted, concretely situated worlds of those who compose, perform, and listen.[35]

But surely, it might be argued, music itself is the best refutation of this postmodernist position. Music is still the most immediate of all aesthetic experiences, however we relativize the concept of immediacy, and words, do what they might, are still unable to capture the character, texture, and force of compelling music attentively heard. If the first clause of this response simply begs the question—different things hold different people spellbound, and the fact of spellbindingness is not in question, only what it involves—the second clause rings true. Its truth, however, says nothing special about music. Language cannot capture musical experience because it cannot capture any experience whatever, including the experience of language itself. Language always alienates what it makes accessible; the process of alienation, the embedding of a topic in supposedly extrinsic discourses, is precisely what produces the accessibility. Describing the experience of reading Proust's *Within a Budding Grove,* with its leitmotif of the sea at Balbec, is just as difficult as describing the experience of listening to Debussy's *La mer* or, for that matter, of passing the time from dawn till noon on the sea.

The emergence of postmodernist musicologies will depend on our willingness and ability to read as inscribed within the immediacy-effects of music itself the kind of mediating structures usually positioned outside music under the rubric of context. These "structuring structures"—locally general dispositions, tendencies, or cultural tropes—would appear as forces both deployed by and deploying music, deployed by and deploying discourse about music.[36] At the same time the differences between text and context, the aesthetic and the political or social, the "inside" and the "outside" of the musical moment, the hermeneutic and the historiographical, would be (re)constituted as provisional and permeable boundaries destined to disappear in and through the heteroglot weaving of musicological discourse. The music "itself," whether studied at the level of work, style, or genre, would be decentered in that discourse—sometimes more so, sometimes less—but not thereby relinquished as an occasion of pleasure, understanding, or valuation.

.　　.　　.　　.　　.

For a productive way to theorize this postmodernist version of musical immediacy, we can return, but with a twist, to Lacanian psychoanalysis. I have suggested elsewhere that musical immediacy behaves like the Lacanian imaginary, "the illusory, if inescapable, immediacy of the ego." Like the process of imaginary identification, music offers a seamless band of pleasure and presence, but nonetheless one "open to disruption by recurrent intimations that the supposedly self-present ego is always already alienated, that its desire is the desire of (desire for, desire determined by) the Other."[37] This suggestion may be developed further with the help of Julia Kristeva's rewriting of Lacan's distinction between the imaginary and the symbolic. Noting that both of these "registers" of signification imply the separation of subject and object, Kristeva focuses on a register of supposedly earlier origin that she calls the semiotic. Its character is given by the experience of drive, or rather of the multiplicity of drives in collision and interchange; it is impulsive, rhythmic, dynamic, plural, untotalized, supercharged. In these respects it is very like music when music excites us most, and Kristeva in fact calls it musical.[38]

Its music, however, is never heard as such. The semiotic appears only to subjects who have already entered the symbolic order of culture, and precisely by the rhythmic-impulsive disruption of that order. The very existence of the semiotic as an independent register is a retrospective hypothesis, as Kristeva is the first to insist. Like Derrida's dissemination, Kristeva's semiotic appears only in the infractions that *mark* the symbolic. One function of the symbolic, therefore, is to bind or channel the powerful currents of semiotic energy, a process that, because it is always unstable, also releases and articulates those energies.

The yield of immediacy that accompanies this process is what Kristeva designates as music and what grounds the metaphorical identity of the musical and the semiotic. Real music, however, *musica practica,* stands apart from this figurative deployment (something Kristeva herself fails to recognize). Music is, after all, a cultural practice. It is

distinctive, even unique, in that its symbolic function includes the signification of the semiotic, but it, too, necessarily binds symbolically
the semiotic energies that it signifies as unbound.

The practical consequences of these interrelationships show up
strikingly in some clinical observations of the neurologist Oliver Sacks.
Playing, singing, and listening to music, Sacks found, or even hearing
it in the mind's ear, could relieve impairments in speech, mobility, and
writing in Parkinsonian patients. Important as this relief was somati-
cally, it was even more important psychically; in the words of one
patient, "It was like suddenly remembering myself, my own living
tune. . . . [What music imparted] was not just movement, but existence itself." In Sacks's terms, what the music imparts is a "naturalness
in posture and action" correlative to "the living 'I'";[39] in Kristevan
terms, the gift imparted is the primordial *jouissance* (quasi-orgasmic,
unrepresentable bliss) of the semiotic, the continuity of presubjective
desire and signification.

Not just any music, though, can accomplish this. "Rhythmic impetus" has to be present, writes Sacks, but it "has to be 'embedded'"
in a formal pattern the listener can grasp unreflectively. Raw "bang-
ing," indeed, could prompt pathological jerking. For Sacks's patients,
schooled in the American popular music of the 1920s, the embedding form was melody.[40] In other words, for these listeners the rhythmic pulsions of the semiotic became available as music only when
they were articulated against and through the discriminate symbolic
bounds of melody, which simultaneously took its own "living" quality
from the pulsions it embedded.

But an articulation of this type has yet a further, and even more
important, dimension. Even assuming that the dynamism of a musical
passage is properly embedded, whether in melody or some other configuration as the listener's musical culture prescribes, not all such passages can become transparent in their semiotic pulsions. Only the music that listeners identify closely with their own lives, music they find
meaningful, can do this. The semiotic is articulated as an immediacy
only through an already-significant symbolic that endows the immediacy of the semiotic with an already-reflective meaning. All musical
styles, accordingly, as well as certain musical works, embody a certain
relationship to the signifying process. This relationship can prompt

and reward interpretation, both in general terms and more abundantly by producing specific sites of interplay between the semiotic (or the imaginary) and the symbolic. These sites are where music, and for that matter visual and verbal discourse, are simultaneously at their most immediate and most explicitly disseminal. The occasions of surplus on which one register overflows into the other, and the occasions of deficit on which one register breaks down into the other, thus form a cardinal source of what I have elsewhere called hermeneutic windows, sites of engagement through which the interpreter and the interpreted animate one another.[41]

What we see or hear at such windows can, of course, always be recuperated for the symbolic order. But by resisting or deferring that recuperation, that perhaps inevitable normalization, we can understand more than the symbolic order allows. And by that means, since no one can do other than inhabit the symbolic, we can learn to inhabit it with a disseminal energy that may in the end transform it. This project, which I would like to claim as the utopian project of postmodernism, treats as emancipatory the principle that subjectivity is, as we now say so easily, "culturally constructed." It seeks to install a credible, value-laden human agency where the irreducibly multiple and heterogeneous determinants of this becoming-constructed engage in their fullest interplay.

To do this for music in particular, we need to venture a series of radical presuppositions. The first begins with the recognition that music participates actively in the cultural construction of subjectivity— an idea popular at the end of the nineteenth century but badly eroded in the twentieth.[42] The process of musical subject formation may involve the conditions of composition, performance, reproduction, or reception; my concern here is primarily with the last, understood as part of the communicative economy.[43]

Deeds of music seek receptive listeners. As part of its illocutionary force, the music addresses a determinate type of subject and in so doing beckons that subject, summons it up to listen. The subject is determined by, or as, a position in relation to historically specific possibilities of discourse, action, and desire. The musical summons may be issued at the level of style, genre, form, or "the work itself"; it may appeal to social, sexual, psychical, or conceptual interests. Listeners agree to personify a musical subject by responding empathetically to the music's summons. Their pleasure in listening thereby becomes a vehicle of acculturation: musical pleasure, like all pleasure, invites legitimation both of its sources and of the subject position its sources address. If I enjoy Beethoven's Fifth Symphony, my pleasure coaxes me to find edification in violent struggle, spiritual value in heroic ordeal. If I enjoy Ice-T's rap revenge-tragedy "Cop Killer," my pleasure coaxes me to find edification in violent scapegoating, social value in ritual sacrifice. That my pleasure may include an appreciation of organic form in the Fifth or visual rhythm in the "Cop Killer" video does not interdict the processes of subject formation, but interacts with them. The character of aesthetic pleasure varies with that of the subject who enjoys it, and vice versa.

To some degree, the act of personifying the musical subject situates the listener within that subject's cultural order. Just what degree depends on how much reciprocity there is between the music's repertoire of communicative actions and the listener's. It should be recognized, however, that the listener's empathy in itself posits a substantial reciprocity, without which the musical summons cannot well be heard, let alone answered. What the listener hears and says from the musical subject's position constitutes knowledge of the music, a knowledge that cannot be contrasted or subordinated to an external norm. The knowledge itself is situational, and necessarily so; claims issued from an "objective," extrasituational position do not count as knowledge here, even if they are conceded to be true.

When Helen Schlegel, protagonist of E. M. Forster's *Howards End,* listens to the transition from the third movement to the Finale of Beethoven's Fifth, she reflects that "Beethoven took hold of the goblins [of the third movement] and made them do what he wanted. He appeared in person. He gave them a little push, and they began to walk in a major key instead of in a minor, and then—he blew with his mouth and they were scattered!"[44] Although Helen is no musicologist, she can hear a turning point as a change of mode. More importantly, she can hear the change of mode as communicative action and connect what she hears to the understanding that appearing in person is the primary technique or figure of human agency in the Fifth, and that the locus of appearing in person is a threshold, a transitional passage. (No one, meanwhile, could fail to observe that in "Cop Killer," Ice-T, too, appears in person.)

Admittedly, this account of the musical subject and its knowledge is overidealized and therefore too simple. For one thing, the possibility of knowledge implies the possibility of error; the listener as personified subject can always listen badly, or listen well and report on it badly. Errors, however, may be dialectical means as well as dead ends. An error may ignite a debate that advances knowledge in correcting the error, or a wrong claim may be made on the right topic, confirming or revealing the pertinence of the topic. When Wagner wants to justify a long hold on the fermata in the second measure of Beethoven's Fifth, he conjures up "the voice of Beethoven . . . from the grave" to enjoin, "Hold my fermata long and terribly."[45] He may be wrong that the held note should be "squeezed dry," but he, too, hears the necessity of Beethoven's appearing in person.

A deeper complication is that different listeners modify the summons to subjectivity in the process of answering it, especially when the answer crosses historical divides. In practice, most listeners personify a subject that the music only partly determines. This partly determinate subjectivity, however, may act less to limit than to enfranchise listening knowledge. A subject fully determined by the summons would be transfixed by it, a condition some music certainly encourages and some listeners seek. The effect would resemble the ideological "interpellation" theorized by Louis Althusser, in which the subject, answering a "hail," yields to a coercion misrecognized as freedom. In contrast, a measure of difference between the summons and answering subject may open a space hospitable to critical understanding, dissemination, negotiations of meaning and value. Across this space, the music acts like what Mikhail Bakhtin calls "internally persuasive discourse." In addressing us, it is "half-ours and half-someone else's. . . . It is not so much interpreted by us as it is further, that is, freely developed, applied to new material, new conditions; it enters into interanimating relationships with new contexts." In practice, musical and otherwise, the persuasive and interpellative modes of subject formation continually alternate, conflict, and intermingle.[46] Helen

Schlegel answers the hail of Beethoven's Fifth by identifying ecstatically with its "gusts of splendour . . . colour and fragrance broadcast on the field of battle, magnificent victory, magnificent death!" But she also makes what is half Beethoven's half her own: "The music summed up to her all that had happened or could happen in her career. . . . The notes meant this and that to her, and could have no other meaning."[47]

The second presupposition holds that the musical subject is not only implicated in broader psychocultural processes of subject formation, but so fully implicated that it cannot be understood apart from them. Put another way, we hear music only as situated subjects and hear *as* music only that acoustic imagery which somehow "expresses" part of our situatedness, our ensemble of ways to be. Music that strikes us as purely extrasituational—abstract, opaque, or alienating—counts, literally or figuratively, as noise.[48] Such musical noise has so much power to disrupt our routines of identification that it commonly provokes rage or visceral disgust—just as music that seems to transfigure those routines can evoke something like *jouissance*. Consequently, it is not enough to say, in contradiction to hard epistemological claims, that music *may* be interpreted in relation to nonmusical phenomena. Rather, music *must* be so interpreted or it cannot even be heard. It must be made interdiscursive in theory because it is always already interdiscursive in practice.

The third presupposition holds that the formative processes affecting the musical subject, like those affecting any subject, include some specifically aimed at supporting certain values or ideologies. The musical subject's legitimacy, its conformity and/or its resistance to legitimizing principles, is always in question. The issue of legitimacy may be raised in terms of a rigid division between allowable and unallowable identities, or in terms of norms against which a variety of deviant identities can proliferate. By the reckoning of Michel Foucault, the normalizing process begins its continuing rule over Western society in the mid eighteenth-century.[49] One conclusion is that the study of music in relation to deviant or illegitimate subjectivities, notably including those identified as feminine, homosexual, and exotic, does not constitute an appeal to special interests but is, instead, basic to the cultural project of music. It is no accident that both Beethoven's Fifth and "Cop Killer" address masculine—and "manly"—subjects. Admittedly, this last statement is risky and suggests that the study of the musical subject's legitimation can become glib and doctrinaire. Even at its most violent, the Fifth can be heard as incorporating important, problematical encounters with the feminine—in the oboe cadenza of the first movement, for example. It is intriguing that Helen Schlegel—or E. M. Forster—ignores or disparages such encounters as if they were impediments to exclusive identification with the musical subject as all-conquering virile youth. One result may be to put a queer spin on the figure of the conquering hero consistent, if not identical, with Beethoven's own idealization of it. No such spin seems likely for "Cop Killer." Like its sexual counterpart in Forster, Ice-T's racial position tethers him to a masculinity that is continually policed, both literally and figuratively. The result in "Cop Killer" is a hail—of bullets, the expressive vehicle of a hypermasculine subject who has virtually become an automaton, the youthful conqueror as killing machine. Beethoven, in short, is not Ice-T, and vice versa. But the contacts and divergences of the two are instructive when taken together, and in any case there is nothing unique in the risk of critical blindness. Any form of study can become glib and doctrinaire—even modernist musicology.

With these presuppositions in place, it should be possible to recast musicology as the rigorous and contestable study, theory, and practice of musical subjectivities. This would be a musicology in which the results of archival and analytical work, formerly prized in their own right, would become significant only in relation to subjective values— which is not to say the values of an atomized private inwardness, but those of a historically situated type of human agency. Such a musicology would satisfy the demand for human interest, not by making good on music's lack of meaning, but by ceasing to entertain the illusion that such a lack ever existed.

．　．　．　．　．

At this point a more detailed example is clearly in order. I offer one partly to set the stage for subsequent chapters and partly to show that music "itself," even in its supposedly most autonomous form, the Viennese Classical style, can sometimes be heard to lead the way in accentuating the mediated character of its own immediacy.

Charles Rosen writes that Mozart's Divertimento for String Trio, K. 563,

is an interesting precursor of the last quartets of Beethoven, in its transference of divertimento form, with two dance movements and two slow movements (one a set of variations), into the realm of serious chamber music, making purely intimate what had been public, and, as Beethoven was to do in many of the short, interior movements of his late chamber works, transfiguring the "popular" element without losing sight of its provenance. In Mozart's Divertimento, the synthesis of a learned display of three-part writing and a popular genre is accomplished without ambiguity or constraint.[50]

The key terms in this paragraph are "synthesis," "transfigur[ation]," and "purely intimate." Their effect is to posit for the music an effortless, exalted immediacy, which Rosen identifies as the product of Mozart's mastery of divergent compositional styles, the popular and the learned. The divergence, a potentially mediating or alienating element, disappears without "ambiguity or constraint"—that is, without a trace—into the higher (synthetic, transfigured) immediacy of "serious chamber music." This same immediacy, coded as "intimacy," also marks the disappearance of a formerly public expressiveness. It is not the culturally resonant process of negotiating between the intimate and the public that appears in the music, but only its homogeneous outcome. Presumably, residual traces of the process would count as aesthetic flaws.

But what if the music were heard, not as the site where its contexts vanish, but precisely as the site where they appear? Not long ago I attended a performance of K. 563. Its texture, which as Rosen suggests includes a great deal of complex three-voice writing, struck me not merely as transparent but as painfully transparent, transparent to excess. The instrumental voices seemed to be entwining and disengaging with something like physical friction—or so I thought until I realized that this figurative idea was close to being literal. The friction *was* physical, or, more exactly, corporeal. By emphasizing both the linearity of each instrumental voice and the textural differentiation among the voices, and by doing so in the spare, exposed medium of the string trio, Mozart was foregrounding the effort required to produce the music in performance. This effort was specifically bodily, conveyed by the bodies of the performers to and through the bodies of their instruments, so that the music became a tangible projection or articulation of bodily energy.

At an early moment of the performance, this recognition added a silent fourth voice to the ensemble. I was no longer simply listening to a string trio, but specifically not-listening to a string quartet. (This moment of Derridean *différance* was enhanced, though in retrospect, by my understanding that the combination of violin, viola, and cello, unlike the quartet combination, was not yet standardized when Mozart wrote K. 563.) Had the work been a quartet, its trio sonority intimated, the bodily labor that went into it would have been effaced. The quartet combination has a sonority resonant enough to envelop its constituent voices without blurring them but open enough to distance any impression of sensuousness—an "intellectual" sonority, perfectly suited for being idealized in Goethean terms as a conversation among four intelligent people. A skillfully managed trio can, of course, approximate the same effect, but Mozart confines that sort of management largely to the trio's two minuet movements, the only ones that offer the sort of light musical entertainment suggested by the title "Divertimento." Most of the rest, the "serious chamber music" that, in ironic contrast to the minuets, lacks overt associations with the body, renders palpable the muscular effort of arms and fingers, the rhythmic sway of the players' torsos.

The body thus represented is not a natural fact but a social figure: the performer's (and by proxy the composer's) body shuttling, with ambiguity and constraint, between labor and pleasure. In revealing that figure, K. 563 opens the question of why it is usually concealed. Adorno's notion that the Festspielhaus at Bayreuth, with its invisible orchestra, embodied a bourgeois disavowal of behind-the-scenes labor may or may not apply to Wagner but seems to fit neither Mozart's historical moment nor his medium.[51] More pertinent is the suggestion by the art historian Norman Bryson that Western representational painting typically conceals the labor that goes into it, in part because the distancing of the *palpable* body has historically served as a cardinal sign for the condition of being civilized.[52] Mozart's Divertimento collapses this signifying structure; it casts its most obviously civilized (and civilizing) feature, its learned three-part writing, as not only compatible with but thoroughly contingent on a heightened corporeality. In so doing, the Divertimento intimates that the artistic and social distancing of the body is fictive at best, fictitious at worst—something resembling what would later come to be called a defense mechanism. Push that thought a bit further and inflect it darkly, and you get the dynamic of delusion and desire that underpins the ambiguities of *Così fan tutte.*

Once recognized, Mozart's staging of the body in K. 563 alters the epistemic value of Rosen's statement that the music seamlessly unites public and private spheres of expression. What seemed to be a historically informed act of criticism becomes an ideologically fraught act of praise. (Not that the two categories exclude each other! But there is a shift of emphasis.) The body figured by the music is decidedly public and specifically artisanal; in this capacity, it is also decidedly masculine and specifically positioned within a fraternal, homosocial order.[53]

There is, however, a single episode, marked by the discontinuity of its presentation, in which the music exchanges this figure of the public, artisanal, masculine body for its contrary. The episode occurs during the second slow movement, a set of variations on a quasi-popular tune. Variations 1 and 2 are ornamental, but not routinely so. Their ornamentation aims at a surplus of both labor and pleasure; its contrapuntal activity and expressive intensity heighten with each reprise in the melodic pattern A B A' B', turning a simple strophic alternation into a kind of fantasia. Intellectual rather than sensuous, "virile" rather than "effeminate," this ornamentation serves not to enhance the theme but to fragment and recast it as if to some higher purpose.[54] The texture is heteroglot in both technique and expression. The A and B strains of the theme, originally all of a piece, become antithetical; brilliant passagework and learned counterpoint jostle and overlap; contrastive voices—lyrical, dry, animated, dramatic—sound simultaneously. The cello, progressively liberating itself from the plodding bass line of the theme's first strain, is especially dynamic. The second strain of Variation 2 brings a climax, redoubled in its extended reprise,

Example 1. Mozart, Divertimento for String Trio, K. 563, fourth movement
(Andante), Variation 2.

as statements of an angular trilling figure pile up in close counterpoint, all but obliterating any trace of the hapless theme (Example 1).

Variation 3 follows like a sleeve suddenly drawn inside-out. Ornamentation disappears, and with it all sense of dynamism; the mode
changes from major to minor; the style becomes uniform, transmut-
ing its earlier play with learned counterpoint into a texture suggestive
of archaic polyphony (Example 2). A pianissimo hush combines with
a warm, tightly woven sonority to produce a tranquil breathing space.
Withdrawing from labor, withdrawing their labor, the performers (the
imaginary performers performed by the real ones) appropriate their
bodily energy by turning it inward. In so doing, they posit a sensitive,
enclosed interiority that is at once private, contemplative, and feminine. They play, though overheard, a passage for themselves.

Nothing seamless here. And nothing long: the variation, slow as it
seems, is painfully brief. Variation 4, last of the series, follows as a
peroration, but one that raises more questions than it answers. Here

Example 2. Mozart, K. 563, fourth movement (Andante), Variation 3.

the plainest melody in the movement is enveloped by the most brilliant passagework. The melody, on viola, still belongs to the withdrawn, archaizing privacy of Variation 3; an inner voice, a simplification of the theme in cantus firmus–like long notes, it is suggestive of an essence bared, a primary truth discovered through introspection. In contrast—whether in synthesis or contradiction—an expansive walking bass on cello and sweeping arabesques on violin carry the extrovert display of Variations 1 and 2 to its peak (Example 3). The mixture is obviously unstable, and in the end it simply comes apart, leaving a tiny lyrical codetta behind to reminisce on the first phrase of the theme.

With Variation 4 the figures of the public and private bodies themselves form a kind of counterpoint—or is it an unrelieved dissonance? Is the public body always a figure of excess, appointed, in line with Jean-Jacques Rousseau's argument in his *Second Discourse,* to disguise by sophisticated workmanship the alienation of civil society from primitive health and vigor?[55] Or is this body in its artisanal form

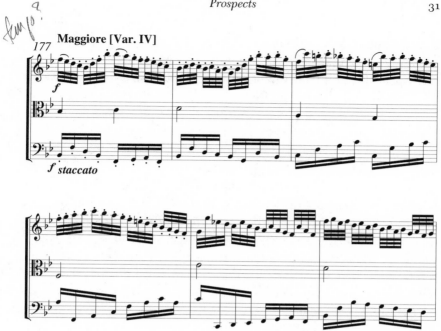

Example 3. Mozart, K. 563, fourth movement (Andante), Variation 4.

a vehicle of reintegration in which vigor and pleasure combine effectively with the technical and mechanical labor characteristic of the arts in civil society? Is the sensitive private body the origin and founding truth from which the public body derives? Is it the artist's body rather than the artisan's? Or is it a secondary formation in which the artisan is deceptively idealized as the modern figure of the artist?

Here, however, I imagine the sound of a skeptical voice. "This is all well and good," it says pointedly, and with some tartness. "But where is Mozart's *music* in this series of questions?" The shortest answer is that the questions are in the music. Mozart provokes them by making his music behave as it does and trusting to the listener to hear the music within a broader field of rhetorical, expressive, and discursive behaviors. The questions engage us, with varying degrees of directness and displacement, whenever something that they bring to the music—the overwrought texture of Variations 1 and 2, the archaizing strangeness of Variation 3, the antipodean rhetoric of Variation 4—arrests our attention, affects our pleasure, or incites us to intermittent, silently verbalized commentary on what we are hearing. The same questions may affect the mind's ear as it replays the music in retrospect. From the postmodernist standpoint I have been advocating here, listening is not an immediacy alienated from a later reflection, but a mode of dialogue. And like all dialogue, it is fully participatory no matter which partner is doing the talking.

It follows that the aim of musicology, ideally conceived, is to continue the dialogue of listening. At stake in the current crisis of the discipline is the participatory scope of that dialogue: the issue of whether and how to (dis)locate the boundary between the musical and the "extramusical." A little over fifty years ago, a similar crisis arose in another discipline, a discipline that, like musicology, is primarily concerned with phenomena strongly felt and semantically indirect. Arguing against the idea that only medical doctors should be allowed to practice psychoanalysis, Sigmund Freud speculated on the curriculum of an imaginary psychoanalytic college:

Much would have to be taught in it which is also taught by the medical faculty: alongside of depth psychology . . . there would be an introduction to biology, as much as possible of the science of sexual life, and familiarity with the symptomotology of psychiatry. On the other hand, analytic instruction would include branches of knowledge which are remote from medicine and which the doctor does not come across in his practice: the history of civilization, mythology, the psychology of religion and the science of literature. Unless he is at home in these areas, an analyst can make nothing of a large amount of his material.[56]

Freud's remarks translate with uncanny aptness into musicological terms. Faced with the question, Where is the music? a postmodernist musicology would—will—reply that wherever it may be, we can only get to it by getting beyond it.

Two

From the Other to the Abject

Music as Cultural Trope

[handwritten: he has co-opted into PM perspective! SK into]

Assume for the moment that my first chapter has told the right story. The loose ensemble of contemporary efforts to understand reason, language, and subjectivity in relation to concrete human activities rather than to universal principles has sparked a classical paradigm shift in musicology.[1] Formalism and positivism, although far from dead, are no longer hegemonic; music, particularly classical music, is increasingly interpreted, not only as an object that invites aesthetic reception, but also as an activity that vitally shapes the personal, social, and cultural identities of its listeners. As we have seen, the epistemic character of this shift derives from a rethinking of several key topics in modernist thought. Postmodernisms resituate reason among its objects, install local generality in the economy of explanation, affirm subjectivity as a decentered mobility, and treat communication as a mode of action, subsuming the constative under the performative and undoing the division of human agency into distinct psychical, social, and cultural subfields.

This epistemic shift, however, is practical as well as theoretical; it has substantial moral and political implications. These implications need to be spelled out, both to show what is humanly at stake in the contention between modernist and postmodernist musical understanding and to make the connections with wider fields of action and value that will be necessary for either the understanding of classical music or the music itself to get much of a hearing in the future.

What follows is a kind of prelude to that hearing, an attempt to theorize the terms on which an invaluable body of music can survive the dissolution of the cultural order that housed it. Classical music and the modern subject have interlocking histories, the crux of which is the formation of the concept of the aesthetic in the mid-eighteenth century. Thereafter, music figures with increasing regularity and importance as a formative element of subjectivity, or more exactly of subjectivity at its extremes. Although socially defined as a mere pastime, music functions both as the paradigmatic means by which the aesthetic elevates and universalizes the subject—this, more than the canonizing of particular works or styles, is what constitutes bodies of music as "classical"—and also as the paradigmatic means by which the subject is humbled and destabilized, even debased and annihilated. Modern representations of music dwell often on these functions and their sometimes conflictual, sometimes cyclical interplay, but modernist thinking about music tends to disavow them—even in the act of invoking them—by focusing on the supposed isolation of music from discursive meaning and therefore from the contingent worlds of its production. What postmodern knowledge offers classical music is the chance to acknowledge and explore, to de- and reconstruct, its relationship to modern subjectivity, and in so doing to form a different relationship to the postmodern subjectivities that may now be in the making.

·　·　·　·　·

By the turn of the 1990s, literary and social theory was laying heavy stress on the discursive logic through which dominant ideologies commonly route their power. We can call this the logic of alterity. It works by setting up oppositions between a normative, unitary self, usually invested with universal significance, and a plurality of deviant or imperfect others. The others are defined by negation; they are everything the self is not, the mirrors in which the self recognizes its own identity. As we will see, this system of oppositionality is far from stable. The other represents not only what the self is not but also what it may wish to be. Furthermore, the identity that the self recognizes through the other is necessarily mystified, imaginary in the Lacanian sense. But the logic of alterity is hard to resist, partly because its field of operation is very wide and partly because its capacity for mystification is endless. Its historical force has been (and remains) to privilege masculinity over femininity, hetero- over homosexuality, whiteness over nonwhiteness, the West over the East, civilization over the "primitive," high over low culture, and higher over lower social classes.[2]

The argument of this chapter is that music has been closely tied to the logic of alterity since the mid-eighteenth century at the latest; that this tie depends on a systematic contradiction in the identification of self and other; and that the production and understanding of music have alike served as cultural institutions for perpetuating this contradiction. "Music" in this context refers not so much to an acoustic phenomenon as to an object constituted in representation. It is music as a cultural trope produced by musical aesthetics, imaginative literature, and, reflexively, by musical composition.[3]

Music scholarship was quick to take interest in the logic of alterity, especially in relation to gender and cultural identity. Recent studies have traced the processes of "othering" in musical historiography, tonality and sonata form, musical genre, the signifying practices of particular compositions, and the definition of "musicality" as a personal trait.[4] Broadly speaking, these studies have figured the musical articulation of self against other as the opposition of form and sensuous plenitude. As Leo Treitler observes, "If there is a single word that can express what is for the modern period the essential attribute of 'Western music' . . . that word is 'form,' flanked by all its qualifiers (rational, logical, unified, concise, symmetrical, organic, etc.)." Form is associated with closure, unity, and—perhaps above all—structure, "the idea that every note is necessary to the whole and no note is superfluous to it." By this account, form is a dynamic principle of containment or regulation, a continual foreclosure of contingent or excessive sonority. And as such it is opposable both to "oriental" luxuriance and to Western "decadence" and "effeminacy."[5]

When music historiography constructs these, or parallel, oppositions, it produces an other within a field of musical practice in order to clear a space within that same field for the self. The same thing can be said to happen when musical compositions unfold through the opposition of stable to unstable or recurrent to nonrecurrent features. It is no accident, suggests Susan McClary, that "chromaticism, which

enriches tonal music but must finally be resolved to the triad for the
sake of closure, takes on the cultural cast of 'femininity.'" For tonal
music in general depends on a "narrative adventure away from and
back to [the] tonic" that must pass through, and ultimately annex or
master, an "alien terrain."[6]

But matters do not end here. The logic of alterity operates not only
internally, within a musical terrain, but also externally, upon music as
a whole. And when the internal logic of alterity yields to the external,
music as a whole stands with the other. McClary observes this process
with specific reference to femininity, remarking that "in Western culture, music *itself* is always in danger of being regarded as the feminine
other that circumvents reason and arouses desire."[7] As we will see,
this association of femininity and music as other is not just one example among many; it becomes paradigmatic at a particular historical
moment. What I want to foreground here, however, is the way this
"othering" of music stands *in contradiction* to the process by which
musical form constructs a musical self. If the self speaks through music when form contains (limits and encloses) sonority, then formally
articulate music cannot stand as other. Yet the very presence within
music of an opposition between form and sonority presupposes that
something in music must be other. The cultural "regard" that sees
music itself as other must be beckoned by that something. And in a
cultural order that regards music itself as other, a musical work or
style cannot overcome otherness by form without, in so doing, overcoming its own musicality.

Far from requiring resolution, this antinomy has been basic to the
modern institution of music as a cultural trope. Tracing this institution
will require a complexly additive argument, proceeding through five
stages: (1) a more detailed characterization of the logic of alterity, a
process less straightforward than it seems in the abstract; (2) a look at
how the logic of alterity overtly constructs the self in two exemplary
texts of nineteenth-century aesthetics, one literary, one musical, and
how the musical instance distinctively involves the antinomy between
the internal and external forms of this logic; (3) a critical look at the
same process working covertly in a major twentieth-century work of
musical history and, correlatively, in a nineteenth-century composition; (4) a theorization of the typical means and ends for the construc-

tion of music as other; and (5) an account of how and why modernist musicology depends on perpetuating the antinomy between internal and external logics of alterity while postmodernist musicologies depend on that antinomy's undoing.

.   .   .   .   .

The logic of alterity is apparently a special case of binary thinking, although, as we will see, it is hard to formulate binary oppositions without delegitimizing one of its terms as other. Although the other is constructed in order to be mastered, it need not be overtly or grossly stigmatized, even though that happens with depressing regularity and a stigma, in any case, is never far to seek. In its most persuasive and therefore most problematical forms, the logic of alterity invests the other with considerable allure and even with a measure of (usually arcane) power and truth. Yet the underlying hierarchical principle remains in force, and even gains in force, when the self gives the other some latitude to play seductively against the norm.

Even gains in force. Except when driven by sociocultural panic or pronounced epistemic uncertainty, the logic of alterity works best more as ground than as figure. Self-other binaries gain in force when they admit ambiguities, hover or withdraw behind a variety of intermediate forms, show that certain terms count as self here and other there, substitute one opposition for another, mix the terms of parallel oppositions, and in general complicate or defer the recognition of their own role. The binaries serve less to generate discourse than to delimit and, finally, to close it. The recognition of self against other is positioned both at and as the end of discourse, both as a source of aesthetic pleasure (in finality, totality, unity) and of critical recognition (the binary as truth, structure, insight).

In the modern era this positioning, and the dynamism and deferral that go with it, derive in part from a discontinuity in the concept of the self. Although the self sets the standard for psychocultural identity, it has little identity of its own; its normative character tends to make it anonymous. As Michel Foucault suggests, modern individualization is "descending":

those on whom [power] is exercised [now] tend to become more strongly individualized [than those who exercise it]. . . . The child [becomes] more individualized than the adult, the patient more than the healthy man, the madman and the delinquent more than the normal and the non-delinquent. In each case, it is towards the first of these pairs that all the individualizing mechanisms are turned in our civilization; and when one wishes to individualize the healthy, normal, and law-abiding adult, it is always by asking him how much of the child he has in him, what secret madness lies within him, what fundamental crime he has dreamt of committing.[8]

By dwelling with the other, mingling with it in an interplay at once inspiriting and threatening, the self can appropriate the fullness, density, and specificity it would otherwise lack. Whether it can do so unaffected is another question.

In general, the self is associated with reason, activity, progression, unity, and the integrity of boundaries, the other with irrationality, passivity, stasis or regression, fragmentation, and the crossing or dissolution of boundaries. Reversals of the privilege that the self draws from this network of dualities are possible, at least rhetorically, and to good effect; hierarchical structures can be deflated by inversion, temporarily or metaphorically escaped, even subjected to critique. But the structure of privilege can accommodate a great deal of reversal without real damage, and many such reversals willy-nilly repeat the key terms of dominant structures in the very act of resisting them.[9]

Self-other dualities do not necessarily display an overtly political content. They can operate in purely conceptual or aesthetic spheres, thereby implying a cultural politics without declaring one. As postmodernist theories insist, seemingly abstract categories always do concrete cultural work, serving social and disciplinary interests and shaping subjectivities. For better or worse, structures of thought cut across and proliferate beyond the appointed boundaries of thought. No wonder, then, as we will see shortly, that certain aesthetic dualities have historically burst the narrow bounds of strictly aesthetic interest to energize cultural politics of the most passionate sort.

Precisely because this is so, it is important to acknowledge frankly that critiques of the logic of alterity can easily slide into glibness, tendentiousness, or myopia. Not all dualities are automatically or consistently oppressive, nor are all historically oppressive dualities readily expendable as elements in art or thought. Nonetheless, binary thinking must clearly be understood as a historical, not just a conceptual, phenomenon, the consequences of which have too often been inhumane or worse. To stay with musical aesthetics alone, it is no accident that Richard Wagner's anti-Semitism, Heinrich Schenker's dream of Germanic political and cultural hegemony, and Charles Ives's misogyny and homophobia all grounded themselves in binary articulations of musical style. Judaic superficiality (bourgeois and melodically discrete) opposes Germanic organicism (revolutionary and motivically seamless) in Wagner; French Enlightenment superficiality (vertical and mechanistic) opposes Germanic organicism (linear and vitalistic) in Schenker; effeminate superficiality (modish and sensual) opposes virile spirituality (recalcitrant and rugged) in Ives. Nor can these dualities be written off as merely blinkered and outmoded; communities of interest persist. Wagner's claim that Mendelssohn could only mimic authentically great art remains the basis of modern Mendelssohn reception; contrapuntal complexity and structural integration are still the stereotypical signs of musical profundity; and the same virility myth purveyed by Ives animates the much-publicized recent discomfiture over the likelihood that Schubert was homosexual.[10] Dualities, like histories, often happen twice: the first time as politics, the second as ideology.

Binary thinking, in short, always has a moral dimension. It has underwritten dubious values far too often, and it has the power to implicate us, whether we like it or not, in those same values. Admittedly, recognizing this will often lead us to resist the suasions of conceptual or aesthetic dualities, including some that seem reasonable or even cherishable. But the same commitment will just as often lead us to make legible the resistances, or, better yet, the positive disseminal energies, that arise within the very works that articulate the dualities we question.

It should be added, too, that binary thinking may already be historical in another sense. In the present era of fiber optics, digital information technology, and global economy, the logic of alterity may be less culturally central than it once was. The old hierarchies are no longer needed to do ideological work now better conducted along all-embracing data networks that transform individual subjects into interchangeable members of a vast "atomized collective."[11] But this "informatics of domination," as Haraway calls it,[12] does not in fact wholly disempower the logic of alterity and in important ways may empower it further. The dualities that once claimed, compellingly but vulnerably, to be present and normal, the very structure of the real, now hover alluringly as nostalgic and prelapsarian. The old adage that the only paradise is the paradise one has lost takes on a troubling new resonance when that paradise lost is the transcendental security of the self against its menagerie of others.

.   .   .   .   .

And now to cases. In 1853, Matthew Arnold wrote a magisterial rejection of all poetry, famously including his own "Empedocles on Aetna," in which sentiment predominates over the representation of action, expressive mobility over linear construction, a passivizing address to the transitory interests of the reader over an energizing address to what is "permanent and the same" in human nature. In thus rejecting the performative for the constative, though more in sorrow than anger, Arnold felt that he was rejecting nothing less than the confusions and corruptions of the modern world itself, with its misguided, merely transitory goals of "progress . . . industrial development, and social amelioration."[13]

Thirty-five years later, Nietzsche diagnosed the problem of Wagner and Wagnerism in much the same terms, linking the malaise of modernity to the temporal laxity and passivizing audience address of Wagner's music. Unable to shape an organic totality, Wagner translates his incapacity into a principle of atomization. His art is performative in extremis, "theatrical" in the most pejorative sense; its pathos "holds its breath, refuses to let go an extreme feeling, achieves a terrifying *duration* of states when even a moment threatens to strangle us." Drawing, like Arnold, on a rhetoric of degeneration, but more in anger than sorrow, Nietzsche castigates Wagner as a neurosis ("une nevrose"): decadent, diseased, castrating, feminizing, and dangerously seductive to youth.[14]

It would be easy enough to dismiss Arnold and Nietzsche as one-sided. Surely dualities can be utilized more dispassionately! It is by no means clear, however, that the intention to be even-handed can neutralize the logic of alterity. Perhaps Arnold and Nietzsche offer only particularly glaring examples of what happens whenever we try to process a particular work or style on the basis of a binary concept. Binary oppositions, as Derrida has argued, are always implicitly hierarchical but never fully stable. They are always threatening to crumble from within, and the effort to stabilize them enhances their hierarchical effect.[15] Concurrently, as Foucault has argued, power, knowledge, and disciplinary discourse continually intertwine with each other; conceptual energies are always also social energies.[16] On both counts, we risk allying ourselves with the cultural agenda of domination whenever we embrace a duality, however abstract or depoliticized, that repeats the logic of alterity. The energies of valuation have high voltage; a duality is a treacherous instrument to ply.

Just how treacherous Arnold and Nietzsche make clear. Arnold calls for a modern poetry subservient to classical Greek models and, therefore, willy-nilly, to the interests of the socially privileged university men whose education was based on the Greek classics. The antidote to modernity is a kind of donnish paternalism. Ideally, that would mean living masters, contemporaries who could be figured as pedagogues on the Greek model, transmitters of both love and wisdom. What the young writer "wants" (wishes and lacks) "is a hand to guide him through the confusion" of "present times" and "a voice to prescribe to him the aim he should keep in view." But such a hand and voice are sadly lacking. The writer can find a "steadying and composing effect" only through "commerce with the classics": "All that can be looked for, all that can be desired, is, that his attention should be fixed on excellent models; that he may reproduce . . . something of their excellence, by penetrating himself with their works and by catching their spirit."[17] In a textbook illustration of Freud's dictum that living, for the ego, means being loved by the superego,[18] Arnold redirects the subject's longing for personal guidance toward a depersonalized authority that becomes the object of an eroticized submission. (Note the unwitting multiple meanings of "commerce" and the suggestive sequence, rhetorically put awry, of desire, penetration, reproduction.) The aspiring modern subject is urged to identify with the "aims and demands upon life" of precisely those exemplary "great men" who judge the modern age to be "impeding and disabling." This "disciplined" subject will then "esteem himself fortunate if he can succeed in banishing from his mind all feelings of contradiction, and irritation, and impatience; in order to delight himself with the contemplation of some noble action of a heroic time, and to enable others, through the representation of it, to delight in it also."[19] High culture becomes a narcotic, to be transmitted—dispensed—through a barely sublimated nostalgia. The ironic result is that the contemplation of classical mimesis does not cure the lyrical stupefying pathos of modern culture but, instead, perpetuates it.

Unlike Arnold, Nietzsche finds no romance in authoritarian ideals and only a dangerous charm in their narcotic properties. Indeed, his attack on Wagner's lyric paralysis is also an attack on the mystified repressiveness of the German Reich, the ultranationalism and anti-Semitism spread by the rampaging "*Reich*-worm, the famous *Rhinoxera*" (punningly, with allusions to Siegfried: Rhinepest). Wagner's stage, he writes, "requires one thing only—*Teutons!*—Definition of the Teuton: obedience and long legs." Yet Nietzsche's text is full of blood and iron, "declar[ing] war" on Wagner the modern Minotaur (he "robs our youth, he even robs our women") and Wagner the "female Wagnerian." The cultural effect of Wagnerism is "an ever growing indifference against all severe, noble, conscientious training in the service of art."[20] At Bayreuth "one renounces the right . . . to one's courage. . . . One is common people, audience, herd, female, pharisee, voting cattle."[21] Wagner's slippery character is even un-German, perhaps a bit Jewish: "His father was an actor by the name of Geyer. A Geyer [vulture] is practically an Adler [eagle; a Jewish name]."[22] In sum, Nietzsche's polemical rhetoric reinstates the ideal of ascetic, bellicose manhood on which both the ideal of the Reich and the antithetical image of its other, the wheedling Jew, depend.

Nietzsche's opposition to Wagner, however, cannot escape and at bottom even depends on an undercurrent of susceptibility, fascination, and love. Reflecting in his autobiographical *Ecce Homo* on polemics past, Nietzsche proudly claims to "know better than anyone else of what tremendous things Wagner is capable—the fifty worlds of alien ecstasies for which no one besides him had wings. . . . That in which we are related—that we have suffered more profoundly, also from each other, than men of this century are capable of suffering— will link our names again and again, eternally." The two men are to be joined in a kind of mystic marriage, a symbolic repetition of the "days of trust, of cheerfulness . . . never darkened by a single cloud" for which Nietzsche says he would "let go cheap the whole rest of my human relationships." And for all Nietzsche's scathing rhetoric about it, Wagner's music remains part of this union. The *Siegfried Idyll,* at least, figures prominently among the small handful of pieces that Nietzsche finds indispensable.[23] And then there is *Tristan.*

"To this day," writes Nietzsche, "I am still looking for a work that equals the dangerous fascination and the gruesome [*schauerlich*] and sweet infinity of *Tristan*—and look in all the arts in vain."[24] A passage from *Beyond Good and Evil,* to which *The Case of Wagner* makes an apparently casual reference,[25] suggests that this comment is truer than it knows. Here Nietzsche imagines a "supra-German" music, "deeper, mightier, perhaps more evil and more mysterious" than any yet composed. Such a music would "be at home" in the amoral world of "great beautiful lonely cats of prey" yet be hospitable to the "last gleams" of a "sinking, almost incomprehensible *moral* world"—Wagner's world— as well. Its "rarest charm . . . would be that it no longer knew anything of good and evil, except that some fleeting sailor's nostalgia, some slight golden shadows and tender regret ran over it now and then."[26] But surely this non-Wagnerian music of the future had been written already—by Wagner. For what fits Nietzsche's description better than the nostalgic sailor's song that opens the first act of *Tristan* and prefigures the "deeper . . . more mysterious" monody, *die alte Weise,* that opens the third?

In constructing and mastering Wagner as the other, then, Nietzsche also sets up a deconstruction and partly undoes the mastery. This reversion to the other has no parallel in Arnold, who testifies to the absolute rule of the self by publicly humbling himself before it with a moral passion that borders on masochism. The case may be extreme, but the difference is telling. Reversion to a supposedly mastered other is above all *musical.* It arises in music and musical aesthetics in order to mitigate the contradiction by which music, being other, can be identified with the self only at the cost of its own musicality. Reversion makes use of the relative freedom enjoyed by what is marginal, secondary, or extrinsic to recoup at least part of that cost.

Although not inevitable, reversion has a strong enough impetus to seem so, especially in the long run. Once the logic of alterity begins to act on music from the inside as well as the outside, something that happens with increasing insistence after the birth of aesthetics in the eighteenth century, the instability of music as a cultural trope becomes almost irrepressible. The rogues' gallery of musical selves I compiled earlier bears out the point.

First, Wagner famously opens the *Ring* cycle by depicting the rippling, undine-haunted waters of the Rhine. The music of the *Das Rheingold* Prelude, he claims, came to him whole cloth in a dream vision. Yet parts of it bear a remarkable—an uncanny?—family resemblance to the depiction of rippling, undine-haunted waters in Mendelssohn's overture *Die schöne Melusine. Parsifal* suggests that the irony in this is more than casual. As Leon Botstein has argued,

It is indeed ironic that at the end of his life Wagner, in *Parsifal,* not only extended musical language but brilliantly demonstrated his own mastery of the Mendelssohnian rhetoric of *St. Paul* and *Elijah.* In his last work Wagner reveals, both ideologically and musically, the lingering power of the image of Mendelssohn, particularly Mendelssohn's ambition to render music an ethical, cultural, and religious force. The contrast between Parsifal, the innocent fool, and Amfortas, the privileged son of a king, and the redemption of the latter by the former are distillations of Wagner's career and ambition.[27]

In this context, the presence in Wagner's grail motive of the same Dresden Amen that Mendelssohn places near the beginning of his *Reformation* Symphony suggests more than just recourse to a common vocabulary.

Second, Schenker generally speaks of music as an "art of connection" in a masculinist language of mastery and procreative power. But when he tries to account for music's "allegorical appeal to the human soul," he feminizes.[28] Just as the "living organism" of music develops from background to foreground, the human being "develops in body and mind as from a background to a foreground, from his first existence in his mother's body, from the first cry at the moment of birth, through all the years of childhood and maturity till old age." In this analogy, the musical background stands in the place of the mother's body; it is, as Schenker says elsewhere, a womb.[29]

Like Wagner's reversions to Mendelssohn, this one carries more than a casual irony. Schenker also claims that "within the mystery of [organic connection between background and foreground] lies the complete independence of music from the outside world."[30] Unlike the human being, the musical organism does not separate gradually from the mother's body to complete its life cycle in the outside world. The musical foreground is never born, no matter how much it develops; it remains as remote from the outside world as the background does. We might even say, since the foreground is what we actually hear, that it is precisely what makes the interiority of the mother's body audible. Originating in a womb, music continuously reproduces the condition of the womb; the art of connection is the art of regression.

Finally, even Ives could not help yielding, at least once, to a music evocative of the "feminine" fluidity and tenderness he generally found anathema. Celebrating a moment of epiphany shared with his wife the summer after their marriage, he fills "The Housatonic at Stockbridge" with the dreamy liquid murmur of maternal nature, borne on multilayered currents of string sonority. Even though the image of this "contented realm" is meant (as we will see in chapter 7) to be secondary in the end, a halo around the emergent self, its independent presence is indelible. This is especially so when, after seeming to lose or repudiate the idyllic string sonority, the music ends by reverting to it in a brief moment of exceptional poignancy and warmth.

The possibility of reversion is also built into certain musical forms. Do sonata recapitulations, as Susan McClary suggests, master "feminine" second-group materials originally heard in the dominant by bringing them under the tonic? Surely many of them do, sometimes as drama, sometimes (perhaps more insidiously) as routine. But then again, the recapitulation of first-group materials is commonly subject to variation, abbreviation, or "secondary development," the last generally involving movement to the subdominant and other "flat" keys. The self may be transformed by the other it masters; or the other, supposedly mastered, may take over the discourse, with the harmony, of the self. Reversion may never be certain, even in the circumstances just described, but it is always more than likely.

In the logic of alterity, then, music is always, ultimately, on the other side. No wonder that musicality often counts as the definitive sign of otherness in general. It is tempting to find in this allegiance a defense of music—always meaning music as a modern cultural

trope—against cultural and political critiques that find it too much
the factotum of the self. But although a feeling for reversion can help
renew both our pleasure and our critical understanding, reversion is
still locked into the logic it opposes. Social and epistemic authority
still gravitate powerfully toward the self, sometimes with a will, sometimes in spite of it. Can we somehow *open out* the logic of alterity so
that our pleasure and understanding are less constrained by it?

.   .   .   .   .

Carl Dahlhaus tries to answer that question affirmatively in his magisterial *Nineteenth-Century Music*. If he fails, as proves to be the case,
it is because he is unwilling to cross the divide that separates the ideal
of form from the unidealizable force of dissemination. A critique of
his project may help make that crossing possible.

Nineteenth-Century Music is a veritable seismograph of the paradigm shift that is, or may, be replacing a formalist/positivist with a
postmodernist musicology. Formidable in the depth and breadth of
its cultural allusiveness, the book is nonetheless a model of "structural
history," an account of "the setting and breaking of norms," of formal
problems and procedures in (d)evolution. It mounts a perhaps last-
ditch defense of formalism, at least as applied to the "inescapable"
canon of German masterpieces. To these works, which represent music as "art in the strong sense," Dahlhaus accords a "relative autonomy"
that exempts them from concrete social-historical understanding.
Their meaning, accordingly, and their interrelationships with the conditions of their production and reception, are affirmatively under-
specified, rendered only in topical or allusive silhouettes. For Dahlhaus, social history becomes salient only to music of doubtful artistic
status.[31]

Nineteenth-Century Music seeks to sort out the century's European art music into "twin styles" identified with Beethoven and Rossini. Dahlhaus's troubles with this project may include misreading
Rossini, as Philip Gossett has suggested, but I believe they run even
deeper.[32] The duality of the twin styles quickly becomes an opposition
of self and other. The Beethovenian style produces "relatively autonomous" musical "works" that develop the consequences of "thematic
ideas." Such works claim a textual power, on a par with works of lit-

erature and philosophy, to embody meanings that require active, "exegetical" listening to be "deciphered." The Rossinian style does not so much produce "works" as "events," "mere recipes for performance" in which "melodic ideas" are reiterated without consequence but to "magical" effect. The magic is utterly immediate; Rossinian "events" do not need to be understood, only passively heard, to captivate their audience.[33]

Dahlhaus does his best to keep this duality from overprivileging narrative and Beethoven; he is, in fact, trying to rehabilitate Rossini's reputation as a mere "prankster" compared to "the titanic author of the Ninth Symphony." But the logic of alterity resists the dispersal of privilege. Whereas Dahlhaus's language about Beethoven is purely laudatory, his language about Rossini tends to follow a rhetorical sequence from sharp depreciation to a somewhat equivocal appreciation. "Beethoven's themes," we are told, "may be terse or almost nonexistent without doing serious damage to the key issue, form." But "the substrate of Rossini's melodies and harmonies . . . is trivial; his rhythms have a sharpness of focus that emphasizes the banal; his formal designs are guilelessly simplistic. . . . Yet all these factors complement each other, forming an aesthetic and compositional unity in which cleverness and primitivity merge in such a way that each element thrives on the other."[34]

More broadly, Dahlhaus casts Beethoven as a heroic, world-historical subject who "thrusts" on his age "a portentous phenomenon of far-reaching significance," the "new insight," of which Rossini is "completely oblivious," that music may have textlike meaning. Rossini, by contrast, is no more than a representative man, a kind of inspired ventriloquist's dummy for the Zeitgeist. His mercurial music "becomes intelligible when, without undue psychologizing, we conceive of [it] as an expression of its moment in history, including the history of the human psyche. Something in his comic operas . . . causes their buffoonery to turn for an instant (an instant is all it takes) into the demonic. And this factor is mysteriously one of a kind with the sugar-coated pathos of his serious operas." Rossini is cast, if not as a prankster, then as a hysteric, the feminized other of the imperious, manly Beethoven. Where Beethoven "claim[s] for music the strong concept of art" by combining emotional expression with intellectual challenge,

Rossini complies with a "pathology" of compulsive, convulsive emotions. Where Beethoven stands magisterially alone as a subject, a Byronic hero with a good conscience, Rossini, like Nietzsche's Wagner, personifies the leveling crowd mentality of the modern age. Thus does the logic of alterity give Rossini equal time.[35]

At least one of Rossini's more notable nineteenth-century listeners prefigures Dahlhaus's representation of the composer as a feminine/ demotic figure. Wilkie Collins, in a memorable passage of his sensation novel *The Woman in White,* describes the archvillain Count Fosco as an itinerant Rossini in drag:

A blue blouse, with profuse white fancy-work over the bosom, covered his prodigious body, and was girt around the place where his waist might once have been with a broad scarlet leather belt. Nankeen trousers, displaying more white fancy-work over the ankles, and purple morocco slippers, adorned his lower extremities. He was singing Figaro's famous song in the Barber of Seville . . . accompanying himself on the concertina, which he played with ecstatic throwings-up of his arms, and graceful twistings and turnings of his head, like a fat St. Cecilia masquerading in male attire. "Figaro quà! Figaro là! Figaro sù! Figaro giù!"[36]

The notorious con man, notoriously fat composer, and patron saint of music fuse into a kind of gypsy queen (in every sense) who is both grotesque and seductive and whose musical voice is compelling enough to impose itself on Collins's text.

On Dahlhaus's, too: for there is, eventually, a reversion to Rossini's magnetism. Lacking a firm boundary between *seria* and *buffa,* Rossini's operas engage in what Dahlhaus identifies as a "switching of genres" that can look "on the surface . . . like a mindless confusion of styles." Although this oscillation has its rationale in a skeptical melancholy "that affected not only Rossini himself but his entire age," the imputation of mindlessness persists: "In Rossini the extremes meet: the farcical takes on catastrophic proportions in the frenzy of the music; the tragic, in its moments of greatest despair, exposes the marionette strings from which the characters are dangling." But a similar mobility between genres, now called "transformation," also counts for Dahlhaus as the major achievement of Beethoven's late style. In late Beethoven, "the meaning of one form seems to emerge precisely from its transformation into another." Amalgams of fugue and sonata, for example, are recurrent, and similarly in the *Diabelli* Variations "two genres, the variation cycle and the character piece, have fused. This fusion may have started in the eighteenth century, but only in Beethoven did it reach a stage that makes it seem appropriate to speak of a transformation."[37] On this reading, the key to being late Beethoven is to do esoterically what Rossini does outright.

What can we do with conceptual-ideological slippages such as these and, more broadly, with the cultural logic they perpetuate? As a historical force, the logic of alterity must be reckoned with, but merely recognizing its operations is as dead (and less satisfying) an end as unconsciously reproducing them. One way past this impasse is to ask how both music and musicology may inventively undo the logic of alterity they are also historically fated to reproduce. What are the possibilities of opening out the categories of self and other so that they appear, like the musicological dualities mentioned in chapter 1, not as the first principles of a conceptual or political order, but as temporary limits in a dynamic, open-ended process?

A willingness to see the disseminal potential in both mastery and reversion alike makes a good place to start. Compliance with the logic of alterity does not preclude resistance to it, nor does resistance preclude compliance. The oppositional or dialectical character of self-other dualities may sometimes be accepted at face value but sometimes treated as terms of negotiation, complexly motivated efforts to restrict a more mobile and plural play of meanings. Sometimes the voice of the self may silence the other, but sometimes the self may be spoken in a voice not quite its own, another voice if not quite the other's voice, deconstructing or resituating the binary order.[38] Sometimes the self's claim to a "god's-eye" perspective may impose itself unyieldingly, but sometimes the self-other relation may produce what Donna Haraway calls situated knowledges, the multifaceted outcome of (re)casting *both* self and other, not just the former, as positive, meaning-producing agents rather than as screens, grounds, or resources.[39]

This multiple or divided actualization of the logic of alterity has nothing to do with the process of breaking and (re)setting norms on which a Dahlhaus-like structural history depends, even though the structural historian and postmodernist interpreter may make their claims on the basis of exactly the same musical events. Outside the logic of alterity, the concept of the normative is empty; observed or defied, norms are vehicles of compliance. Indeed, one of the strongest anti-interpretive moves available to the structural historian is to muffle resistant material by classing it as the observance or defiance of a norm. The interpreter's responsibility, therefore, includes the specification of the exact terms on which a resistant configuration can be said to empty out the norms that impinge on it.

A musically obvious example of divided actualization is the surprise comic-opera coda to the Finale of Beethoven's *Serioso* Quartet (F minor, op. 95). This ending, thumb firmly on nose, stands to the preceding Allegretto agitato as caballeta to cavatina. Its effect is perfectly described by one of Dahlhaus's deprecatory remarks about Rossini's genre switching: "Sometimes, in situations dominated by a mood of oppression or tragic pathos, particularly in the caballetas, [Rossini] strikes a note of tuneful, almost merry brio that seems oblivious of the characters and their plights."[40] The coda is so disconcerting because it seems to give us Beethoven saying, "Oh, friends, not these tones! You've got it all wrong; I *am* Rossini." In Dahlhaus's terms, the autonomous musical work reveals itself to be an event in disguise, thoroughly contingent on the sociability and theatricality that surround any actual performance of a string quartet.

Beethoven's coda may seem an extreme gesture, but only because it exposes, by flouting, the exclusionary impulse latent in all codas, all rituals of enhanced rather than casual closure. Structurally, the coda is as orthodox as it is expressively bizarre. As Joseph Kerman observes, its increasingly prominent chromatic motive, F♯–G–G♯–A, is "a reflection of the F–G♭–G♮ of the opening movement, and at the same time a way of resolving it into the clear major 3rd, F and A."[41] By trumpeting this contradiction of structure and expression, the coda proclaims that full closure is really *foreclosure,* a generic and therefore a social device by which lowly performance events are transformed into realizations of high art. Extremity, no doubt of it, surfaces in the Finale of op. 95: the extremity, not of the "frivolous" coda, but of the "serious" norm of authenticity that the coda deconstructs.

At the same time, the coda is a highly marked moment of reversion, virtually a cathartic release of reversionary energy. From a generic perspective this energy marks a sudden turn to what Dahlhaus identifies as the "catastrophe" of Rossinian *opera buffa*, the sudden eruption ("an instant is all it takes") of riotous laughter or demonic frenzy. Scorning even a "flimsy" Rossinian pretext, the coda openly courts the staging of hysteria, the "women's malady" of which the unaccountable eruption of mirth from gloom, or vice versa, is a classical symptom or rhetorical topic.[42] From the perspective of subject construction, Beethoven's coda is an act of unmasterable feminization. It revalues hysteria not only as a force of affirmation, a means of getting outside the bonds of reason without breaking them, but also as a species of critique.

. . . . .

This reading of Beethoven's coda relies on principles of performativity and plurality. It tracks how the terms of self and other *behave* in the music, and it glosses their behavior through a multiplicity of discourses, structural, generic, social, psychical, and sexual. The reading is also disseminal. It presupposes a dynamic interplay among its terms that may, but need not, resolve into a hierarchy. The result is to show the coda opening out the music's internal logic of alterity far enough to implicate a different, more plural, more multiply situated cultural logic. Another piece, of course, might hesitate over the same venture, or limit it, or clamp down on it altogether. But the possibility of alternative internal logics has been set in place, not to be dislodged. Can the same thing be done for the external logic of alterity that takes music as its other? If so, it might also be possible to open out the whole structure of antinomy and to transform the character of music as a cultural trope. We need to know more, then, about what that character is and where it comes from.

Even where its work ethic and self-control have been strongest, music in the modern era has supplied verbal and visual modes of communication with their culturally mandated other: fluid, irrational, passivizing, indefinite. *Music*, indeed, has often been simply the name given to any conjuncture of these qualities, sonoric or not, especially in association with another name for the same thing, *woman*.

The synonymy is no accident. The development of aesthetics in the eighteenth century produced the once triumphant and still-compelling principle that the function of art is to promote the "mutual determination of subject and object in the act of perception."[43] Under the regime of this principle, music assumed a new ideal dimension that supplemented its aging associations with cosmic harmony and eventually led to its nineteenth-century status as the paradigmatic art. As Kevin Barry has shown, music became an "empty sign," the meanings of which are equally remote from determinate concepts and phenomenal intuition:

When eighteenth-century epistemology noticed that the signs of music evade the categories of distinctness and clarity of ideas, it became possible (1) to locate the significance of music in its composition, in its structure . . . and (2) to locate the significance of music in its emptiness, in its absence of meaning, and therefore in the act of listening, in the energy of mind which its emptiness provokes. . . . Instead of replacing a source which they would imitate or express, [musical signs] would turn the listener's attention toward his own inventive subjectivity.[44]

Music thus enters what has come to be known as the specular economy: it assumes the function of mirroring the identity of the self, but only by means of a radical lack that can blur or even obliterate the identity it mirrors.[45] As Hegel put it, music makes "the inner life . . . apprehensible" to itself, but only in the form of "an undeveloped subjective concentration," an "abstract generality." Music is therefore "capable only to a relative extent of harbouring the . . . broad expanse of a richly filled conscious life." Worse yet, even this imperfect token of the normative subject's "actual existence" is fated to be partly lost in the resistant materiality of musical sounds, the "sensuality [Sinnlichkeit] of the notes." The actual existence (*wirkliches Dasein*) is like a property (the richly filled expanse) that paradoxically loses value the more material it becomes. The "new-won wealth" (*neu gewonnenen Reichtum*) of conscious life cannot wholly be expressed as sonorous presence. In relation to music, the subject is like a man who has made his fortune but dissipates half of it in dubious pleasures.[46]

As Hegel intimates with his contrast of self-possession and sensuality, the one figuratively masculine, the other stereotypically feminine, the place that music assumes in the specular economy of the modern era is also the place long since assigned to woman. Music, *like woman,* is the bearer of a lack that both threatens and articulates the identity of the normative masculine subject.

This convergence employs the traditional association of music with femininity and feminization to new ends.[47] It originates together with an ill-matched pair of cultural changes identified with the Enlightenment. First, there is the elevation of a traditional social hierarchy, male over female, into a transcendental principle, the masculine over the feminine, aligned with foundational hierarchies of subject over object and reason over nature.[48] Second, there is the increasing identification of subjectivity in general with qualities of sensitivity, sensibility, variability, and volatility once regarded as inherently feminine.[49]

In the lack borne by music, these conflicting trends can find a degree of reconciliation. Music shares, by embodying, the feminine subjective qualities of sensitivity and so on, but it does not signify them. When music, as empty sign, turns the listener's attention inward, what it reveals is, not those qualities themselves, but a creative "energy of mind" that subsumes them. Men contemplating music can freely claim this active, synthesizing faculty as a distinguishing mark of their gender; women (officially, at least) cannot. Precisely, then, by *not* harboring the Hegelian "broad expanse . . . of a richly filled conscious life," music allows the subject to discover *in himself* the underlying principle by which that expanse is possessed and filled. Through the coalescence of the musical empty sign and feminine lack, the self secures its proper masculine position. At the same time, the division between music-induced introspection and "the sensuality of the notes," insofar as this unstable division can be maintained, becomes a pleasurable confirmation of the transcendental polarization of masculine and feminine principles. Strictly speaking, there can be no feminine listening, which is why, in this dispensation, women (and effeminate men) are represented as performing, embodying, or succumbing to music, but rarely as contemplating it. Even Forster's Helen Schlegel answers the summons of Beethoven's Fifth as a kind of young man. Thus in the modern or, as we can now call it, the aesthetic era, the nexus music-woman emerges as the paradigmatic other.

And this nexus does not emerge in the arts alone. In 1784, the French government appointed a scientific commission to investigate the phenomenon of animal magnetism and the magnetic therapies of Franz Anton Mesmer. The commission concluded that the "active and terrible power" responsible for mesmerism was not magnetism but imagination, a faculty localized in the eye and in the uterus. When

Commissioner Jean-Sylvain Bailly, reporting these results, needed a figure to clarify the effect of unreason on the body, the figure he found was the equation of woman and music. For Bailly, the exemplary site of mesmeric effects was the female body, which was so suggestible that it was effectively mesmerized in advance: "In touching [women] in one part, one might say that one simultaneously touches them everywhere. . . . Women . . . are like sounding strings perfectly tuned in unison."[50] The resonance of this touch is explicitly erotic; as another commissioner, Antoine Lavoisier, observed, the masculine observer is vulnerable to the patient's desire, and the experimental situation "does not entirely allow us to escape from the other's power."[51] The line of influence runs from the woman's uterus to the man's eye; the music of desire is made, or released, from woman by the controlling/desiring master('s) hand, only to prove itself impossible to grasp.

From Bailly's day to ours, music has operated within the symbolic order on terms much like these. It has served as the preeminent measure of the self's relation to a generalized otherness, the means by which the other is brought, or fails to be brought, under discursive control. As the figure of the other, music may address the normative subject of culture in any number of terms ranging from the transcendentalizing to the demonizing. These terms, however, do not work in opposition but in continual mutual implication, interchange, overlap, latency.

Flaubert captures the resulting indeterminacy very well in a passage from his novel *Sentimental Education:*

The company of these two women made as it were two melodies in [Frédéric Moreau's] life: the one playful, wild, amusing; the other grave and almost religious. And the two melodies, sounding at the same time, swelled continually and gradually intermingled; for, if Madame Arnoux merely brushed him with her finger, his desire immediately conjured up the image of the other woman . . . while if in Rosanette's company his heart happened to be stirred, he promptly remembered his great love.[52]

The musicality of the other blurs the familiar nineteenth-century opposition of madonna and prostitute, a self-other binary in its own right, and blends the two women named here into a continuous object (the other) set against Frédéric Moreau as representative subject (the self). Frédéric's identity is defined by the counterpoint between his two feminine "melodies." But the counterpoint, however lucid at first, is itself defined by an eroticized (swelling and intermingling) fluidity into which all distinction, all contrapuntal structure, eventually dissolves. The result is to transfer to Frédéric the same receptivity to an infinitely mobile sexual desire that Bailly reads in the female body. And that receptivity dissolves still further the boundaries between sexual and romantic love, between the women correspondingly loved, and, more broadly, between the low (wild, playful, amusing) and the lofty (grave and religious).

The signifying range of music under the logic of alterity is well represented by the literature of the aesthetic era, which routinely invokes music as the other of language, of conceptual thought, and of conscious self-possession. This "othering" has a wide range in its own right; it can appear in the most casual usages, such as references to the music of a (usually female) voice, and in the most deeply considered, such as Proust's remarkable suggestion that music represents a lost alternative to the self-affirming voice of language and reason, "the unique example of what might have been—if the invention of language, the formation of words, the analysis of ideas had not intervened—the means of communication between souls."[53]

"Music," wrote Thomas Mann apropos Heinrich von Kleist's story "St. Cecilia,"

> is at the same time [an] enchantment and [a] supremely sinister power—an attitude illustrated by the casual yet significant remark of the poet [Kleist] concerning "the feminine gender of this mysterious art." . . . Kleist once employed the phrase, "the full horror of music." When I read this I thought of the description of Tolstoi's face when he listened to great music: an expression of *horror* came into it.[54]

> Music is sinister and enchanting alike because it has the putatively feminine power to combine promiscuously with any other expressive modality and to exceed whatever it combines with. At its most alienating, as Mann suggests by conjoining the "feminine gender" of the art with Tolstoy's expression of horror (or *horror*), music is symbolically castrating for the normatively masculine subject. At its most involving, this same music acts like what psychoanalysis calls a transitional object, an object that, charged with charisma, temporarily crosses, blurs, and may even dissolve the listener's ego boundaries.[55]

Put in Kristevan terms, the transitional object positions the subject undecidably between the semiotic and the symbolic. Hence T. S. Eliot's equivocal praise of

> music heard so deeply
> That it is not heard at all, but you are the music
> While the music lasts.[56]

Eliot understands this state of fusion as a low-level approximation to the self-abnegation by which the saint or mystic intuits the Godhead. For those, such as Kleist, Tolstoy, and Mann, who see horror there, the same state suggests a high-level loss of identity bordering on automatism or madness. The listener once more inherits the uncontrollable subjectivity of the always-already mesmerized female body. "Music," says the narrator of Tolstoy's "The Kreutzer Sonata,"

> causes me to forget myself and my true state; it transports me to another state that is not my own. Under the influence of music I fancy I feel things I really do not feel, understand things I do not understand, am capable of things I am incapable of. . . . Is it permissible that any chance person should [thus] hypnotize another (or even many others) and make him do what he likes? . . . How dare anyone play this *presto* in a drawing room where there are women sitting about in *decolleté?*[57]

The later Tolstoy, a pleasure-hating moralist, would seem to be worlds apart from an aesthete such as Oscar Wilde, but Wilde, speaking through Dorian Gray, shows himself Tolstoy's double as a listener:

> [The words] had touched some secret chord that had never been touched before, but that he now felt was vibrating and throbbing to curious pulses.
> Music had stirred him like that. Music had troubled him many times. But music was not articulate. It was not a new world, but rather another chaos, that it created in us.[58]

Music is other, it always belongs to another, and when heard it makes the self vibrate and throb as something other (a tuned string, the female body, the womb of nature before the intervention of divine intelligence). "A song," wrote Rimbaud, is seldom "a thought sung and comprehended by the singer. For *I* is someone else."[59]

The ultimate form of this alienation of identity is a regression to the "oceanic" state of undifferentiation associated with the maternal body.[60] According to Walt Whitman, the totality of music is like the sound of a "tremulous" organ, beneath which

The strong base stands, and its pulsations intermits not,
Bathing, supporting, merging all the rest, maternity of all the rest,
And with it every instrument in multitudes,
The players playing, all the world's musicians . . .
And for their solvent setting earth's own diapason,
Of winds and woods and mighty ocean waves.[61]

Locating the maternal in a fundamental bass ("base") cross-gendered from masculine to feminine, Whitman celebrates as vital a regression that most nineteenth-century writers, following Wagner in *Tristan und Isolde,* associate with ecstatic death. Kate Chopin's Edna Pontellier, returning, a disappointed Venus, to the "soft, close embrace" of the sea invoked by "Isolde's song"; Ibsen's Peer Gynt rocked and crooned to sleep on the lap of his mother/bride Solveig; Mann's Frau Klöterjahn, the consumptive mother who, in the story "Tristan," becomes an Isolde whose song figuratively doubles her fatal hemorrhage ("'She has brought up so much blood, such a horrible lot of blood. . . . She was sitting up quite quietly in bed and humming a little snatch of music . . . and there it came . . .'"): all tell the same story of the self dissolved, ebbing or gushing away.[62]

In less drastic form, the regressiveness of music manifests itself as the arrest or paralysis, whether pleasurable or painful, of the listener's will. The narrator of Proust's *The Fugitive,* taking a lonely drink by a Venetian canal, hears a boatman sing "O sole mio." The result is a paralysis "like a sort of numbing cold," laden with "a despairing but hypnotic charm":

My mind . . . was entirely occupied with following the successive phrases of *O sole mio,* singing them to myself with the singer, anticipating each surge of melody, soaring aloft with it, sinking down with it once more. . . . Each note that the singer's voice uttered with a force and ostentation that were almost muscular stabbed me to the heart. . . . Thus I remained motionless, my will dissolved.[63]

Proust's metaphors depict a trancelike regression that, like its more mortal counterparts, conflates pleasure with pain and conforms itself to an invasive/enveloping music with a passivity that borders on—in this case, with the imagery of muscular stabbing, no doubt crosses into—masochistic self-surrender.[64]

If we follow this discourse one step further, we come upon a defensive rhetoric by which the music that encroaches on the self is cast as an object of visceral blockage or disgust, sometimes mixed with pleasure, which the listener must reject or expel. Music thus becomes what Julia Kristeva calls an *abject*, something within the subject that belongs to the sphere of fusion with the mother and must thus be cast violently out in order to maintain the subject's intactness.[65]

The rhetoric of musical abjection is more typical of criticism than of literature; the first examples that come to mind are Nietzsche calling the Wagnerian leitmotif an "ideal toothpick, an opportunity for getting rid of *remainders* of food" or, again, equating the effect of listening to Wagner to that of "continual consumption of alcohol: blunting, and obstructing the stomach with phlegm."[66] Or there is Hugo Wolf, who once boasted of writing a song that could "lacerate the nervous system of a block of marble," commenting on the indigestibility of Brahms's B-Flat Major Piano Concerto: "Whoever can swallow this [work] with relish may look forward with equanimity to a famine; it is to be supposed that he . . . will be able to help himself excellently with food-substitutes such as window-panes, cork-stoppers, oven-screws, and the like."[67]

Mann and James Joyce, however, do offer important literary treatments of the musical abject. In "Death in Venice," Mann's Gustav von Aschenbach embraces abjection in the same parallel forms, drink and song, that paralyze the will of Proust's Venetian narrator. Aschenbach drinks from "a glass of pomegranate-juice and soda-water sparkling ruby-red before him" at the same time as "his nerves dr[i]nk in thirstily" a series of "vulgar and sentimental tunes." For "passion," Mann observes, "paralyzes good taste and makes its victim accept with rapture what a man in his senses would either laugh at or turn from with disgust."[68]

Likewise, the "Sirens" section of Joyce's *Ulysses* recurrently takes up the possible identification of music with the abject. At one point, listening to the ballad "When Love Absorbs My Ardent Soul" while eating "with relish . . . inner organs, nutty gizzards, fried cod's roes," Leopold Bloom vacillates between a conscious desire to merge with the "flood of warm jimjam lickitup secretness [that] flowed to flow in music out, in desire, dark to lick flow, invading" and a displaced, unconscious desire to render the music repellent and thus recoup his distance from it:

> .... *my ardent soul*
> *I care not foror the morrow.*
> In liver gravy Bloom mashed mashed potatoes.

Music as the vehicle of the ardent soul undergoes a metonymic slippage; the vocalic sob that distends "for" to "foror" elides into the glutinous mass of potatoes and liver gravy. And it is not long before the same elision takes a coprophagic turn: "Only the harp. Lovely gold glowering light. Girl touched it. Poop of a lovely. Gravy's rather a good fit for a. Golden ship."[69] The "lovely" is one of the "lovely seaside girls" named in another song that flits across Bloom's day; the "poop" for which the gravy's rather a good fit is both music of a sort and its abject material embodiment: the tooting sound of a horn (Bloom has earlier recalled a horn player emptying spittle), the sound of a fart, and, of course, loose feces (note the submerged phonemic pun: golden ship/ golden shit).[70]

The conclusion seems clear: for the modern subject, to hear music made is *dangerous*. Being dangerous, but not insuperably dangerous, to the wholeness, detachment, self-possession or normative masculinity of that subject, to the privacy of his property, is a cardinal cultural function of music in the modern West. To modify an earlier formulation, the division between music-induced introspection and "the sensuality of the notes," insofar as this unstable division can be *put at risk* without collapsing, becomes a pleasurable confirmation of the transcendental polarization of masculine and feminine principles. Or, in stark, psychoanalytic terms: in music the self appropriates the phallus by risking castration.

An intriguing, if obviously speculative, possibility plays about this last point. Roland Barthes once observed that the Romantic Lied, with its emphasis on unfulfilled desire, developed "*precisely* when the castrati disappear from musical Europe . . . The publicly castrated creature is succeeded by a complex human subject whose imaginary castration will be interiorized" in the Lied.[71] "Castration" here, as in my paragraph above, carries the Lacanian charge of signifying a constitutive lack within the human subject. Is it possible that the "castrated" subject Barthes finds in the Lied also functions, historically, to epitomize aesthetic-era musical subjectivity in general, the subjectivity of music as other?

Regardless of the answer, the demand for musical risk affects not only the way in which listening is constituted in representation but also the practical venues of listening. Sound recording, for instance, tends to domesticate and demystify music, to turn it into a listener-operated commodity. As John Corbett has suggested, however, the disembodied quality of recorded music may also provoke anxiety. The visual void between the music and the performer's body can unnerve some listeners and impel them to seek fetishistic compensations: the opulence of record jackets or CD "jewel boxes," the technological quest for perfect recorded sound, the avocation of the collector-aficionado.[72] But the same void may also offer the self the pleasures of risk. Some avid listeners will "go with" the music by closing their eyes, or staring into space, or turning up the volume so that sound overcomes vision.

Paradoxically, the risk evoked in separating music from the performer's body is exceeded only by the risk evoked in conjoining the two. Music in live performance promises a special excitement that can readily overflow into sheer self-abandonment. Or at least we act as if it does, and not only at the high-tech stadium-filling rock concerts designed to simulate rather than to contain the eruption of musical otherness. Most "classical" concertgoing is still familiarly governed, for audiences and performers alike, by rigid decorums left over from the late nineteenth century, the golden age of the bourgeois self. These decorums function in part as ritualized defense mechanisms. They serve, although nowadays with strained credibility, to invest music with the hypnotic and invasive power of the other by conspicuously providing the means to contain it.

Certain performance practices serve a parallel function. Prominent here are the prohibitions, only now eroding a little, on improvisation and ornamentation in the cadenzas, arias, and repeats that can accommodate them, and the more inclusive limitations placed on expressive fluctuations in tempo, intonation, and articulation. Such interventions by the performer(s) are, of course, basic to popular music and jazz, where they serve listeners as signs of irresistible impulsiveness, the anarchic energies of the other. In classical-music performance, the constraint on performer interventions serves, perhaps no longer viably, as what might be called an absent sign of the same energies. The otherness of the music is constructed, and at very high voltage, by its defensive positioning between two modes of disciplinary control, the letter of the score and the training of the performer.[73]

When electrifying performances cause defensive practices to "fail" or their simulated failure to become "real," audiences respond with a frenzy that both reflects and reenacts the positioning of music as the other. Institutionalized, such frenzy becomes cult-level fandom, the outer limit of which is the kind of superstar craze that begins in the nineteenth century with figures such as Liszt and Gottschalk. With the progress of mass culture, the character of the superstar evolves; figures such as Jenny Lind, Enrico Caruso, and Leopold Stokowski, who straddle high and popular art, are replaced by purely popular figures such as Frank Sinatra, Elvis Presley, and the Beatles. But one need only mention Arturo Toscanini, Maria Callas, Van Cliburn, and Glenn Gould to mark the persistence of the superstar role among "classical" performers. Performer cults can even be understood in Dahlhaus's terms as the specific other of composer cults, the social vehicle for posing the ex-centric energies of the event against the concentric monumentality of the work.

.   .   .   .   .

What applies to the institution of music as a cultural trope also applies to its disciplinary construction, but with a critical difference. Like "music" itself, the modern study of music rests on the contradictory workings of the logic of alterity. At one level, the logic works "inside" music to divide the self from the other and to generate value and intelligibility from that division. At another level, the same logic operates "outside" music to divide it as other from the self and to generate value and mystery from that division. For music as a cultural trope, movement from the internal to the external logic of alterity has been primary throughout the aesthetic era. For music as a disciplinary object, the reverse holds true.

In the disciplinary sphere, the internal logic of alterity appropriates a portion of music for a self that the external logic establishes as the always extramusical. In other words, the internal logic recuperates music for truth and reason. It allows (some) music to become the object of (limited) disciplinary study and makes this privileged (or denatured) music available for idealization and the associated formation of a canon. Music outside this sphere can be either enjoyed or disdained as a "lower" pleasure, appropriate for emotional or erotic stimulation but not for aesthetic contemplation.

Yet the music of the aesthetic canon holds, and is meant to hold, its higher status only in the most equivocal terms. Confronted with the dense referential and symbolic capacities of language or visual imagery, even the most "classical" music collapses instantaneously into the inarticulate, emotionally loaded, and erotically charged character of the more demotic forms. In the language of the music-woman nexus, analysis or structural history can silence the feminine otherness of music, but only in terms that grant unspeakable power to that otherness, that render it the figure of the unrepresentable, source of a wound or ecstasy that cannot be survived by the self. Strikingly, however, such reversions to the other are not allowed to undo the idealization of the music and may even be courted as evidence of the composer's esoteric mastery. The reversions are necessary; they belong to an institutional cycle. The internal logic of alterity reverts to the external, from which an appeal to form will recuperate it until the next reversion. Music as a disciplinary object becomes music as a cultural trope until music as a cultural trope becomes music as a disciplinary object until . . .

This state of affairs is not without its advantages. One often-noted feature of the logic of alterity is a cultural version of the Freudian return of the repressed: what is banished to the place of the other returns to the place of the self in the form of desire. As Peter Stallybrass and Allon White formulate it, "The 'top' attempts to reject or eliminate the 'bottom' . . . only to discover, not only that it is in some way frequently dependent upon that low-Other . . . but also that the top *includes* that low symbolically, as a primary eroticized constituent of its own fantasy life."[74] The desire for the other, the desire to be other, is, however, unavowable; it comes fearfully hedged about with prohibition, re-repression, secrecy, violent reaction formation. In this context, music begins to look like the modern cultural institution by which this desire can be satisfied with impunity. Music is pocket carnival. For the normative subjects of culture, it is the site of permitted deviance, of release from the demands of their self-policing normality. For those appointed as deviant, it is the site of collective affirmation, of the great reversal in which it is the dominant culture that must say, "But if, baby, I'm the bottom, you're the top."

As the site reserved for deviance—the normative site for departures from the norm—music helps produce the very category of deviance. As the art of otherness and the other's art, music helps construct the very category of otherness. These functions give underlying continuity to the cycle in which music appears now as a cultural trope, now as a disciplinary object. In the cultural trope, the self deviates into music, which, as we've seen, continually mixes and separates terms of abjection and transcendence. In the disciplinary object, music inhibits—protects, restrains, redeems—the self from that very deviation. Either way, the division between top and bottom, normal and deviant, is upheld.

Modernist musicology gradually evolves an aesthetic ideal in which that division is reenacted in the activity of listening. The ideal depends on the familiar premise that music is essentially self-enclosed, "mute" about its concrete human interests.[75] This premise need not be absolute; the "relative autonomy" claimed by Dahlhaus, in his pained awareness of the force of culture, is enough. It follows that truly musical listening must rest on solely musical considerations. Such "structural listening" (which Rose Subotnik has submitted to a rigorous critique)[76] cannot be contingent on "extramusical associations" even if the music is texted or programmatic. The listener is enjoined to follow the music closely, subordinating the recognition of concrete human interests to the perception of organizing patterns. In a reversal of the effect, discussed earlier, of taking music as an empty sign, the listener does not identify with "his" own ability to hear but with the music's ability to direct his hearing. Involvement with what is communicative, expressive, or sensuous in the music occupies the position of controlled deviance. It is allowable, even in abundance, as long as it lacks discursive specificity and does not threaten to become part of the music "itself." The result is a yawning gap between musical knowledge and musical response that nothing seems able to bridge.[77]

But it is the gap, not the bridging of it, that defines the ideological project of music in the aesthetic era. Modernist musicology maintains that gap by constructing the material and expressive force of music as the other of musical form. It does so whenever it brackets most living experiences of music as subjective, ineffable, or irrational in the name of a normative experience of music *qua* music; whenever it minimizes the formative action of musical expression and the expressive action of musical form; whenever it "takes account" of musical meaning by granting emotive descriptions, critical judgments, and indications of "context" a small place on the fringes of discourse about style, form, structure, and technique. The result, in Lacanian terms, is to constitute musical expression as subimaginary and musical structure as supersymbolic. As expression, music takes on the intensity of imaginary signification without the definite content that feeds into an intersubjective imaginary order. As structure, music takes on all the unyielding rigidity of the symbolic order without the compensatory fluidity of language. Expression, so conceived, rationalizes the cultural trope of music as other. Structure, so conceived, rationalizes the musicological claim to retrieve a uniquely privileged space for the self from that otherness.

This conceptual apparatus has proven to be virtually inescapable, even for those who have tried most and best to escape it. Two factors seem particularly responsible for its tenacity. The first is the failure of modernist discourse to provide workable alternatives to its own formulations. The second is the success of modernist discourse in providing accounts of music's effect on the listener which apply with equal facility to the equivocal sphere of "othered" response and the ideal sphere of "selved" knowledge.

In the nineteenth century these accounts were typically metaphysical; in ours they have been phenomenological. Musical time has come to be figured as numinous. What Edward Said calls "the tyranny of its forward logic or impulse" and Carolyn Abbate its "fundamental and terrible" inescapability is said to have, prescribed to have, a wholly involving effect.[78] The listener is endowed with a submissiveness that, as Said acknowledges, borders (Proust-like) on the masochistic, the reward for which is a certain deliverance from worldliness. The question of musical time is too complex to be argued here, although as my last sentence already begins to suggest, the idea(l) of music as wholly involving is consistent with ideologically and politically fraught motives. But at least submissive listening, which certainly occurs, at least sporadically, at least with certain kinds and examples of music, can be challenged as an instituted norm. Is my not listening that way really a "deviation?" Am I failing to experience the music when I vary my attention level or simply let it fluctuate, when I interrupt a sound recording to replay a movement or a passage, when I find myself enthralled by a fragment of a piece that I hear on my car radio without losing concentration on the road, when I intermittently accompany my listening by singing under my breath or silently verbalizing commentary on what I hear, when I perform some part of a piece in my mind's ear, perhaps vocalizing along, and perhaps not?

These questions all point to a mode of musical experience that subsumes the logic of alterity but can never be subsumed by it. The character of this experience is irretrievably pragmatic, unmystified, and heterogeneous, but it is not the less compelling for that. It is a mode of experience in which presymbolic involvement, symbolic understanding, and keenness of pleasure or distress can all coexist, precisely because there is no imperative to reconcile them or order them hierarchically. It is a mode of experience that cannot be regulated by unitary ideals or norms, because it can emerge, can disseminate itself, from any situation in which the involvement, understanding, and keenness, in whatever combination and whatever medium, engage us in the communicative economy. Listening, in this dispensation, becomes a performative activity in its own right, and one that does not necessarily require all—or any—of the music "itself" to be materially present. The postmodernist musicology for which I am pressing in this volume is ultimately an attempt to transfer disciplinary value from the logic of alterity to such performative listening. Not that that logic will cease to operate: but it will operate in a mode of acknowledged fantasy, capable at any moment of being opened out into the more flexible, more plural, more contingent logic of postmodern musical experience.

From a modernist viewpoint, such experience may seem chaotic, and therefore other, and in a sense that is exactly what it is: not the traditional sense with which we will see Haydn grappling in the next chapter, but the contemporary sense supplied by chaos theory. Musical experience in this sense would not admit of being centrally organized by familiar structural and aesthetic principles, but it might—speaking figuratively—admit of being regulated by a "strange attractor":

> It is possible for a system to behave in a "chaotic," irregular way . . . and still be capable of formalization by means of an "attractor" that regulates it—an attractor that is "strange," i.e., that acquires the form not of a point or a symmetrical figure, but of endlessly intertwined serpentines within the contours of a definite figure, an "anamorphically" disfigured circle, a "butterfly," etc.[79]

The image of a butterfly seems especially felicitous, a signifier flitting unconstrainedly among traditional signifieds that specify, it just so happens, the three primary media of music: transience, metamorphosis, and subjectivity. Ancient representations touch on this connection when they show the psyche (mind or soul) emerging in the form of a butterfly from the mouths of the dead: no doubt like something uttered (logos, word), but also like something sung.

Schumann and "Papillons":—

Three

Music and Representation

In the Beginning with Haydn's *Creation*

It would be fair to say that music criticism becomes postmodernist when it proceeds by deconstructing the concept of the extramusical. As the polarization of music and language erodes, and the participation of music in the communicative economy gains recognition, the distinction between music in itself and an external conceptual or narrative "substrate" becomes increasingly arbitrary.[1] This chapter proposes a test case on the notorious subject of musical representation. It aims to show "internal" and "external" meanings intertwining closely and widely in the very kind of music commonly held to make their separation most obvious.

For most of the aesthetic era, representation in music has been much practiced and little valued. Tone painting has typically been regarded as an expressive extra, acceptable only in small doses and, at that, only when it can be overlooked in favor of a self-sufficient musical structure. Music that represents too much risks becoming unmusical. A hostile contemporary critic of Haydn's *The Creation* had virtually the last word on this subject several years before Beethoven nervously insisted that the *Pastoral* Symphony is "more the expression of feeling than painting."[2] "What can one say," wrote Johann Karl Friedrich Triest, "to a natural history or geogony set to music, where the objects pass before us as in a magic lantern; what to the perpetual pictorializing? . . . Truly, the author of the old Mosaic story of the seven days of creation probably did not dream it would make such a great hit again at the end of the eighteenth century!"[3]

Triest's attitude is strikingly protoformalist. His irony takes aim at both the inadequacy of musical representation and its usurpation of proper musicality. In making his point he tacitly makes the chain of assumptions that would later come to seem nearly indisputable: that music is radically inferior to language as a bearer of meaning; that intelligibility in music must itself be purely musical; and that any definite meaning attached to a composition is in principle detachable as "extramusical"—or if not, that the music is somehow trifling. Triest's rhetoric characterizes musical representation as an unwitting travesty of verbal representation, in particular of written narrative. Music slackens the coherent creation story told by various books—a natural history, a geogony, Genesis—into a mere series of pictorial images, or rather the musical images of images. (Since such books were typically illustrated, the music in effect anthologizes their pictures and deletes their texts, placing the auxiliary in the place of the primary.) The music's secondhand images are not even firmly drawn or painted. They belong, rather, to an illusionistic device often associated with trickery and sensationalism, the magic lantern.

Still, as Triest is the first to concede, the old Mosaic story as retold by Haydn certainly made a hit with its audiences. The purpose of this chapter is to suggest that the audiences knew something—knew something *musical*—that Triest didn't. My claim is that musical representation has significant, definite, interpretively rich ties to both musical processes and cultural processes. Far from being a slightly embarrassing extra, musical representation is one of the basic techniques by which culture enters music, and music enters culture, as communicative action. The case for this claim rests on a postmodernist hermeneutic that understands representation less as a relationship established between a sign and a referent than as the dynamic, culturally conditioned process of affirming and deploying such a relationship.

.   .   .   .   .

To begin with, a working definition of representation—in the strict sense of pictorial, reproductive, imitative signification—is in order. Signs become representational in this sense when we take them to constitute an intentional likeness, whether of a real or imaginary, specific or generic referent. Whatever else it may do (and it may do a good deal), such a sign must operate by means of a resemblance formed expressly to enable its operation.[4] Generic representations can usually meet this condition just by utilizing signs that are iconic by convention. More definite or individualized representations usually require something more: a designator, as we can call it, that implicitly or explicitly identifies what is being represented. Virtually anything can function as a designator, from a title or allusion to a nearly subliminal detail—even a bit of accumulated lore. Whatever form it takes, however, the designator is never extraneous to the representation. It does not occupy an "outside" in relation to a representational "inside." If Edvard Munch's painting *The Scream* were entitled *The Toothache*, it would be quite a different work.

The role of the designator determines the character of representation on at least two counts. First, representation is in principle (if not always in practice) antinormative; there can be no criteria for resemblance that all representations must satisfy. The designator serves, not to report on a generally valid resemblance, but to postulate a situationally contingent one. Second, although the content of a representation is referential, the representational function is performative. Once designated, a representation may be judged true or false to its object in varying degrees, but any such judgment presupposes representation itself as a given; a misrepresentation is still a representation. On both counts, representations appear to be first cousins of the classical performative utterances of J. L. Austin's speech-act theory, which are also situationally contingent but not contingent on being verified or falsified. Performatives are successful or unsuccessful; representations are accepted or refused.[5]

In music, the most common designators consist of texts for vocal setting; titles, epigraphs, score annotations, and programs; and musical allusions both typical (to styles, genres, forms, or characteristic sonorities) and individual (to tunes, with or without associated words, or particular compositions).[6] Alerted by the designator, the listener is empowered to find likenesses between specific features of the music and the designated object(s) of representation. Once such likenesses have crystallized, the same listener can go on to make interpretive connections between the music as likeness and the music as pattern or process.

How would such an interpretive practice work? The answer depends on a further characteristic of representation. While the ascrip-
tion of intention to a likeness establishes the function of representation, and the designator establishes a referent, neither is sufficient to
establish meaning. In all but the most rudimentary cases, and especially where representation seeks the status of art, some signifying ele-
ment(s) exceed or default on the terms of likeness. In so doing, they
begin an open-ended process of commentary and interpretation. As
Mary Ann Caws puts it, "Presumably the 'water' of a mirror should
not deform, nor the 'mirror' of a water, or they would not be called
upon to mirror; art, on the other hand, deforms in order to be, for it
begins where deformation begins and ceases where deformation
ceases."[7] The action of this constitutive deformation is tropological, a
"turn" that reorients the field of signification. When the terms of a
representation are homogeneous, as in a still life or portrait, the tropological effect may be latent, at least at first sight. Where the terms
are heterogeneous, as in rippling music for a rippling stream, the effect is usually manifest and typically metaphorical.

On this understanding, musical representation is a mode of metaphor, a statement that is itself meant literally rather than metaphorically. The conjoining of disparate terms forms a metaphor if it can be
interpreted as an elliptical comparison. As a communicative act, metaphor opens the possibility of two-way transfers of meaning between
its constituent terms, each of which appropriates elements from the
other's characteristic spheres of discourse. It is this opening, more
than any logical or syntactical relationship among signifiers, that generates the trope; as Derrida observes, metaphor necessarily "risks disrupting the semantic plenitude to which it should belong. Marking the
moment of the turn . . . from the truth that attunes it to its referent,
metaphor also opens the wandering of the semantic."[8] In a tradition
stemming from Aristotle, metaphor is a type of pictorial rhetoric, but
its defining conditions can clearly be met by nonlinguistic forms of
expression, music among them. If, say, I hear a wintry bleakness, op-
pressing both eye and heart, in the constantly repeated rhythmic motive of Debussy's "Des pas sur la neige" [Footsteps in the Snow], what
I have done is not all that different from remarking, as Debussy did in

the score, "This rhythm should have the sonorous value of a sad and icy background landscape."

The tropological aspect of a representation is the immediate source of its meanings, its hermeneutic window. The trope "opens the wandering of the semantic" by placing the representation in the thick of the communicative economy, affiliating it with a wide variety of discourses and their social, historical, ideological, psychical, and rhetorical forces. Debussy's metaphor, for example, has poetic resonances from Villon to Mallarmé, and those are just the beginning. The interpretation of such a metaphor involves the correlation of its discursive affiliations with the characteristics of the representation it informs— in this case with musical figures and processes. Like the internal structure of metaphor itself, this correlation moves in two directions. It "condenses" the discursive field into the music and at the same time reinterprets the discourse by means of the music. The music and the discourse do not enter into a text-context relationship, but rather into a relationship of dialogical exchange.[9] In the process, both the symbolic and disseminal possibilities of the representation come into view, along with the general conditions of the representation's meaningfulness. The latter, as Charles Altieri has suggested, include both "what [actually] gave intelligibility to the given, and what might have remained inchoate as tension and as potential within the [historical] agent's efforts to establish intelligibility."[10]

· ■ · ■ ·

For an illustration of musical representation and its interpretation, I turn to Haydn's *The Creation,* and in particular to its Introduction: an instrumental movement that Haydn calls "The Representation of Chaos" [*Die Vorstellung des Chaos* (mm. 1–59)] followed by a recitative and chorus on the opening lines of Genesis (mm. 60–96).[11] Both Heinrich Schenker and Donald Tovey, from their different vantage points, found representational meaning in the impelling processes of this music. Schenker identifies Haydn's chaos with a series of orchestral "thrusts" [*Stöße;* dramatic *forte* or *fortissimo* attacks] that are gradually mollified [*gesänftigt*] by the "composing out" of musical order. Example 4 outlines and comments on this process; for

Example 4. Registral sinking and linear motion in Haydn's "The Representation of Chaos." The graph shows an underlying "background" pattern "composed out" or "prolonged" via intermediate ("middleground") forms into the musical surface or "foreground." Basic to the background is the "fundamental line": a descent, by diatonic steps in an upper voice, from any tone of the triad to the tonic. Numerals with carets refer to the scale degrees of this descent; its constituent tones, and those of similar "linear progressions" at other levels, are grouped under slurs. Except where phrases of music are quoted, note values indicate structural importance, not rhythm; the longer the note, the higher its importance.

nonspecialist readers, the graph's caption offers explanations of key terms and symbols. Three waves of underlying melodic motion (middleground linear progressions) traverse the movement in tandem with a continual sinking [*Senkung*] in register. The registral process at first cuts across and finally coalesces with the linear one; as the coalescence advances, solo passages at first ornament it from above and finally mirror it at the upper octave.[12]

Where Schenker finds expressive thrusts and structural mollifications, Tovey finds formal sense and nonsense. He identifies chaos with the music's continual arousal and contradiction of expectation,

and cosmos with its underlying rationality and "symmetry." "The
universe," however, "is not going to show its symmetry to a first
glance"; although the musical order is immanent, its presence is revealed only by slow stages and not confirmed until the very end. Tovey
finds the model for this gradualism in the evolutionary paradigms of
eighteenth-century science, citing in particular the nebular hypothesis of Kant and Laplace: the conjecture that the solar system evolved
from a swirling cloud of gaseous matter.[13]

Tovey's suggestion, which can be said to historicize Schenker's, is
the place to begin. Haydn's chaos is unmistakably conceived as an incipient cosmos; the music begins in mystification and slowly expli-
cates its underlying coherence. This conception, however, cannot rest
merely on its scientific laurels; as an element of *The Creation*, it must
also fit into a religious narrative. Haydn essays the fit by drawing on
the ancient concept of *harmonia mundi*, which not only has historical
links to astronomical and cosmological speculation but also, more important, provides a model of creation founded on both biblical authority and something very ready to Haydn's hand: music.

The idea that cosmic order coincides with musical harmony derives
from Pythagoras, enters Western literature in Book 10 of Plato's *Republic*, and passes into music theory through Boethius's concept of
musica mundana.[14] As the concept of world harmony becomes Christianized, creation narratives emerge that combine biblical creation
imagery with the Pythagorean imagery of the music of the spheres.
Both the creating Word and the created world come to be represented
as forms of music. These representations were already commonplace
by the time that Isidore of Seville compiled his highly popular encyclopedia in the seventh century. "Nothing exists," writes Isidore,
"without music; for the universe itself is said to have been framed by
a kind of harmony of sounds, and the heaven itself revolves under the
tones of that harmony."[15] As early as the second century, Clement of
Alexandria identifies "the heavenly Word . . . the divine beginning of
all things" as "an all-harmonious instrument of God, melodious and
holy." Even incarnate, the Word still echoes the music of creation:
Christ himself is "a new Song."[16]

Later, I will have occasion to cite revivals of this complex of ideas
by Milton and Dryden. Meanwhile, it is worth noting that the meta-

phor of *harmonia mundi* was very much alive for Haydn's audience. *The Creation* inspired several eulogistic poems, most of which are alert to the figurative tie between harmony and creation. Gabriela von Baumberg, for example, explicitly transfers the power of the Logos to Haydn's music, in which she hears a second creation emulating the first:

Jüngst schuf *Dein* schöpferisches *Werde!*
Den Tonner durch den Paukenschall
    Und Himmel Sonne Mond und Erde,
Die Schöpfung ganz zum zweyten Mahl.[17]

[Lately *thy* creative *fiat!* / Made thunder through the kettledrums, / Made heaven, sun, and moon and earth / Compose Creation a second time.]

It is also worth noting that the idea of a musical creation lingered in scientific discourse at least into the seventeenth century. In his *Harmonice Mundi* (1619), Kepler argued that God gave the planets elliptical orbits because the concentric spheres imagined by Pythagorean cosmology would have yielded an aesthetically defective monotone, whereas the elliptical orbits yield a polyphony. For Kepler, God the creator is God the composer.[18]

Haydn's "Representation of Chaos" opens with a sullen thrust by the bulk of the orchestra on an unharmonized C. As Tovey observes, this sonority is strictly speaking the most chaotic element in the movement.[19] We would expect an unharmonized tone at the beginning of a Classical composition to be a tonic or dominant, but this tone opens a designated representation of chaos, so we must hear it as raw material: an *Urklang*, not yet intelligible, not yet even music. The vehicle of this primordial feeling is, famously, Haydn's orchestration: mixed timbres, muted strings, heavy brass on middle C, a timpani roll. Writing on behalf of the first listeners to *The Creation*, Haydn's biographer Giuseppi Carpani described the opening C as "a dull and indefinite surge of sound."[20] The oppressive sensation was probably compounded, as A. Peter Brown has shown, by the use of muted trumpets and timpani in performances under Haydn's own direction—a practice not reflected in the published score.[21] A further compounding comes from the only fermata in the whole "Representations of Chaos." Haydn's *Urklang* is as indefinite in duration as it is in sonority.

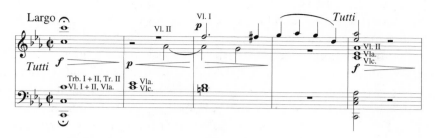

Example 5. Haydn, "The Representation of Chaos," mm. 1–5.

After the opening *forte* attack, the *Urklang* gradually fades to black. What follows (see Example 5) requires detailed description.

Measure 2 quietly begins motion in tempo by adding tone to tone, assembling the raw materials of harmony. The middle C at the core of the *Urklang* reappears as a bass, first of a minor interval (c^1–$e^{\flat 1}$), then of a major chord (c^1–$e^{\flat 1}$–$a^{\flat 1}$). Neither tonic nor dominant nor in root position, this first chord—call it the chaos chord—is a model of instability. It progresses to dissonant polyphony around the dominant of C minor in measure 3, which in turn leads to a bare phrase swelling and subsiding on first violins in measure 4. The unharmonized phrase rather grimly echoes the texture of the *Urklang*, but it also consolidates the dominant of C minor. The next measure will bring disruption—a new orchestral thrust that fades into the chaos chord—but a horizon of consonance has been traced, a cadence promised. Tonal harmony has evolved from unharmonized tone.

With this gesture, Haydn forms the nucleus of everything to follow. He at once invokes the classical / Christian metaphor of *harmonia mundi* and makes that metaphor evolutionary, scientific, modern, by deferring its realization in a cadence, projecting the cadence forward as the outcome of a more comprehensive process.

The movement proceeds by repeating the basic action of the opening (mm. 1–5^2) in expanded forms. Three large cycles fill out the whole, the end of each overlapping the beginning of the next (mm. 5–40^2, 40–50^2, 49^3–59). Each cycle begins as the chaos chord, which is fixed in pitch and tone color, answers an orchestral thrust. Dissonant polyphony then wends its way sinuously to a precadential dominant of C minor (mm. 39, 44–49, 57), from which cycles 1 and 2 close

into their successors, and cycle 3 closes into the C-minor cadence deferred since measure 5. In the long and highly checkered cycle 1, the
polyphonic impetus combines with movement to and from a secondary tonality, in this case the E-flat major customary in C minor works.
Hints of impending cosmos begin to emerge as the turbulent cycle 2
yields to the gentler cycle 3 and as both these cycles reinterpret the
initially refractory chaos chord in terms that subordinate it to the ensuing dominant (Example 6).

The harmonic motion of the three cycles is matched by their linear
motion. Each cycle coalesces with one of the three cardinal linear
progressions that "mollify" chaos in Schenker's analysis (Example 7).
Chaos finally "expires" [*atmet aus*], in Schenker's phrase, when the
registral sinking associated with this structural pattern arrives at the
same middle C that resonates from the *Urklang* to the chaos chord.
The arrival coincides with the C-minor cadence at the close of cycle 3.

Haydn also represents chaos as incipient cosmos by melodic means.
The operative metaphor here is the traditional visualization of the
cosmos as spatial / spiritual hierarchy, an ascending scale of being.
Melody in "The Representation of Chaos" is appropriately fragmentary, but what melody there is incessantly ascends. Uprushing scales
and arpeggios that span more than an octave are recurrent; these tend
to grow more mercurial as the music proceeds, as if to suggest a progressive "quickening" of vital forces. More constricted but even more
pervasive is something we might call the chaos motive: three notes
ascending a minor third in double-dotted rhythm.[22] On two emphatic
occasions (mm. 22–24, 45–47), the chaos motive itself ascends se-
quentially through three steps, the second time decorated by a parallel group of ascending flute arpeggios.

This accumulation of ascending figures endows chaos with an urgent impetus, almost a desire, to be lifted into cosmos. The urgency is
partly a product of insistence, but even more of frustration: the most
dramatic ascending gestures rush headlong to greet the cadences that
fail to arrive at the end of cycles 1 and 2 (mm. 39, 49). The treatment
of the chaos motive likewise both reveals and thwarts the aspiration
to cosmos. In the chief polyphonic passage of cycle 1 (mm. 31–40),
the motive first overlaps an ascending two-octave run on solo clari-

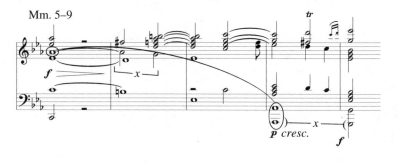

Mm. 5–9

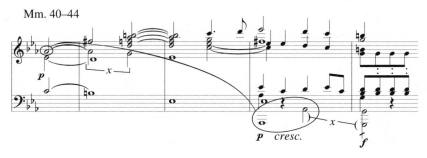

Mm. 40–44

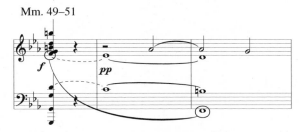

Mm. 49–51

Example 6. Reinterpretations of the chaos chord. An incipient subdominant of E flat in cycle 1 (mm. 5^3–9), the chaos chord dwindles to an incipient C-major German sixth in cycle 2 (mm. 40^3–44, recapitulating mm. 5^3–9) and to a mere chromatic auxiliary of the dominant in cycle 3 (mm. 49–51).

net, itself rises three octaves in three overlapping entries from low solo doublebass to high violins, then gradually contracts in registral breadth as its always-overlapping entries continue. (The motivic density of this passage can plausibly be taken to represent the motion of atoms in a void, an ancient image important to seventeenth- and eighteenth-century science, which tried to reconcile it with immanent

Example 7. Schenker's graphic analysis of "The Representation of Chaos" (abridged).

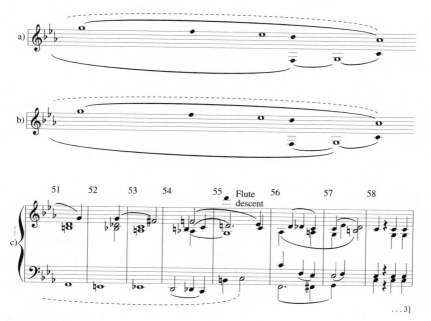

Example 7. (*continued*)

principles of cosmic order.)[23] And on both its sequential ascents, the chaos motive as model (spanning a minor third) is contradicted by the linear melodic projection of the sequence (spanning a major third: E♭–G♭ vs. E♭–G♮ at mm. 22–24; C–E♭ vs. C–E♮ at mm. 45–47, Example 8).

The hierarchical model of the cosmos also aligns height and depth with light and darkness. In *Paradise Lost,* Milton traces this linkage to the original Word of creation:

> at the voice
> Of God, as with a mantle, [did light] invest
> The rising world of waters dark and deep,
> Won from the void and formless infinite.
>
> (3, 10–13)[24]

On these terms, Haydn's failed ascending figures betoken a plea for the voicing of the Word as the *lux fiat.* This plea assumes dramatic impetus at the end of cycle 1, when the first flute sweeps through a two-octave run to the registral apex of the movement, a brilliant g^3,

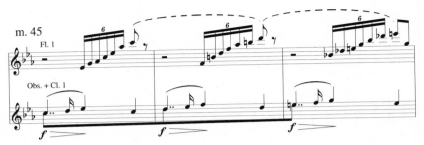

Example 8. Model/sequence contradiction, "The Representation of Chaos,"
mm. 45–47.

Example 9. Close of (1) flute descent ("The Representation of Chaos," mm. 57f.)
and (2) choral setting of "Und der Geist . . . Wasser" (mm. 79f.).

only to be contradicted by a brutal tattoo on the sonority of the
Urklang.

The registral gap thus opened is symbolically filled in, and a transition to cosmos effected, in the closing measures of cycle 3. Here a solo
flute emerges *pianissimo* high above sustained string harmonies and
slowly descends by step to the cadence (mm. 55–58). I do not think
it is fanciful to hear this phrase as a representation of the descent of
the unvoiced Word "far into *Chaos,* and the World unborn" (*PL* 7,
220). The melodic descent by the flute answers and resolves the urgent rising figures that precede it; the chaos motive in particular is
sublimated in the flute melody, which begins with an inversion of the
motive in dotted rhythm. When the chorus subsequently takes the
text, "Und der Geist Gottes schwebte auf der Fläche der Wasser"
(mm. 76–80), the lyrical brightening of color and harmony ushers in
a second C-minor cadence as the flute's did the first (Example 9).

Linked by a distinctive falling octave (c^2–c^1; recall Schenker's association between c^1 and the *Ausatmung* of chaos), the two passages effectively frame the interval of "brooding"—Milton's term[25]—that separates the divine descent from the creation of light.

The style assumed by the strings during the flute solo bears a certain resemblance to elevation music, the slow, soft polyphony improvised during the mass from the sixteenth to the late eighteenth centuries to accompany the elevation of the Host. Beethoven would use a similar style, and a similar solo descent, to precede the Benedictus of his *Missa Solemnis*.[26] Haydn's liturgical allusion draws a parallel between the descent of Christ to the altar at the close of the Consecration and the original descent of the creative but unvoiced Word. Suggestive enough in its own right, this link between communion and creation serves here primarily to mark a turning point in the music. As chaos retreats, hints of Christian mystery emerge for the first time. Sacramental ritual supplements cosmological speculation; revelation supplements natural religion.

The reason for these supplements quickly becomes apparent. Haydn's flute solo is not set in high relief like its violin counterpart in Beethoven. As the flute completes its descent, it loses definition, gradually blending into the rest of the instrumental texture. When the long-awaited C-minor cadence follows, the accompanying tone color is disconcertingly neutral. Worse, the cadence itself is neutral: Haydn attenuates it by dropping the fifth of the tonic chord, representing the tonic only by an expanded form of the C–E$^\flat$ interval that forms the germ of the chaos chord (m. 58, Example 7). A brief closing figure does add the missing tone after a rest, but the impression of a lacuna remains. The Word is still silent, and chaos, evolve as it might, cannot transcend itself.

The consequent need for the voicing of the Word, to be represented by a perfect(ed) cadence, is also implicit in the formal plan of "The Representation of Chaos." The form of this music seems to be undecidable, as well it might. Haydn, who ought to know, calls it an Introduction; Landon a "vague ternary form"; Brown a ricercar; Charles Rosen a slow-movement sonata form.[27] Still, certain formal tendencies are unmistakable here. The most important of these are recapitulation, as one might find it in a sonata form, and movement toward an extended dominant, the characteristic goal of a slow introduction. The two processes, however, cause more problems than they solve. Each of them contradicts itself, and the two contradict each other.

In establishing an extended dominant, the Classical slow introduction assumes the value of a large-scale upbeat. Something of this sort does happen in Haydn's chaos music—but then again it doesn't. At measure 44 a dramatic dominant pedal begins, but at its peak of intensity the pedal tone shifts and the music veers sharply toward the subdominant, the arrival of which curtails the pedal (mm. 47–48) for good. The effect is disquieting; the new harmonies are technically predominant but feel like contradictions. Measure 49 regains the dominant per se, but the passage that follows (mm. 50–54) imposes a degree of local harmonic obfuscation that has led more than one commentator to murmur "*Tristan.*" This is the sort of music with which a slow introduction is supposed to precede a dominant pedal, not follow one.

Admittedly, from an analytical standpoint there is nothing problematical about all this. The entire passage from the onset of the pedal to the verge of the closing cadence unmistakably hinges on the underlying presence of the dominant (Example 7). The tensions and contradictions, even the whole of cycle 3, are no more than foreground effects, a surface turbulence over a calmer depth. Structure bounds expression as ultimate determinacy bounds the randomness of chaos.

This formula, however, should not automatically be preferred to its contrary, that chaos subverts the boundaries meant to contain it. There is a sense in which the life of this music lies precisely in the split between surface and depth. The essential thing about the dominant of a Classical slow introduction is that it *is* a foreground effect, a perfectly manifest dominant. Tonic, subdominant, and neighbor-tone sonorities may all be involved, but the dominant is the focal point; it commands immediate expectation. Eleven of Haydn's twelve London symphonies have slow introductions; nine of them follow this principle. As for the two that do not—nos. 99 and 103—they are the exceptions that prove the rule. Both of them complicate expectation by juxtaposing the home dominant with the dominant of the relative minor. In Mozart's Symphony No. 39, the last third of the introduction veers away from the dominant, but with ample compensation. The middle third is devoted entirely to a dominant pedal, and on a time scale that makes the dominant arrival almost premature. Haydn's "Representation of Chaos" drives the intelligibility of the dominant into the structural background, and in so doing it effectively deconstructs the rhetoric of the Classical slow introduction. As its lack of dominant feeling confronts the necessity of dominant function, a rift opens between the two that cannot easily be bridged. Where the digression in Mozart's 39th extends a well-established expectation, the surface turbulence in Haydn's chaos renders expectation merely nebulous—or nebular, confined to the realm of incipience that is the chosen territory of the music.

The recapitulatory process in "The Representation of Chaos" is no less perplexed. Measures 40–48 plainly constitute a sort of recapitulation, though a notably constricted one. This passage treats the chaos motive like the second theme of a sonata movement. Played first off the tonic (mm. 22–24), the motive must be repeated and resolved at the tonic (mm. 45–47). The only trouble is that we never hear the motive in tonic harmony! Its recapitulation begins with a harsh dissonance and ends with a harsher. From an initial combination of the dominant pedal with the chaos chord (sonorously enhanced), the motive passes through the dominant per se to a minor-ninth chord built on a tonic pedal—a chord that invokes the tonic only as itself a dominant, $V^{9\flat}/iv$, and more particularly as the most plangent, most dissonant, of dominants. Deploying the tonic only in this unstable form, the "recapitulation" of the chaos motive is little more than a simulacrum. It literally renders inchoate what a Classical recapitulation is supposed above all to accomplish, the resolution of the large-scale dissonance typically introduced by the second theme.

More important—to repeat my last point with a difference in emphasis—the dominant pedal(s) and the recapitulation of the chaos motive become *one and the same*. In Classical practice, a dominant pedal often leads to a recapitulation, but the pedal is supposed to stop where the recapitulation starts. To displace a pedal into the recapitulation itself, as Beethoven made a point of showing in the *Appassionata* Sonata, can be profoundly destabilizing—and Beethoven disrupts only the relatively expendable first theme. To do such a thing to the second theme, and to do it while at the same time evoking the expectant aura of a slow introduction, where no recapitulation belongs in the first place, is to form precisely what Haydn's contemporaries most often designated as chaos: a crazy mixture, a *Mischmasch*.[28] A sonata-style recapitulation discharges tension, recalls the past, precipitates a definite end; an introductory dominant pedal accumulates tension, delineates the present, precipitates a definite beginning. Superimposed, the two processes create a temporal snarl.

This impasse emerges with great exactitude. The chaos motive first appears in a key (D flat) unusually remote from the tonic. For that reason, as Rosen observes, something like the recapitulating pedal is necessary: "A transposition to the dominant is, in fact, the only way that Haydn could have resolved the earlier passage and prepared his [subsequent] dominant/tonic cadence." *Pace* Rosen, however, the earlier passage is not a natural fact whose tonal peculiarity forced Haydn's hand and thereby gave the recapitulating pedal a rationale. Rather, as part of the representation of chaos, this D-flat passage jars violently against the music around it; like a warring mass of Lucretian atoms, it embodies a force of negativity that cannot be recuperated within the regime of chaos itself. The recapitulating pedal is indeed rational with respect to the D-flat passage. Its rationality is what makes it futile.[29]

At the point of its greatest organization, then, Haydn's chaos music also reaches the point of its greatest perplexity. In rhetorical terms, the recapitulating pedal might be said to form an *aporia*: the figure of irreducible doubt, impassability, being at a loss. As representation, this aporia gives the measure of the distance that divides a still incipient cosmos from God, particularly from the God of Revelation who affirms: "I am Alpha and Omega, the beginning and the end, the first and the last" (21:6). In confounding the beginning and the end, the misshapen temporality of chaos amounts to a parody of the eternal present. As expression, the aporia sounds in the weight and turbulence of the passage that embodies it: in the wailing trombones, portentous drumbeats, agitated flute arpeggios, and thrumming string repercussions alternating *piano* and *forte*.

From another standpoint, the same aporia places the chaos music at the outer limit of representation as such. Haydn's contemporaries worried over the obvious but inescapable dilemma that the representation of chaos might itself have to court the chaotic, with results that are more muddle than metaphor.[30] Haydn's aporia explicitly accepts this dilemma and, more, compounds it, raises its stakes. The recapitulating pedal declares that "The Representation of Chaos" does not rest on mere confusion but on a lucid and principled process of deformation. The music seeks to model what exceeds representation through a scrupulous logic of antinomy, imperfection, blockage. The full rigor of this logic may be gauged from a "fearful symmetry" comparable to that of William Blake's roughly contemporary Tyger.[31] Of the four measures with pedal (mm. 45–48), the first, on the dominant, stands outside the motivic recapitulation, and the last, motivically recapitulating, stands outside the (foreground) dominant—*and* completes the climactic contradiction of the chaos motive as model by its sequential projection.

The negativity of the recapitulating pedal, in Kantian terms its "outrage on the imagination," is typical of what eighteenth-century aesthetics recognized as the sublime. Indeed, "The Representation of Chaos" shows a striking affinity throughout for the sublime as Kant, in particular, understood it. With its cyclical structure, the music continually approaches a closed totality it never quite achieves. In that respect, it forms an exemplary provocation to the Kantian sublime: the mental state that occurs when one is forced to recognize a representation of limitlessness, but with a "superadded thought" of totality.[32]

To invoke the sublime, however, whether we do it or Haydn does it, may be to overidealize or overcontrol what is most negative about this music. One step beyond sublimity is monstrosity, a purely irrecuperable meaninglessness that arouses both fascination and dread. Sounding so close together, the great tattoo on the *Urklang* and the recapitulating pedal surely carry us to the border zone between these two modes of extremity. In literary tradition, monstrosity is a familiar means of personifying chaos; witness Milton's image of an "Anarch old / With falt'ring speech and visage incompos'd (*PL* 2, 988–89).[33] Haydn's climactic images, to the degree that they approach monstrosity, recast the literal defacement imagined by Milton in specifically Enlightenment terms. It is well known that the late eighteenth century spawned a whole menagerie of monsters: "an eruption of the uncanny strictly parallel with bourgeois (and industrial) revolutions

and the rise of scientific rationality—and, one might add, with the
Kantian establishment of transcendental subjectivity, of which the uncanny is the surprising counterpart."[34] As we noted in chapter 1, Slavoj Žižek suggests that the transcendental subjectivity of the modern
(initially the Enlightenment) subject manifests itself as a resistance to
being bound or contained by any "symbolic tradition." ("Symbolic"
here carries its Lacanian sense.) Žižek also suggests that the surprising, the nightmarish counterpart of this resistance is monstrosity,
which gives the negative freedom of the subject a material form. "The
monster is the subject himself, conceived as Thing."[35] Heard as monstrous, Haydn's "negative" passages might be just this sort of Thing:
both formally, in the "incompos'd" structures that resist the musical
symbolic, and expressively, in the visceral violence of the tattoo and
stabbing dynamics of the pedal passage, where chaotic "thrusts" repeatedly sound, fade away—and return.

Whether monstrous or "merely" sublime, the representation of
chaos as deformation implies the representation of cosmos as reformation. Haydn accepts this logic, which conforms both to the paradigm of cosmic evolution and to a long hermeneutic tradition that
associates divine wisdom with the "order[ing] and disposition of that
chaos or mass" antedating the *lux fiat*.[36] The representation of the first
day accordingly consists of a lucid ordering and disposition of the materials that make up "The Representation of Chaos." The first-day music begins with an extended passage that retraces the broad harmonic
outline of the chaos music, including its lengthy deferral of a cadence
(mm. 60–80). The same passage also amounts to a fourth evolutionary cycle based on the opening measures. The first phrase of recitative, essentially unaccompanied, calls forth unharmonized string octaves that lead once more to the chaos chord, its color softened by the
addition of a clarinet. Episodes on E-flat minor (recuperating the notorious D-flat passage) and E-flat major follow, leading to a tentative
dominant (V$_3^4$) and a premonitory cadential pause on the tonic. Missing here is the friction of dissonant polyphony, its absence part of a
progressive emphasis on consonant sonority within the new cycle. As
Haydn models it, the creation arises by repeating its own prehistory
in "harmonious" form.

In keeping with this model, the climactic *lux fiat* (mm. 81–89) both
repeats and revises the movement from unharmonized tone to tonal

harmony traced at the opening. The passage forms yet a fifth evolutionary cycle, but a cycle pared down to its essence, free not only of polyphonic distractions but also of the at last exhausted chaos chord and the "flat" sonorities associated with it. Unaccompanied, the chorus embarks on a series of three climactic phrases: "Und Gott sprach," "Es Werde Licht," and "Und es ward Licht" [And God said, Let there be light, and there was light]. Each phrase moves from unharmonized octaves to primary C-minor harmonies. After the divine *fiat*, pizzicato strings interject a single soft dominant seventh chord, like a Biblical "siehe!" The chorus then sings "Und es war" on three unharmonized Gs, consolidating the dominant on the model of the unison in measure 4. That earlier unison had been swept aside by the full orchestra with a mute-choked *forte* enclosing the chaos chord. This time, the chorus and orchestra join in an unmuted *forte* to proclaim the birth of light with a full cadence on the tonic—or rather on the brighter and more stable tonic major.

This sonority has nowhere been prefigured and indeed has almost been interdicted. From Raphael's announcement of the beginning to the descent of the Holy Spirit, the music arches from C minor to E-flat minor; from the Spirit's hovering to the voicing of the Word, the music arches back from E-flat major to C major. The modal shift on E flat imparts a sense of impending brightness that the enveloping shift on C will confirm. Yet the turn, or turn back, to E-flat major also seems to anticipate the persistence of the tonic minor. The birth of light in the major, although a stabilizing gesture on the largest scale, *Urlicht* to *Urklang,* is in local terms a structural shock. The representation of the Logos thus appropriates but does not fully escape from the disconcerting logic of the sublime that governs the representation of chaos.

Not that any other outcome would be credible, either in mode or in key. In Haydn's frame of reference, to represent the dawn of creation is inevitably to stage a first sounding of the primal consonance, the C-major triad: traditionally the chord of nature, the chord of light, and, for Haydn's Austrian audience, the tonic triad of the solemn Mass.[37] The multiple shock of the creation cadence in harmony, dynamics, and orchestration functions to defamiliarize the C-major sonority so that it may be heard, with a sense of the miraculous, as if for the first time.

Considered as representation, the creation cadence seems to be modeled closely on a pair of thrice-famous biblical verses: "Make a joyful noise unto the Lord, all ye lands. . . . Come before his presence with singing" (Psalm 100:1–2) and "Where wast thou when I laid the foundations of the earth . . . when the morning stars sang together, and all the sons of God shouted for joy?" (Job 38:4–7). These joyful noises are the prototypes of hymnody, and in the discourse of *harmonia mundi* they have a cosmological resonance. In the Christian cosmos, the music of the spheres inscribes hymnody in the order of nature; it constitutes a festive liturgy to guide the "mystic dance" of the planets and "resound / His praise, who out of Darkness call'd up Light" (*PL* 5, 179). In their treatments of this topic, both Dryden and Milton conflate celestial motion with the primal hymn sung at the creation. Dryden alludes to the Platonic myth that the spheres are moved by Sirens, Christianized as hymning angels: "from the power of sacred lays / The spheres began to move, / And sung the great Creator's praise / To all the blest above" ("Song," ll. 55–58). Milton condenses the parallel terms of Job 38:7, the morning stars singing together and the sons of God shouting for joy, into one packed phrase, "the sons of morning sung" ("On the Morning of Christ's Nativity," l. 119). The metaphorical value of Haydn's creation cadence is similarly double. The awesome peal of C major invokes the dawn of the *harmonia mundi,* while the choral outburst on "Licht" praises the Creator by repeating the *lux fiat,* the musical Word, as both a song and a shout for joy.

The creation cadence also expresses an identity between light and harmonious sound, something implicit, too, when Milton calls on the "Crystal spheres" to "Ring out" with their "silver chime" ("On the Morning of Christ's Nativity," 125–28). In a celebratory poem that reportedly delighted Haydn, Christoph Martin Wieland mirrors this equation of light and harmony:

Wie strömt dein wogender Gesang
In unsre Herzen ein! wir sehen
Der Schöpfung mächtgen Gang,
Den Hauch des Herrn auf dem Gewasser wehen,
Jetzt durch ein bliztend Wort das erste Licht
     entstehen.[38]

[How streams thy surging song / Into our hearts! We see / The Creation's mighty going-forth, / The breath of the Lord upon the waters breathe, / Now through a lightning Word first light arise.]

For Wieland, Haydn's song enables his audience not to hear but to *see* the process of creation. The creation cadence is a "lightning Word," a condensation of sound, light, and Logos, that makes primal light visible to the mind's eye. Behind this metaphor there may hover a long-standing iconographical tradition. As Warren Kirkendale notes in relation to Beethoven's *Missa Solemnis,* paintings from the second to the sixteenth centuries often show the Annunciation being carried to the Virgin's ear on rays of light.[39] The (literally) enlightened ear becomes the site at which divine truth (again literally) incarnates itself by penetrating the body with quasi-erotic force.

This mystical tradition of "hearing the light" has a significant counterpart in the discourse of musical cosmology. The *musica mundana* is normally inaudible to human ears, and there is a Renaissance tradition that its inaudibility is a consequence of fallen human nature. In a famous passage from *The Merchant of Venice,* Shakespeare suggests that the corruptible body renders the cosmic spirit mute:

Such harmony is in immortal souls,
But whilst this muddy vesture of decay
Doth grossly close it in, we cannot hear it.
              (5, 1, 63–65)

In *Pericles,* however, Shakespeare also makes the contrary suggestion that states of special blessedness or moral renovation may make the music of the spheres briefly audible. This idea derives from an extended family of metaphors in which the "well-tuned" soul is said to be in harmony with the celestial music.[40] In a school exercise on the subject, Milton writes: "If our hearts were as pure, as chaste, as snowy as Pythagoras' was, our ears would resound with that supremely lovely music of the wheeling stars" ("On the Music of the Spheres").[41] This same utopian vision finds expression in the nativity ode when Milton calls on the "Crystal spheres" to "Once bless our human ears, / (If ye have power to touch our senses so)" (126–27).

Haydn's creation cadence makes the same invocation: or, more ambitiously, it tries to touch our human senses with a metaphor that figures, and to some degree confers, the blessing of hearing the light. Certainly the music was received in these terms—among others by Haydn himself, who was once so moved by his own cadential outburst that he gestured heavenward and said, "It came from there." One of the distinctive elements in the contemporary reception of *The Creation* was the conviction that the work could somehow form a ritual nucleus for the renewal of spiritual community. Gabriela von Baumberg, with the creation cadence clearly in mind, likens the effect of hearing Haydn's musical Word to a renewal of prelapsarian bliss:

> Wie Adam einst in Paradies
> Am Arm der Eva hingesunken
> Zwar sprachlos den Erschaffer pries[,]
> So hören wir entzückt die[se] Tone.

[As Adam once in Paradise / Into the arms of Eve sank down / Speechless in his Maker's praise, / So we in rapture hear these tones.]

Heinrich von Collin, with similar utopian fervor, assigns *The Creation* an explicitly liturgical power:

> Wie nun in dieses Musentempels Hallen
> Erwartungsvoll sich frohe Schaaren drängen;
> So sieht man einst die späten Enkel wallen
> Zu deiner Schöpfung hohen Himmelsklängen.[42]

[As to the Muse's temple of this hall / Expectant happy multitudes now throng, / Our grandchildren too will gather at the call / Of thy *Creation's* high and heavenly song.]

To put this in other terms, the creation cadence intertwines the tradition of hearing the light with eighteenth-century representations of spiritual harmony that speak of human perfectibility, the recovery of nature as unfallen and divinely ordered, the creation of amity through idealizing the work of civilization. The role of *The Creation* as a utopian ritual is the real significance of the bursts of applause that, in Haydn's day, regularly used to greet the annunciation of light.

.   .   .   .   .

Looking back over the musical processes that culminate in that annunciation, we can observe a tacit duality in the way Haydn relates chaos to cosmos. The turn from C minor to C major that accompanies the creation cadence is so abrupt, so startling, that the creation seems to be represented as a radical discontinuity, God's primal *fiat* as an unplumbable mystery. Haydn suggests as much when he sets the first appearance of the word "Gott," during an otherwise unaccompanied recitative, to an isolated diminished-seventh chord on the strings (m. 61). In its sublime aspect, the creation cadence presents light itself as a sacred mystery, a "quintessence pure / Sprung from the Deep," as Milton puts it (*PL* 7, 244–45). Yet the representation of chaos as a germination, an evolution from incipient to imminent cosmos, is unmistakable. The evolution even continues right through the music for the first day, which, as we have seen, reenacts certain vital features of "The Representation of Chaos." From this standpoint, creation is a supremely intelligible process, and Haydn's creation cadence, which crystallizes the meaning of everything heard before it, can be taken to celebrate, not only the light of what Milton called the "Birth-day of Heav'n and Earth" (*PL* 7, 256), but also a much later conception: the Cartesian "natural light," the "light that lighteth . . . understanding," the light of reason.[43]

This dual representation marks the confluence of the two metaphorical streams on which Haydn draws: one from traditional cosmology, with its discourse of music and mystery, and the other from eighteenth-century science, with its discourse of regularity and immanent world order. Historically, these two models of the cosmos came into ever-increasing conflict with each other and so helped to create the split between religious and scientific understanding that would haunt the nineteenth century. Haydn, however, brings the two models together as genially—as naively, if you like—as he combines Classical melody and Baroque recitative, Classical harmony and Fuxian polyphony. His unruffled attitude belongs as much to the seventeenth as to the eighteenth century. Like Sir Thomas Browne, Haydn finds the metaphor of the music of the spheres more revealing than the truth that the heavens are mute. "Thus far," writes Browne, "we may maintain the musick of the Sphears: for those well-ordered motions, and regular paces, though they give no sound to the ear, yet to the understanding they strike a note most full of harmony."[44] Browne's position is developed in a hymn by Joseph Addison, "This Spacious

Firmament on High" (1712), that was later set in the Episcopal hymnal to some music from *The Creation*. Writing about as many years after Browne as before Haydn, Addison strikingly anticipates—literally prefigures—the latter's trope of musical light:

What though in solemn silence all
Move round the dark terrestrial ball?
What though no real voice nor sound
Within their radiant orbs be found?
In reason's ear they all rejoice,
And utter forth a glorious voice,
Forever singing as they shine,
"The hand that made us is divine." [45]

The eye of reason may, it is true, reveal the traditional cosmology to be a mere fiction. But the ear of reason, hearing the light, reinstates the lost cosmic music as a metaphor—a metaphor for the divine truth inscribed in the order of nature. Haydn's music makes Addison's radiant orbs, the heirs to Milton's crystal spheres, touch our human senses as a primary image for Enlightenment itself.

   This image even has its political side, which bears once more on the utopianism of *The Creation*. Though the *harmonia mundi* was a common, even a commonplace topic in traditional creation narratives, its relationship to common life in the created world was marginal, esoteric both by definition and in practice. Outside of literature, the topic figured primarily in learned debates—did such music really exist?—and in the arcana of Renaissance magic, which took "the recovery of cosmic harmony . . . [as its] persistent, supreme end." [46] Haydn's music, with its show-stopping C-major cadence, brings the music of the spheres into public life, where its metaphorical sounding becomes the introit to a great communal occasion, a performance widely understood to be a quasi-religious festivity. In this role, the cosmic harmony becomes popular as well as public: democratic, if you will, or at least a vehicle for the Enlightenment ideal of universal sympathy. Anyone who wished to could hear the primal consonance and applaud it like one of the sons of God.

   The first great event in *The Creation,* then, is a choral speech-act in which music's summons to the listening subject becomes an all-embracing offer of human solidarity. Beethoven's chorus on "Seid umschlungen, Millionen, / Diesem Kuß der ganzen Welt" [Be embraced, you millions, / This is a kiss for all the world] in the Finale of his Ninth Symphony is a later—more explicit, more extreme—version of the same thing. Haydn's offer of solidarity is reinforced by the choruses that close each part of the oratorio, all of which emphasize the one-ness and humility of an awed humanity confronted with the works of God. Yet *The Creation* also forms a celebration of rigid social hierar-chy. Underwritten by a consortium of aristocrats, composed by a man whose enormous success was inextricable from his unprotesting sub-ordination, the music could hardly do otherwise. Haydn's libretto takes up this theme in terms that would have seemed both natural and emblematic to his audience: the subordination of Eve to Adam. The subject comes up both in Uriel's aria, "Mit Würd' und Hoheit angetan" ["Erect, with native Honor clad," *PL* 4, 289] (no. 24), and in the recitative "Nun ist die erste Pflicht erfüllt" [Now the first duty is fulfilled] (no. 31), for Adam and Eve themselves. A full discussion of the way the music subscribes, indeed oversubscribes, to the hierar-chical theme would lie outside the scope of this chapter.[47] Suffice it to mention that in the recitative Haydn's Adam repeats the imperative "folge mir" in his concluding phrase, "Komm, folge mir, ich leite dich" [Come, follow me, I'll guide you]. In response, Eve repeats "dir ge-horchen" in her own concluding phrase, "Und dir gehorchen bringt / Mir Freude, Glück und Ruhm" [And to obey you brings me Joy, good fortune, and renown]. Eve is also given an elaborate celebratory me-lisma on "Freude"—a gesture that resonates throughout the oratorio. By diverting emphasis from obedience to pleasure, Haydn smudges the contradiction between the communal ideal invoked by his cosmic harmony and the social conservatism fixed in his garden of Eden.

Not even the creation cadence is wholly exempt from conservative pressures, or at least from the uneasy commingling of emancipation and authority. The chorus's joyful noise on "Licht" overlaps with a rising orchestral arpeggiation of the C-major triad, which ends by voicelessly seconding the vocal cadence (mm. 86–89, Example 10). Borne on a wave of repercussive string attacks, the *fortissimo* arpeg-giation is vigorous, insistent, and majestic. And as Schenker observes, it is this arpeggiation, not the choral outburst, through which light in C major "lifts itself aloft," "overtopping" the E♭ of C minor with an E♮

m. 86

Example 10. Creation cadence and C-major arpeggiation, "The Representation of Chaos," mm. 86–89 (chorus and strings only).

in the highest register.[48] As I have suggested elsewhere, it is possible to hear the arpeggiation, though not the vocal cadence it supplements,

as a little overstated, a little forced. This is especially so in the interior of the four-measure phrase: in m. 88, where [tonic and dominant fuse to suggest] a brimming over or momentary knotting up of luminous energy, and in m. 87, when the massed instrumental forces take over after only a single measure on the cardinal word "Licht." It is as if the word, despite the climactic cadential voicing that allies it with the scientific and religious Word, were in need of an instrumental or tonal supplement: as if some external authority, or rather some external power, were being introduced to support a truth that ought to need no support but its own self-evidence.[49]

Presumably it is just a coincidence that the first private performances of *The Creation* at the Schwarzenberg palace, attended by "the flower of literary and musical society of Vienna" (Carpani's phrase), was nearly mobbed by uninvited onlookers, so that a detachment of police was called out to maintain order.[50] But it is no coincidence that the discourse of Enlightenment could apply the figure of *harmonia mundi* with equal facility to both the ordering of the creation and the policing of society. According to the *Universal Police Dictionary,* published in Paris in 1787, "all the radiations of force and information that spread from the circumference culminate in the magistrate-general. . . . It is he who operates all the wheels that together produce order and harmony. The effects of his administration cannot be better compared than to the movement of the celestial bodies."[51]

For a final perspective on the ideological value(s) of *The Creation,* we can turn to a pair of comparisons. In his "Ode for St. Cecilia's Day," composed in 1692, Henry Purcell also depicts the creation. His representation both begins and ends with a deep organ point, which draws a link between the words "Soul of the world" and "one perfect harmony." Milton's image of "the Bass of Heav'n's deep Organ" ("On the Morning of Christ's Nativity," 130) may well hover behind this expressive choice. The music also depicts the binding of primeval atoms into "one perfect harmony" by a shift from imitative counterpoint to homophony. In the next number of the ode, Purcell sets a couplet that praises God for tuning the music of the spheres. This music is simply a stately dance in the French style, with dotted rhythms. What is striking about the representational resources at work in these pieces is their easy accessibility. Purcell has no need to stretch his musical vocabulary as Haydn does; the material he needs comes ready to hand. Writing just five years after the publication of Newton's *Principia Mathematica,* Purcell still finds the figure of *harmonia mundi* both viable and obvious—impossible, really, to avoid. For Haydn, who lives in a fully Newtonian world, the same metaphor embodies an awesome mystery that arises at the crossroads of human reason and transcendental truth. By articulating a natural alliance between these terms, *The Creation* voices a principal Enlightenment ideal. Yet the extravagance of Haydn's expressive means, and perhaps of their reception, too, suggests a certain strain, a penumbral acknowledgment that the ideal is already breaking down.

If so, the Finale of Beethoven's Ninth Symphony is built upon the ruins. With this music, Haydn's progression from naked tone to harmony is radicalized as a movement from cacophony to voice. In a typical Romantic reversal of traditional religious imagery, Beethoven's humanized Word does not descend from the heights but rises from the depths, as the recitative of the double basses is "incarnated" in the bass voice that calls out in appeal to a community of friends.[52] The music of the spheres has become the still, sad music of humanity. No other prelude is possible to Beethoven's "Ode to Joy," music that is compelled to seek the assurances that *The Creation* can still simply find. The subsequent great performative on "Seid umschlungen, Millionen, / Diesem Kuß der ganzen Welt" similarly tropes on Haydn's movement from tone to harmony, reenacting it from an alienated position. First intoned in medieval ecclesiastical style by unharmonized male voices and trombones, the proclamation immediately receives a modern reprise in which the full chorus sings in harmony against a backdrop of orchestral melody. What Haydn claims as a utopian immediacy, Beethoven distances through historical self-consciousness.

In these compositions by Purcell, Haydn, and Beethoven, the music becomes a site on which cultural forces converge in considerable numbers. In terms that are important to recognize, the opening of *The Creation* takes this convergence as basic to its design. As we have seen, the movement from chaos to creation proceeds in cycles. By continually reinterpreting the cardinal features of its first four measures, the music achieves a progressively fuller clarification until the creation cadence refashions Haydn's *Urklang* as the root of a C-major triad. From one standpoint this cyclical structure forms an extended representational metaphor; it suggests the circle as a traditional symbol of perfection, the "compass" or circular boundary that God in the beginning "set . . . upon the face of the deep" (Proverbs 8:27), the circular shape of the heavenly spheres, the celestial sphere of astronomy, the swirl of planetary nebulae. More important than any of these associations, however, is the larger action that embeds them. With each new structural cycle, a greater density of allusion comes to bear upon the music. What is clarification or resolution at the level of musical structure is complication and interpretive provocation at the level of discourse. Haydn's chaos thus becomes cosmos by enveloping the *Urklang,* the epitome of what is meaningless, with gradual accretions of meaning. Logos in this music becomes a process: cultural, hermeneutic, open-ended.

I would claim that what Haydn does here is emblematic of musical representation as a whole, and implicitly of musical meaning as a whole. If the claim holds good, a summary view of musical representation would run about as follows. First, music becomes representational not in direct relation to social or physical reality but in relation to tropes. A musical likeness has the "sonorous value" of a metaphor, and more particularly of a metaphor with a substantial intertextual history. Once incorporated into a composition, such a metaphor is capable of influencing musical processes, which are in turn capable of extending, complicating, or revising the metaphor. Thanks to this reciprocal semiotic pressure, musical representation enables significant acts of interpretation that can respond to the formalist's rhetorical question, "What can one say?" with real answers.

Four

Musical Narratology

A Theoretical Outline

Early in the mock dedication to Lord Byron's comic epic *Don Juan,* the raconteurish author/narrator slips in a footnote about a rhyming contest between Ben Jonson and one John Sylvester:

[Sylvester] challenged [Jonson] to rhyme with—
"I, John Sylvester,
Lay with your sister."
Jonson answered—"I, Ben Jonson, lay with your wife."
Sylvester answered—"That is not rhyme." "No," said Ben Jonson; "but it is *true.*"[1]

Interestingly, Byron tells this anecdote to make a point, not about sex, but about narrative—though the overlap of terms is no accident. Narrative, he suggests, begins in infidelity; narrative abrogates form, social or aesthetic, to accommodate experience. And, in so doing, it simultaneously claims truth and produces pleasure.

Byron's anecdote is worth keeping in mind when confronting the recent flurry of narratological activity among musical critics and analysts. As discontent with the conceptual and ideological impasses of formalist approaches to music has grown—and it has grown spectacularly in a very short time—narratological models have come to seem increasingly attractive as means of endowing untexted Euro-American art music with human content. The musical application of these models, however, has been conspicuously un-Byronic. As usual in musical studies, where the ideal of unity still retains the authority it has largely lost in literary criticism, the idea has been to totalize. As one recent essay forthrightly claims, "Studies in narratology have identified syntagmatic or combinatory structures in narrative for which parallels can be discerned in music."[2] Drawn prevailingly from literary structuralism, the models of choice have understood narrative preeminently as a source of structure rather than as a preeminent means of resisting structure. Narratology has acted as a kind of methodological halfway house in which musical meaning can be entertained without leaving the safe haven of form.[3]

This totalizing approach has met with skepticism from several quarters. In an overview of recent work on musical narratology, Jean-Jacques Nattiez argues compellingly (though one might balk at the word "superfluous") that *"in itself,* and as opposed to a great many linguistic utterances, music is not a narrative and that any description of its formal structures in terms of narrativity is nothing but superfluous metaphor." At best, Nattiez suggests, music "has the semiological capacity of imitating the allure of a narrative, a narrative style or mode" that historical hermeneutics may connect to the "reservoir of philosophical, ideological and cultural *traits* characteristic of a particular epoch."[4] In her *Unsung Voices,* Carolyn Abbate claims that the effect of moral distance basic to narrative, the division of the teller from the tale embodied in the past tense of narration, is at odds with the mimetic immediacy of music, the communion of the hearer and the heard embodied in "present experience," "the beat of passing time." Narrative effects in music are accordingly both occasional and disruptive.[5] Similarly, although unwilling to invoke a precritical notion of musical immediacy, I have elsewhere argued that music normatively overcomes the temporal disjunctions and epistemic uncertainties typical of narrative. Narrative effects in music are accordingly both occasional and disruptive—and deconstructive.[6]

If these arguments are right, then any theory of the relationship between music and narrative must start with the cardinal fact that music can neither be nor perform a narrative. In the strictest sense, there can be no musical narratology. At the same time, the theory must assume that music is not limited to the function assigned by Nattiez (and Abbate, too) of imitating narrative modes.[7] If such imitation is really a semiological capacity, then the protean, inveterately ramifying character of signification all but guarantees that other capacities are also in play. In the "outline" that follows, I propose to identify three of those other capacities, each of which corresponds to a different element of the narrative situation generally conceived. The terms chosen for these elements—narrative, narrativity, and narratography—suggest my intention to short-circuit the notion of narrative structure in order to clarify narrative as a mode of performance.

.   .   .   .   .

Definitions first. Commonsensically enough, a *narrative* is an acknowledged story, whether typical (an abstract sequence of events repeatedly and variously concretized within a given historical frame) or individual (one of the concretizations). *Narrativity* is the dynamic principle, the teleological impulse, that governs a large ensemble of narratives, up to and including the (imaginary) ensemble of all narratives. Narrativity is the impetus that powers (what counts culturally as) narrative itself. Finally, *narratography* is the practice of writing through which narrative and narrativity are actualized, the discursive performance through which stories actually get told. Narratography can be said to govern two broad areas of representation: the temporal disposition of events within and between narratives on the one hand, and the sources of narrative information—from narrators, characters, fictional documents, authorial agency—on the other.[8]

And the semiological capacities of music in relation to these elements of narrative? In relation to a narrative, music is a supplement, in the deconstructive sense of the term. In relation to narrativity, music is a performative, in the sense of the term developed by speech-act theory. And in relation to narratography, music is something like an embodied critique of discursive authority. It will prove convenient to take up these relationships last to first.

The most important characteristic of narratography, and the one most often forgotten in musical applications, is that it is not only the vehicle of narrative and narrativity but also—more so—their antagonist. Narratography can be understood as a principled means of resistance to continuity and closure. As the literary theorist J. Hillis Miller suggests,

Each story and each repetition or variation of it leaves some uncertainty or contains some loose end unraveling in effect, according to an implacable law that is not so much psychological or social as linguistic. This necessary incompletion means that no story fulfills perfectly, once and for all, its [cultural] function of ordering and confirming. And so we need another story, and then another, and yet another.[9]

We may choose to give more weight to social and psychological motives than Miller does. In particular, we can, whether as writers or readers, utilize the destabilizing effects of narratography to resist too much "ordering and confirming"—to counter ideological suasions with critical intelligence.

Musical narratography is no less subversive than its textual counterpart, though it is less pervasive. As I have argued in detail elsewhere, narratographic effects are hard to produce in music, and they reward the work that produces them by destabilizing, in terms at once formal, aesthetic, and ideological, the musical order of things. (Abbate has made a parallel argument for scenes of narrative in opera.)[10] From one standpoint, this difficulty and instability are reciprocals of each other. Since music as a medium depends, at least locally, on enhanced forms of continuity—the musical processes of ordering and confirming—music can produce narratographic effects only in relationship to strategies of principled disruption: either as those strategies themselves or, reactively, as strategies of containment. This is not to say, of course, that all musical disruptions and recuperations have narratographic value. To speak credibly of narratography in music we need to relate musical processes to specific, historically pertinent writing practices. The same holds for narrative and narrativity: music enters the narrative situation only in relation to textuality, even when the music itself overtly lacks a text. The salient claim, then, is that music becomes *narratographically* disruptive when it seeks to jeopardize (or unwittingly jeopardizes) the dominant regimes (or what it fictitiously represents as the dominant regimes) of musical composition and reception. To use Nattiez's terms, music provokes us to the narrative metaphor precisely when it seems to be undercutting its own foundations.

For an exemplary glimpse of narratography at work, we can turn, but with a certain demurral, to Anthony Newcomb's essay "Schumann and Late Eighteenth-Century Narrative Strategies," the critical text that has done more than any other to stimulate the discussion of music and narrative.[11] Writing of Robert Schumann's *Carnaval*, Newcomb adverts to its famous motivic cells, which constitute anagrams on the musical letters of Schumann's name. He suggests persuasively that the recurrence of anagrammatical motives throughout the otherwise motley collection of miniatures reproduces a narrative strategy "beloved of Jean Paul [Richter] and [Friedrich] Schlegel." The strategy at hand depends on what these authors called *Witz*, which Newcomb defines as the faculty of discovering underlying connections in a surface of apparent incoherence. *Carnaval*, Newcomb writes, "applies this technique to the musical analogy to the Romantic fragment. A series of musical fragments is held together by framing narrative devices and by the buried interconnections of *Witz*." And it is precisely these interconnections that make Schumann's "structural method" in *Carnaval* "truly original" and "more than just titillating."[12]

Here as throughout his essay, Newcomb's critical practice is totalizing; it produces insight by bidding up the value of organization and coherence in the musical work. Problematical in any context, this practice is especially problematical when it is applied recuperatively, that is, used to install a latent order amid manifest disorder. Carnival, Schumann's guiding idea, does not suggest buried interconnections; it suggests flagrant anarchy. We should at least question, as Schumann may have questioned and Schlegel certainly did, the assumption that "witty" repetition constitutes a unifying force.

Schlegel's remarks on aesthetics tend to be framed rhetorically rather than conceptually; they do not presuppose a hierarchical schema in which chaos is mediated by structure, but a figurative (usually chiasmatic) schema in which chaos is structural, structure chaotic. "It is equally deadly," he claims, "for the mind to have a system or to have none. Therefore it will have to decide to combine both." True to the spirit of this aphorism, Schlegel's *Witz* is a deliberately baffling hybrid. On the one hand, it represents a gregarious sociability trans-

lated into conceptual terms. It is "absolute social feeling, or fragmentary genius"; its effect is often "like the sudden meeting of two
friendly thoughts after a long separation." On the other hand, *Witz*
is a violent dispersive force, "the outward lightning bolt of the imagination," "an explosion of confined spirit." It represents "a disintegration of spiritual substances which, before being separated, must have
been thoroughly mixed." Its essence lies in "the quality of rupture,
and emerges from the ruptured, derivative nature of consciousness
itself."[13]

If *Witz* is really at work in *Carnaval*, then we need to recognize it,
not as the principle that binds the unruly collection of miniatures into
a formal whole, but as the force that arbitrarily breaks down a prior
musical whole into bits and pieces. Our critical approach should subordinate the invariant pitch content of Schumann's motivic cells to
their role in leading a motley parade of expressive variants. Hermeneutic attention should go to the shape changes that occur as one anagrammatical motive follows another, and to the figure-ground ambiguity produced when a motive merges into a larger melodic phrase.
Our critical practice should also be responsive to the mixture of ar-
bitrariness and festivity in the anagrammatical impulse itself. The
same mixture may well extend to other, apparently more high-minded
forms of structural continuity within the collection. Schumann's version of *Witz*, indeed, may turn out to have retransposed Schlegel's
version from intellectual to cultural and material sociability; it may
function as the sign of a transgressive social energy that both criticism
and performance can choose either to further or retard.

Listen, for example, to the way the initial As.–C.–H. motive
(A♭–C–B) contributes to the character of "Aveu" and "Promenade,"
adjacent pieces placed near the end of the collection (Example 11).
In "Aveu" the motive is impassioned, split up by agitato rhythms in a
first phrase running from tonic (F minor) to relative major. The same
motive in "Promenade" is almost swaggering, borne whole in dance-
like rhythms in a first phrase circling from tonic (D-flat major) to
tonic. "Aveu" presents the motive's A♭–C as a stammering rising third,
"Promenade" as a striding falling sixth. "Aveu" tenses with the erotic
fervor underlying romantic "avowal"; "Promenade" releases—or does
it disavow?—that tension in the press of the street or ballroom. This

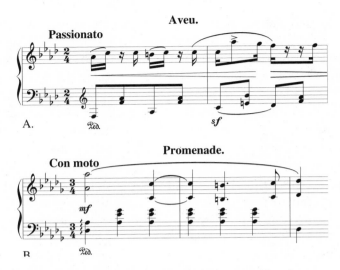

Example 11. Schumann, first phrases of "Aveu" (a) and
"Promenade" (b) from *Carnaval*.

motivic and expressive shape-shifting is *Witz* at work—or play: the
startling "explosion" of the confessional, intimate, internal "Aveu" into
the costumed, sociable, external "Promenade." (Startling but inevitable, as "Aveu" hints twice over: by a wide leap in the melody and by
D-flat-major harmony in m. 2 anticipating the tonic of "Promenade,"
of which the harmony closing "Aveu"—the relative major again—is
the dominant.)

When "Aveu" flips upside down to start "Promenade," the "absolutely sociable spirit" of *Witz* takes on the indeterminacy of Romantic
irony. Just what happens in the "explosion?" Does the private, passionate, confessional self give its authentic identity a social face, protect it under a social mask, or betray it behind a social facade? Or,
given the ease with which the motive, as signifier, travels between inner depths and outer surfaces, does subjective authenticity confess
that it is itself only a mask, no less heartfelt for that but still no more
than an imploded sociability, always already a part of the carnival?

Although *Carnaval* revels in these questions, it ends by appealing
for order from a master hand, an authentic controlling self. When
Witz strings the miniatures together, it acts like a whirligig; to restore
order—carnival, after all, is tolerated because it is temporary—Schu-

mann resorts to the sturdiest of narratographic devices, the frame structure. But the frame is too ponderous to be trusted: first a lengthy "Préambule" and last a still lengthier "Marche" in which the same material from "Préambule" is recapitulated not once but twice. Like Haydn's chaos, Schumann's carnival does not break its frame but may well leave it permanently awry.

．　　．　　．　　．　　．

Narrativity is the next item on our agenda, and here we encounter the use of narrative as a vehicle for both acculturation and resistance to acculturation. By regulating the underlying dynamics of the stories it encourages, mandates, or prohibits, a cultural regime perpetuates itself in at least two ways. First, it prescribes an array of normative character types for its members. Second, it places the prescribed types, each assigned its own mode of subjectivity and range of action, within comprehensive networks of power and knowledge.[14] In relation to the narrativity that impels them, sometimes conceived of as a latent master narrative, the stories themselves function along the lines of performative utterances; they *do* something (or fail to do something) in being told. In this case, what the stories do—or fail to do, sometimes wittingly—is the cultural work of modeling, of symbolically enacting and enforcing, the process of prescription and placement, or what Miller calls ordering and confirming.[15]

Musical narrativity is still a little-explored topic. On two occasions, however, I have been prompted to outline a model of narrativity, based mainly on knowledge networks, that might be applicable to music. The first model is derived from the work of Frank Kermode and brought to bear on Brahms's Intermezzo in B Minor, op. 119, no. 1. It constructs a narrativity that seeks to impart human significance to the uncertain interval between beginnings and endings. Narrativity from this standpoint is a defensive effort to prevent the always indeterminate middle interval from emptying itself out to become (or reveal itself as) arbitrary or mechanical. The second model, poststructuralist in inspiration and alert to the involvement of power networks, is directed to Beethoven's "La Malinconia," the Finale to the String Quartet in B-Flat Major, op. 18, no. 6. It constructs a narrativity that seeks to define and inhabit the gap between knowledge and belief, certainty and surmise, identity and difference. From this standpoint, narrativity may emerge either as the impulse to close the epistemic gap or as the countervailing impulse to prevent the gap from closing.[16]

With regard to power networks, Susan McClary has utilized feminist models of narrativity to argue that music since the seventeenth century has been regularly engaged in the cultural work of constructing gender identities and the ideological work of enforcing them. Feminist theorists, notably Teresa de Lauretis, have shown that Western narrative typically models the efforts of a masculine protagonist to gain cultural entitlement. To win that entitlement, the protagonist must confront and master a feminine antagonist who sometimes appears as a person and sometimes as a space or condition culturally encoded as feminine. (Power here maps onto knowledge when rationality becomes the vehicle of mastery.) McClary shows how the dynamics of tonal composition, especially in big public genres such as nineteenth-century symphony and opera, can be read against this master narrative, whether in compliance, contestation, or a mixture of both.[17]

The Finale of Beethoven's last string quartet (op. 135 in F major) offers a ready illustration of musical narrativity. The narrative element of this music has always been recognized; Beethoven insisted on it. The movement is famously entitled *Der schwer gefaßte Entschluss* [The Hard-Won Resolution] and prefaced by a matched pair of verbal and musical mottos: "Muß es sein?" [Must it be?] inscribed under a short chromatic motive and "Es muß sein!" [It must be!] inscribed under the first motive's diatonicized inversion (Example 12). The "Muß es sein?" motive rules the Grave introduction, which recurs, varied and extended, to preface the recapitulation; the "Es muß sein!" motive gives both the exposition and recapitulation their start.

DER SCHWER GEFASSTE ENTSCHLUSS.

Example 12. Beethoven, String Quartet in F Major, op. 135. Epigraph to Finale.

Critics have differed over how seriously to take the "hard-won resolution," the Grave sections striking some as fervid and others as par-
odistic.[18] But in one respect, at least, the resolution is plainly a sham,
if not a scam. True to its type, the Grave introduction forms an extended upbeat on the dominant, apparently anticipating a structural
downbeat on the tonic at the point where the Allegro starts and "Es
muß sein!" replaces "Muß es sein?" That is not what happens. The
exchange of melodic motives occurs on schedule, but the harmony
lags behind; the Allegro begins on the dominant and scurries to the
subdominant as fast as it can get there. When the recapitulation subsequently answers the second Grave, "Es muß sein!" still sticks to the
dominant, over a dominant pedal no less, although here the obligatory
tonic hastens to make a token appearance in the middle of the fourth
measure. Mapped onto our first model of narrativity, these events
show the dominant becoming disoriented, directionless, emptying itself out as a passageway to the tonic. The result is to make Beethoven's
hard-won resolution seem a bit overwrought, too narcissistic to be a
parody and too capricious to be taken straight. It would seem to follow
that any narrative impetus in the music would be aimed at refreshing
the sense of resolution by somehow replenishing dominant-to-tonic
movement as the means of formal articulation on the largest scale.

And so it is. The replenishment evolves from a dialectical process
in which the "Es muß sein!" motive gradually assimilates itself to the
musical character of "Muß es sein?" The process begins in the second
Grave and concludes in yet another introductory (or transitional) passage, this one set between the recapitulation and coda.

Near the end of the second Grave, the "Es muß sein!" motive embraces the tempo of "Muß es sein?" and engages with it contrapuntally
and antiphonally (Example 13). The motivic interplay proves to be
transformative. The "Muß es sein?" motive appears in several new
forms, all of them lacking its characteristic closing interval of a diminished fourth; the cello harps on one of these, while the viola invents a
series of extravagant variants—they are more like contortions—that
close on wide leaps. Punctuated by tremolos, this mixture of insistence and dynamism exerts a strong dialectical attraction. The "Es
muß sein!" motive responds by taking a chromatic turn in the second
and third of its three statements, exchanging its characteristic closing

Example 13. Beethoven, String Quartet in F Major, op. 135. Finale: end of second *Grave* section.

interval of a perfect fourth for the diminished fourth that "Muß es sein?" has left hanging.[19] Harmonically, however, the two motives remain at odds, "Es muß sein!" proposing diatonic triads and "Muß es sein?" countering antiphonally with diminished ones.

The dialectic continues after overlapping statements of the "Es muß sein!" motive, in vigorous tonic-dominant harmony, close the recapitulation with a rock-solid cadence that feints at ending the whole piece on its own. The rhythmic energy of the motive, however, carries the music onto strange new terrain. Catching at fermatas and eventually dropping in tempo to Poco adagio (not to Grave, true, but in context, close enough), the "Es muß sein!" motive goes on sounding,

Example 14. Beethoven, String Quartet in F Major, op. 135. Finale: "introduction" to coda.

reverberant, transforming itself quietly, lyrically, pensively. More overlapping statements twice settle into chromatic harmonizations, then come to rest through another diminished fourth on a lingering E-flat-minor triad (Example 14). In this way the dialectical circle closes. Poignantly combining the chromatic shape it embraced in the second Grave with the chromatic harmony it embraces here, the formerly declarative "Es muß sein!" motive yields itself fully to the character of the questioning "Muß es sein?"

In so yielding, as Christopher Reynolds has suggested, "Es muß sein!" becomes a literal acknowledgment that what any German musician would call *Es*, the sonority of E flat, must be.[20] Unstable in the home key of F major, *Es* has acted as a sore note throughout the quartet as a whole; the Finale seeks a reckoning with it. The dialectic between "Muß es sein?" and "Es muß sein!" takes *Es*, in the form of E-flat minor, as both its origin (mm. 4^3–5^1, Example 13) and its end. The hard-won resolution is, it turns out, the willing enhancement of a dissonance. Structurally as well as expressively, the resolution proves to be an act, not of self-assertion, but of concession, of pliancy, of resignation. And it is precisely the generative interval in which that resolution is won—won by losing—from which the coda springs forth in high spirits to prolong the tonic reached by the emphatic cadence.[21]

From the standpoint of musical structure, the passage preceding the coda is a reflective detail, a reminiscence of tensions safely under control. From the standpoint of narrativity, the same passage is a surplus of feeling or energy over the logic of the cadence, and as such a moment of cardinal importance. This dual gesture is readily glossed by a familiar series of parallel self-other binaries: masculine/feminine, form/feeling, totality/detail, even a highly refined form of the Beethoven/Rossini binary met with in chapter 2. Expressively weighted in favor of the "lower" term, the dual gesture suggests a moment of reversion, a "feminine" turn or attitude. The suggestion is fairly tacit, but distinct enough to offer a new hermeneutic window onto the music's narrative character.[22]

To open the window requires a shift in emphasis, along the feminist lines suggested by Susan McClary, from knowledge to power in our construction of narrativity. Given the polar opposition of the "Muß es Sein?" and "Es muß Sein!" motives, the yearning chromaticism of the one and vigorous diatonicism of the other readily assimilate themselves to the normative cultural polarity of feminine and masculine. If we recognize this further gender-typing, we can hear the course of Beethoven's hard-won resolution as a critique of the hegemonic master narrative of masculine cultural entitlement. From this standpoint, the lyricizing chromatic evolution of "Es muß Sein!" rests on a narrative impetus to identify with, not against, the feminine. The resolution, hard won and soft voiced, consists in the choice to forgo mastery in favor of desire (the chromatic expressiveness) and pleasure (the piquant coda). From this standpoint, too, the lack of harmonic opposition between the "Muß es Sein?" and "Es muß Sein!" motives at structural junctures becomes an opportunity rather than a problem. The lack, itself coded as feminine, becomes a pleasurable surplus. It dallies with the stern claims of the master narrative and fosters the counternarrative that will later be realized in the mysterious, off-center moments of affinity between the declarative and questioning motives.

.   .   .   .   .

The last item on our agenda, narrative proper, is at once the simplest and, in terms of music, the most problematical. To restate the cardinal point: the very premise of musical narratology is the recognition that music cannot tell stories. This defect—or virtue—is not affected by the ability of music to deploy narratographic strategies or to perform narrativistic rituals; both the strategies and the rituals are migratory, easily displaced from the venues of storytelling. Nonetheless, music since the Renaissance has been used incessantly to *accompany* stories. The usage forms a common thread among otherwise dissimilar musical genres: ballads and other narrative songs, lyrical songs with narrative elements, melodramas, operatic narratives, program music, and what might be called virtual program music, music that, like Beethoven's symphonies in the nineteenth century, compels audiences to find originary stories where the composer has left them unspecified. As an accompaniment to narrative, music assumedly does what all accompaniments do: it adds something extra. But there must be more involved than that, someone will argue. Surely the most memorable thing about the genres just listed is their music, not their narratives. And the truth in this rejoinder leads straight to the semiotic logic that joins music to narrative, namely what Jacques Derrida calls the logic of the supplement.

As Derrida notes in *Of Grammatology*, the term *supplement* is intriguingly ambiguous. On the one hand, a supplement is an excess, a pertinent but inessential item added to something complete in itself. On the other hand a supplement is a remedy, an item called on to make good a fault or lack. For Derrida, this ambiguity poses a choice far less than it defines a rhythm, which he calls a logic. By taking on a supplement, a presumed whole puts its wholeness into question. The act of addition exposes an unacknowledged lack that the supplement is needed to counter. And in countering that lack the supplement exceeds its mandate and comes to replace the whole it was meant (not even) to repair. In his essay "The Pharmacy of Plato," Derrida shows how the account of speech and writing in Plato's dialogues is governed by the logic of the supplement. For Plato, writing is a poison [*pharmakon*], a deceptive and artificial mechanism that blights the natural immediacy of speech. But writing is also a medicine [again *pharmakon*] that cures the ills of speech, especially the inability of speech to create an archive, a storehouse of memory. Philosophy itself, Plato's highest good, depends on the dangerous drug, the supplement, of writing.[23]

Music and narrative obey the same logic of *bouleversement*: music is the supplement of narrative. Emotionally suggestive and technically arcane, music adds itself to the closed circle—apparently all self-sufficiency and self-evidence—of an acknowledged story. The result would be sheer bemusement if we were not so used to it. The narrative circle breaks; the music becomes the primary term and the story its mere accompaniment. Why bother to follow all that stuff Wotan is saying to Erda when we can just listen to the doom-laden procession of the leitmotifs?

Before tracing the supplemental relationship of music to narrative in a specific piece—Schubert's song "Geistes Gruß"—I would like to dwell for a moment on its general cultural importance, as manifested in one of the most pervasive of modern musical institutions: the use of music to accompany narrative film or television. Without engaging in a full-fledged discussion, it can credibly be suggested that the music on a sound track, which we so often think of as an annoyance, a musical elbow in the ribs, is a supplement needed to remedy a medium-specific lack.[24]

The screen for both film and television is a depthless, textureless plane. Without the addition of sound, its sheer flatness can quickly alienate the spectator, deflating and distancing the projected images or, worse, allowing them to develop a disconcertingly amputated quality. Recorded speech—or, in silent movies, the use of often superfluous intertitles as speech simulacra—supplements the images and inhibits alienation. Where speech must be minimized or lost, in lyrical montage or narrative situations of action, suspense, or passion, music is conscripted as a further supplement. In turn, this conscription destabilizes the function of speech; at peak moments, music typically exceeds speech in supplemental force, welling up to suffuse and envelop the image.

 Even at its most banal, sound-track music connects us to the spectacle on screen by invoking a dimension of depth, of interiority, borrowed from the responses of our own bodies as we listen to the insistent production of rhythms, tone colors, and changes in dynamics. (Melody, I suspect, has relatively little importance here, except insofar as certain styles of melody may invoke cultural codes.) Hegel's theory that "the figurations in inwardly reverberating sound" are what make "the inner life . . . something for apprehension by the inner life" here becomes a technical or technological fact.[25] Granted, film does not usually promote the kind of full displacement of narrative by music so common at the opera, not even at peak moments. Once our distance from the screen collapses, the rhetoric of the camera is altogether compelling. But the power of the supplement is more than evident in the rhetorical command exercised even by music that, heard out of context, would strike us as shabby or indifferent.

To return to specifics: Schubert's early song "Geistes Gruß," a Goethe setting, is brief, strikingly varied in texture given its brevity, and not monotonal (Example 15). Goethe's text is a lyric, not a narrative, but the lyric speaker does *quote* a narrative, part of the spirit's greeting of the title:

Hoch auf den alten Turme
Steht des Helden edler Geist,
Der, wie das Schiff vorübergeht,
Es wohl zu fahren heißt.

"Sieh, diese Senne war so stark,
Herz so fest und wild,
Die Knochen voll von Rittermark,
Der Becher angefüllt;

Mein halbes Leben stürmt' ich fort,
Verdehnt' die Hälft' in Ruh',
Und du, du Menschen-Schifflein dort,
Fahr' immer, immer zu."

[High on the ancient tower stands the hero's noble spirit, who, as the ship passes by, bids it a good voyage. "Behold, these sinews were so strong, heart so firm and wild, my bones full of knight's-marrow, my goblet brimming full; half of my life I stormed on, drew out half in rest, and you, you little ship of humanity there, voyage always, always on."]

The poem can be said to pivot on the contrast between the heroic spirit, who narrates, and the lyric speaker and voyaging listeners, who only report and receive narration. The spirit is enabled as a narrator less by his life than by his death. Coinciding with narrative closure, death permits him to represent his life as a finished pattern, a coherent whole composed of two complementary halves. His rhetoric, a quasi-chiasmus, underlines the point, joining the movement of action and repose within the enclosing halves of a life completed: "halbes Leben"—"stürmt'"—"verdehnt'"—"die Hälft'." With the spirit as his mouthpiece, Goethe anticipates the concept of narrative voiced by the literary theorist Walter Benjamin in a classic essay, "The Storyteller":

Death is the sanction of everything that the storyteller can tell. He has borrowed his authority from death. . . . [A man] who died at thirty-five will

Example 15. Schubert, "Geistes Gruß."

fest und wild, die Kno - chen voll von Rit - ter - mark, der Bech - er an - ge-

füllt; mein hal - bes Le - ben stürmt' ich fort, _____ ver - dehnt' die Hälft' in

Ruh, und du, und du, du Mensch - en - Schiff - lein

dort, fahr' im - mer, im - mer zu!"

appear to remembrance at every point in his life as a man who dies at the age of thirty-five. . . . The nature of the character in the novel cannot be presented any better than is done in this statement, which says that the "meaning" of his life is revealed only in his death.[26]

Reading from Benjamin's vantage point, we can identify Goethe's spirit with the spirit of narrative itself. In greeting the living, he urges them to seek the goal of the past tense, the tale told, a goal that will always be found in the distance while they live on.

The poem, however, uses its handling of quotation to counteract this recession to the distance. The spirit's narrative, not merely the gist of the story but its very language, conforms lyrically to the stanzaic pattern set by the speaker. The spirit, indeed, exceeds the speaker in lyrical involution, rhyming his stanzas *abab* as against the speaker's looser *abcb*. The spirit narrates in and through an intensification of the speaker's lyric voice; he has no voice of his own. Given that the spirit's oracular authority depends on the restriction of narrative coherence to the dead, the speaker utilizes a rhetorical device—a form of prosopopoeia, the lending of a face or voice to things faceless and voiceless, among them the dead—to appropriate that coherence and claim that authority on behalf of the living.[27]

Schubert redresses the balance on behalf of the dead. His specific supplement to the text, the musical representation of the speaker's and spirit's different voices, obscures and even revokes the speaker's rhetorical efforts. Schubert endows the speaker and spirit with different tonalities, E major and G major respectively, backed by different accompanimental textures, continuous tremolos versus intermittent dotted rhythms. The act of quotation occurs when the speaker's voice, with neither tonal nor textural transition, gives way to the spirit's. This rather self-abnegating form of quotation turns to a kind of dispossession, a literal revoking of one voice by another, when the music ends in the spirit's G major instead of the speaker's E. Where the poem unites the two voices on behalf of the speaker, the song divides them on behalf of the spirit. The spirit irrevocably claims—or reclaims— the distance from the living that is proper to him and with it his imposing oracular mantle. His music has virtually nothing in common with the speaker's except a harmonic preference for the sixth scale degree, and even this serves as a sign of the spirit's recession to the distance. When vi of G, E minor, emerges near the close of the song (m. 26), it represents the speaker's E major in attenuated form, the tonic-that-might-have-been. Its presence, coming as the spirit hails the voyagers, informs us that the speaker will not be closing his quotation. He cannot do so; he has lost his voice.

More unreservedly than Goethe, Schubert prefigures Benjamin's view of narrative; his setting of "Geistes Gruß" reaffirms that narrative addresses the living but empowers only the dead. This idea is developed further through the handling of both cadences and melodic deep structure. The cadential technique could not be simpler. After establishing E major as the apparent tonic, the speaker's music travels through a circle-of-fifths progression to a cadence on the dominant and there breaks off (mm. 9–13). The speaker departs voicing an expectation that will never be satisfied. Tonal closure comes only in another key, another voice, when the spirit completes his narrative address with a V–I cadence in G major (mm. 30–31). A piano postlude concludes the song with two echoes of this cadence over a tonic pedal, as if the spirit's narrative and its implications were reverberating on— "immer, immer zu"—in memory.

These cadential processes work in tandem with the deep structures shown in Example 16, an abbreviated Schenkerian graph.[28] The speaker's music would seem to begin a fundamental line on $\hat{5}$, but the line thus begun is frozen, unable to descend; at this level the speaker's melodic action consists only of the decoration of the initial $\hat{5}$ by its upper neighbor. Ironically, the foreground vocal line begins with a phrase that consists of a complete descent from $\hat{5}$ to $\hat{1}$, as if to show what shape the fundamental line would take if only there were one (mm. 4–5, Examples 15 and 16). And indeed, the fundamental line that the song eventually provides does take that very shape. But the line, of course, belongs to the spirit, not to the speaker. The living lyric voice is immobile, powerless; the dead narrative voice begins anew, on a different $\hat{5}$, and descends to its alien $\hat{1}$ with perfect aplomb.

The midpoint of this descent is especially worth noting. It occurs a little more than halfway through the spirit's section and coincides with the completion of a quasi-symmetrical foreground image of narrative

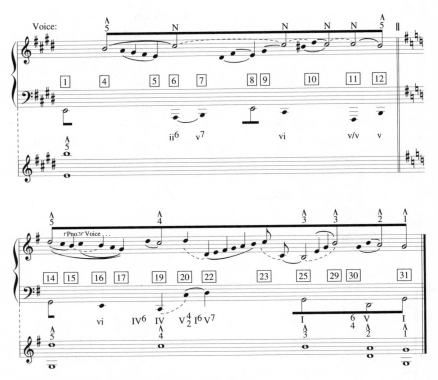

Example 16. Schubert, "Geistes Gruß": analysis.

complementarity. The image consists of the phrase "mein halbes Leben stürmt' ich fort" sung to a dominant scale ascending to c^2, followed by the phrase "verdehnt' die Hälft' in Ruh'" sung mainly to a
dominant arpeggio descending from c^2 (mm. 21–25). The second
phrase ends with a cadence as the spirit sings "Ruh'" on $\hat{3}$ of the fundamental line over a tonic octave in the bass (m. 25). With these materials Schubert issues a reciprocal pair of claims on the spirit's behalf.
By using a microcosm of narrative totality to produce a root-position
cadence, he makes musical closure a function of narrative authority
and projects that authority forward to the cadence that ends the song.
And by meshing the narrative microcosm with a major structural
node, he invests narrative authority with a dynamic impetus that con-
cretizes itself in the desire for musical closure.

    With "Geistes Gruß" we come to the end of this outline of musical narratology. Of the possible conclusions to be drawn from it, the one I would single out as primary is that narrative elements in music represent, not forces of structure, but forces of meaning. That meaning may be read in terms principally social and cultural, as in the case of Beethoven's last quartet, or in terms principally epistemic and self-reflective, as in "Geistes Gruß," or in terms that explicitly address the intersection of social, cultural, epistemic, and self-reflective formations, as in the case of Schumann's *Carnaval.* Anyone looking to narratology as a means of illuminating musical structure and musical unity had better look somewhere else. The condition of narrative, as Byron was trying to tell us, is fractious and disorderly. Structure and unity are its playthings, and its claims to truth are strongest where most contingent, most mixed up with the perplexities of identity and power, sex and death.

Afterword: Music, Writing, Voice

The foregoing "outline" has remarkably little to say about the figure (meaning both "trope" and "person") of the musical narrator. To some degree, this is a pointed omission. If music can indeed stand to narrative as critique, performative, or supplement but cannot narrate in its own right, then the musical narrator is an impossibility and an irrelevance. Musical criticism has traditionally short-circuited this problem by using the name of the composer to adumbrate a narrator and flesh out his shadowy presence. Edward T. Cone's concept of "the musical persona" stands as an influential idealization-rationalization of this practice. Not that the practice should stop, an unlikely outcome in any case. But it should be recognized for what it is: a rhetorical strategy meant to humanize the impersonal agency that we hear in music. Even with textual support, the subject who speaks in a musical work, "persona" or not, narrator or not, is frustratingly impalpable. This subject fully expresses itself in our listening, we could hardly have a sharper or more immediate sense of it, yet when we try to describe it we are stymied. Even in the most literal-minded program music, the musical narrator is, as Fred Maus observes, a "shadow" cast by the listener, an agency as featureless as "the silent, invisible intelligence that guides the montage of a film."[29] Or, as I have suggested elsewhere, the musical subject speaks with the kind of anonymous voice typical of literary discourse set in the ongoing present: the depersonalized yet intimate voice of lyric poetry or the uncannily blank voice of third-person present-tense narration.[30]

The imponderability of the musical narrator has been a latent theme throughout this chapter. Although the agency of narration, or narrative voice, is a basic narratographic effect, voice has figured here only in connection with a particular narrative, the one embedded in Goethe-Schubert's "Geistes Gruß." And the text that embeds this narrative is striking precisely for the lack of a definite narrative voice. The text gives no sign of its source as an utterance; when we ascribe a lyric speaker to it, we are at best invoking one possibility among others, at worst engaging in a questionable prosopopoeia. (We can justify this prosopopoeia only after the fact, when we find it repeated between the "speaker" and the spirit.) The text of "Geistes Gruß" might be pure writing, even writing traced on the cliff face under the spirit's feet, an inscription never spoken and forever unspeaking. Singing this text is indeed an act of prosopopoeia, and a revealingly empty one: the voice that personalizes the text is itself depersonalized by it, drawn into its anonymity. The tonal disjunction in Schubert's setting reproduces this process. The embedded voice of the spirit may be borrowed from the embedding voice of the text, which is itself borrowed from the singer. But the spirit has a definite identity ratified by tonal closure. The embedding voice does not. In articulating this difference, "Geistes Gruß" becomes an allegory of music as "greeting": a literally marvelous greeting, but one offered through a shadowy spirit by someone more shadowy still.

Shadow or not, however, the figure of the musical narrator must somehow be reckoned with. The will to humanize this figure, to make it the vehicle of what Cone calls the composer's voice, is resilient. And it is not just a critical will, as the music discussed in this chapter will attest. The spirit in Schubert's "Geistes Gruß" personifies, even as it supplants, the unknowable subject of the text; the primary motives in the Finale of Beethoven's op. 135 envoice the written words of their composer; and the cyclical turn of Schumann's *Carnaval*, a reprise of the first number within the last, lets the composer "speak" as a frame narrator even though the carnival practices evoked and mirrored throughout the piece subvert any such concentration of subjective authority.[31]

Criticism can afford neither to ignore processes such as these nor to accept them at face value. The composer's voice, narrative or otherwise, is, and needs to be heard as, a cross between rhetoric and history.[32] When Cone presents this voice as the immanence of the composer's authoritative, monological intelligence in the music, what he fails to recognize is that this supposed immanence is both a rhetorical effect—sometimes urged by the music, sometimes by the protocols of listening—and a historical formation that seeks to exclude other voices: the voices, precisely, of the other. In her work on operatic narrative, Carolyn Abbate tries to speak for those excluded voices, but in doing so she, too, overlooks the historicity of their exclusion. She writes as if she and Cone were simply advocates of different models:

There are two ways in which my definition of "voice" differs from that proposed by Cone. First, I do not postulate a monophonic, single "voice" associated with the utterance of a virtual author. . . . Second, I do not hear entire pieces, at every moment, as the utterances of a virtual-author voice. The moments of enunciation are set apart, and in many cases disrupt the flux of the piece about them, and decenter our sense of a single originating speaker.[33]

But for our sense of a single originating speaker to become decentered, it must first have been at the center; if it is decentered by disruptions of immediacy ("the flux of the piece"), it must have been centered by "our sense" of that immediacy; and if it has been decentered it has undergone alienation but not annihilation. Abbate's language thus acknowledges that to hear the unsung voices of music requires listening *through* the virtual-author voice that has historically acted as the agent of exclusion.

Few of the voices we hear (or construct) in this listening-through (or multiple prosopopoeia) will sound much like a narrator's. But many of them will be voices whose imaginary speech acts we can recognize and answer. And to the extent we can speak with them as well as for them, they will be voices that speak credibly, and musically, through ours.

Five

Felix Culpa

Mendelssohn, Goethe,
and the Social Force of Musical Expression

There is *no* such thing as an excess of emotion; what goes
under that name is in fact a lack of it.

—Felix Mendelssohn

The scherzo [to *A Midsummer Night's Dream*] ends with
an astonishing *tour de force* for the flute. Listeners who
wish to appreciate what this involves may be recommended
to pronounce two hundred and forty intelligible syllables
at the uniform rate of nine to a second without taking a
breath.

—Donald Francis Tovey

Since the early nineteenth century, Western art has perhaps been valued most for its opposition to everyday life, a life typically symbolized
by the bourgeois social order.[1] The likeliest reason for this is the cultural paradigm shift by which the bourgeoisie replaced the aristocracy
as the normative, value-defining class in modern Europe. When the
heroic and mythological image repertoire of aristocratic culture dominated high art,[2] artistic distance from the ordinary could be assumed
without question and embodied in real social forms that subordinated
but also validated the commonplace. With the loss of authority suffered by that image repertoire in the nineteenth century, and the concurrent assumption of social authority by a bourgeois order anchored
in, and definitive of, the ordinary, the same distance became redemptive. Lacking an a priori, it had to be *won,* wrested from the fractures
of bourgeois life or found on its fringes.

The result has been an oppositional trope of artistic identity, circulated by populist and elitist, pro- and anti-modern modernists alike.
Either the artist is a client, unwitting or cynical, of repressive social

formations, or the artist is a vehicle of luminous negativity in whom creativity and alienation are at one. Among aesthetic theorists, the most rigorous advocate of this trope was Theodor Adorno, a musical elitist struggling on behalf of a populist cause. Among composers, the most famous impersonator (*sic*) of the trope, as elitist and populist both, was Richard Wagner—an intriguing fact in a chapter devoted to Mendelssohn, whom Wagner did more than anyone else to demean precisely on the basis of the trope in question. My concern in the ensuing pages is both to urge a social and aesthetic reconsideration of Mendelssohn and to challenge the dominant trope of oppositionality. Perhaps it is time to stop thinking that the energy of art is genuine only when it disfigures ordinary life and to stop thinking, or rather talking as if we thought, that social transformation—the overcoming of injustice, inequality, and dystopic community—can come of such disfigurement. Little enough has come of it to date; perhaps what we need is just the opposite.

In an essay on literary abjection and Saturnalia, Michael André Bernstein turns a cold eye on what he, too, sees as the historical tendency to celebrate in art the violent emotions and extreme mental states that would generally bring discomfiture in life. "Already in the Renaissance," he writes,

in Shakespeare's magical land of Illyria, there is no one, on stage or in the stalls, to side with Malvolio . . . although [his antagonists'] jokes are singularly unfunny and their characters ignoble. . . . At times one has the feeling that were Malvolio to read Dostoyevski, he, too, would refuse to recognize where his real kinship of mind and temperament lies and begin to cheer for the success of a mob of frenzied anarchists.

Art, Bernstein suggests, is too often or at least too unreflectively assigned the role of challenging the "normative quotidian rationality" that grounds the dominant social order. Ironically, he adds, such rationality might be said to have wielded all too little influence on a modern history shot through with the deplorable results of extremist and utopian thinking.[3]

·   ·   ·   ·   ·

The critical reputation of Felix Mendelssohn has been both made and marred by the association of art with irrationalism. Since his music generally lacks the rhetorical extremity typical, say, of Beethoven's, which he of course took as a model, or of Robert Schumann's, which he consistently championed, Mendelssohn has been damned with faint praise as the most Classical of Romantic composers. Suspected of harboring too much technical perfection, his music is regarded as just not transgressive enough. So entrenched is Mendelssohn's reputation as a prig of genius that rhetorical extremity can hardly be heard in his work when it does appear, and the pieces marked most signally by it, notably the F-Minor String Quartet, op. 80, and C-Minor Piano Trio, op. 66, have trouble finding their way into the standard repertoire. Mendelssohn remains the composer of a "fairy music," the real implications of which are never thought out, and of a popular violin concerto squashed between the "greater," more serious behemoths of Beethoven and Brahms.

Thus fabricated, Mendelssohn's Classicism, understood as a form of defensiveness or timidity, is linked with a number of unpleasant traits. These include sentimentalism (too many *Songs without Words*), respectability (no one admired by Victoria and Albert can be all good), and middle-class Philistinism (George Bernard Shaw said that the *Scottish* Symphony "would be great if it were not so confoundedly genteel").[4] At the same time, and rather oddly, Mendelssohn's Classicism is allotted a formidable model in the famous Classicism of the elder Goethe, who from 1821 until his death in 1832 served the young Mendelssohn as a mentor.[5]

The oddity I speak of has two sides. First, there is Goethe's Classicism itself, which no one ever spoke of as confoundedly genteel; love of Goethe was popularly supposed to save one from bourgeois tepidness, not damn one to it. Second, there are the compositions that Mendelssohn actually based on works by Goethe, a surprisingly small group given the resonant effect of Goethe's mentorship, which is not in doubt. These works, the overture *Calm Sea and Prosperous Voyage* [*Meeresstille und glückliche Fahrt*, 1828], op. 27, the cantata *The First Walpurgisnight* [*Die erste Walpurgisnacht*, 1831–32, 1842], op. 60, and a handful of songs, do not advertise self-restraint or court a defensive formalism. They form, instead, explicit assertions of exuberance, heterodoxy, and passion.

I don't mean to suggest by this that Mendelssohn's reputation can or should be recuperated by showing that the supposed Victorian gentleman is really a wild man in disguise, a Captain Sir Richard Francis Burton in Prince Albert's clothing. That would be merely to repeat the sentimentalization of wildness, that backhanded form of bourgeois propriety, which underwrites the ruling critical paradigm. What is distinctive about Mendelssohn's assertive energy is that it is revisionary without being adversarial or aggressive. It represents a liberatory dynamism that is not automatically at odds with what Bernstein calls "prudential, rational, and antiapocalyptic modes of cognition."[6] And that dynamism does, indeed, find a model in Goethe, both in Goethe's philosophical aesthetics and in the popular figure of Goethe as an ideal type, the personification of (German) cultural achievement.

A major source of Goethe's cultural authority was the perception, among his contemporaries, that his work embraced the restless self-consciousness but not the attendant alienation of modernity. If, in August Schlegel's memorable phrase, "the contemplation of the infinite [had] destroyed the finite" for the modern West, Goethe approached matters infinite with a cosmopolitanism, an energetic worldliness, that continually rehabilitated finitude. For Novalis, he was "altogether a practical poet" who "accomplished in German literature what Wedgwood did in the world of the English arts." This practicality, downright enough to resemble the material production of the Wedgwood workshop, was the key to Goethe's supremacy. "He abstracts," Novalis continues, "with a rare precision but never without at the same time constructing the object to which the abstraction corresponds." Similarly, if less dauntingly, Wilhelm von Humboldt found in Goethe's work the prototype of an art that combines the "highest ideas" with "the simplicity of what is natural." Goethe led the way in showing that "there is absolutely nothing so extraordinary that it cannot be brought into association with the relationships and conditions proper to the human character." Goethe himself characterized the dynamism that intertwines objects and abstractions, natural experience and high ideas, with a metaphor that locates sacred truth in the pulsations of secular life: "the eternal systole and diastole . . . the breathing in and out of the world in which we live, move, and have our being."[7]

Mendelssohn's music, with its combination of formal clarity and

restless, at times even hectic, melodic vitality, takes this Goethean am-
bience as its own. A reconsideration of Mendelssohn, accordingly,
might well begin with a look at his major Goethe-inspired pieces,
which can be taken as musical credos or manifestos that articulate
Mendelssohn's brand of dynamism against the originary background
of Goethe's. In the remainder of this essay, I will offer a fairly intensive
reading of the ideology of dynamism in *Calm Sea and Prosperous
Voyage* and a necessarily more generalized reading of the less com-
pact *First Walpurgisnight*.

Before we proceed, however, it is important to recognize that Mendelssohn's antiapocalyptic dynamism supplies the impetus, not for
these pieces alone, but for most of his major chamber and orchestral
compositions. (The relative glibness of the lyrical piano pieces and
choral religious works, the venues of sentiment and piety, can be conceded, with an exception reserved for *Elijah*.) Mendelssohn's dynamism declares itself most directly in the melodic impetuosity of his
up-tempo writing: the strong rhythmic and registral profiling, the
agitated or repercussive countermelodies and accompaniments, the
love of sheer high velocity. Attracted to static slow music as a counter-
weight, this impetuosity famously outdoes itself in mercurial scherzos
and propulsive finales where melody is articulated at a breakneck pace
over long musical spans, recurrently dancing on the border that separates melody as such from figuration.

At certain cardinal moments, moreover, Mendelssohn's dynamism
declares itself reflectively. It becomes dialectical in the Overture to *A
Midsummer Night's Dream,* where scampering melody is polarized
against figures of stasis and mystery, glimmering nocturnal motion
traced against hints of chthonic power embodied in the groaning of
the ophicleide, the recurrent drone of the tonic minor six-four chord
garlanded with fantastic dissonances, the subdominant minor chord
in the "gleaming" woodwind progression that frames the whole. The
same dynamism mythifies itself as bardic and archaic in the main
theme of the *Hebrides* Overture, the instability of which—the down-
swing of the melodic phrase to the fifth scale degree—not only or-
dains the theme's own haunted restlessness but also reverberates from
within the halcyon lyricism of the second theme. And it allegorizes its
own genesis, this dynamism, in the first movements of both piano trios
(opp. 49 and 66), the development sections of which, with little pre-

cedent, begin with an entropic gesture that they proceed by reversing. (Perhaps the pattern of Goethe's "Calm Sea" and "Prosperous Voyage" acts as an implicit paradigm here.) These sections begin by rushing precipitously to a statement of the second theme, in which motion and energy drop almost to zero, a condition of pure potentiality, its blankness both threatening and promising. From here each development unfolds, originates itself, by gradually recovering an intense animation that has earlier impelled the exposition. This structural rhythm of de- and reanimation then proceeds to shape the course of the recapitulation and extended coda. Mendelssohn's dynamism, then, may not be aggressive, but neither does it represent the prattle of a repressive tolerance. Like Fingal's Cave to nineteenth-century travelers, it signifies a problematical crossing of the natural and the magical, the socialized and the legendary. It is not, in any sense, to be denied: not by sentimental criticism masquerading as unorthodoxy, and not by performances that—a little too slow, a little wanting in crispness— prettify Mendelssohn's music.

. . . . .

Turning to *Calm Sea and Prosperous Voyage,* we can begin with Goethe's texts, the seeming simplicity of which masks a sophisticated blend of description and allegory:

Tiefe Stille herrscht im Wasser,
Ohne Regung ruht das Meer,
Und bekümmert sieht der Schiffer
Glatte Fläche rings umher.
Keine Luft von keiner Seite!
Todesstille fürchterlich!
In der ungeheuren Weite
Reget keine Welle sich.

[Deep stillness rules the waters,
Without motion rests the sea,
And aggrieved the steersman sees
A flat plane everywhere.
No wind from any quarter!
Fearsome death-stillness!
In the monstrous waste
Not one wave stirs.]

Die Nebel zerreisen,
Der Himmel ist helle
Und Äeolus löset
Das ängstliche Band.
Es säuseln die Winde,
Es rührt sich der Schiffer.
Geschwinde! Geschwinde!
Es teilt sich die Welle,
Es naht sich die Ferne;
Schon seh' ich das Land!

[The mists tear asunder,
The heaven is bright
And Aeolus unties
The eager band.
The winds rustle,
The steersman rouses.
Quickly! Quickly!
The waves part,
The distance nears,
Already I see land!]

First published in a literary almanac edited by Schiller, these texts can most effectively be read in relation to Schiller's famous essay of 1795, "On Naive and Sentimental Poetry" [Über naive und sentimen-talische Dichtung]. The essay develops a contrast between the unre-flective unity with nature evident in classical poetry (the naive) and the self-conscious alienation from nature evident in modern poetry (the sentimental or romantic). As Goethe tells it: "I had in poetry the maxim of objective procedure and would tolerate no other. But Schil-ler, who in his work was wholly subjective, thought his way the right one and wrote his essay in order to uphold himself against me. . . . He proved to me that I was romantic against my will."[8] "Calm Sea" and "Prosperous Voyage," also written in 1795, form a case in point. The poems are sentimental (i.e., reflective) because they perceptibly seek the naive. More exactly, they artfully disguise the sentimental as the naive in the hope of endowing modern experience with the aura of unself-conscious ideality that late eighteenth-century German classi-cism found in classical Greece.[9]

The poems achieve this mimicry of unself-consciousness by tacitly confusing literal and figurative, descriptive and allegorical meanings. The exclamation "Todesstille fürchterlich!" may figure the becalmed sea as an allegory of engulfing death—"Tiefe Stille" collapsing rhetorically and phonetically to "Todesstille"—or it may merely add panic to the immediately preceding statement that in every quarter the wind is still: "Keine Luft von keiner Seite!" The statement that the waves are parting—"Es teilt sich die Welle"—may merely state a fact, or it may allude to the biblical account of the parting of the waters on the second day of Creation and thereby trace parallel allegorical paths from death to life and chaos to cosmos. The remark that Aeolus is untying the winds may be a fancy bit of eighteenth-century rhetoric, or it may place what could be an eighteenth-century voyage in ancient Greece, playfully reversing, perhaps, Odysseus's mishap with the Aeolian winds and the unprosperous voyage that ensued. In sum, without actually committing the reader to a reflective interpretation, Goethe makes a range of such interpretations tacitly available within the process of reading. Exiled from nature by modernity, he tries to cast what he writes as a second nature: to give "his work such a content and form that it will seem at once natural and above nature."[10]

Goethe understands such "spiritual-organic" [*geistig-organisches*] form as the outcome of what he calls *Steigerung*: ascent or increase, enhancement, evolutionary process. *Steigerung* is a dynamic principle that characteristically seeks to repeat originary conditions at higher levels of development.[11] "Calm Sea" and "Prosperous Voyage" can be taken, not only to presuppose this principle as a cause, but also to celebrate it. The semiallegorical movement from the stasis of the first poem to the eager motion of the second is inclusive enough to suggest an ascent from paralytic self-consciousness to the liberatory energy of *Steigerung*. This reading is concretized most strikingly in phonetic terms. Given the content of "Calm Sea," the tight rhyme scheme of the poem (*abab cdcd*) presents itself as the embodiment of an involuted and mechanical energy. "Prosperous Voyage" limbers this energy up, throwing off rhymes in an intricate, irregular pattern (*abcd ef ebgd*) that seems both vital and spontaneous.

Both *Steigerung* and indirect reflection figure largely in Mendelssohn's overture, but on terms that differ significantly from Goethe's. More than either Beethoven, in his miniature cantata *Calm Sea and*

Prosperous Voyage [Meeresstille und glückliche Fahrt], op. 112, or Schubert, in his song "Calm Sea" [Meeres Stille], D. 216, Mendelssohn takes the loose suggestiveness of Goethe's allegory as a model rather than as an interpretive provocation.[12] Although he assumes Goethe's aesthetic as a premise, he alters its focal points. Where Goethe's paired poems are redemptory, Mendelssohn's overture is progressive; where Goethe's *Steigerung* is housed within the dialectics of subject and object, Mendelssohn's is intersubjective, a vehicle for the enhancement of social energy.

The overture falls into three parts, the first and third of which freely exceed or contradict the poetry. There is an Adagio for the calm sea, an Allegro molto e vivace for the prosperous voyage, and an Allegro maestoso epilogue. The Adagio portrays a sea that is more halcyon than becalmed. Although Mendelssohn follows Beethoven in painting the motionlessness of the waves with pedal points, he combines the pedals with slow, steady melodic motion to create a dominant impression of motion in embryo, motion impending. A homogeneous texture heightens the effect; both the motion and the stillness are primarily etched by the strings, with minimal echoes and underlinings from the other choirs. (The string texture is also borrowed from Beethoven, who, however, uses it entirely to create a sense of strangulation.) The Allegro molto, which is closest to Goethe in feeling, forms the main body of the overture and subordinates the tone painting of the Adagio to the constructive interplay of three animated melodies. The Allegro maestoso, another piece of painting, is exuberantly ceremonial, suggestive of a great public festivity. Where Goethe's text closes with an act of individuation—the speaker first says "I" in his last line, "Schon seh' ich das Land!"—Mendelssohn's overture closes with an act of collectivization.

The three sections of the overture are all impelled by a single, strongly profiled melodic process. The music finds a memorable primary motive and continually enhances it and evolves from it. This musical *Steigerung* is what transforms the indeterminate potential energy of the Adagio through the articulate dynamism of the Allegro into the triumphant sociability of the Maestoso. All of this, it is important to add, happens with consummately "naive" clarity, in broad daylight. Like Goethe, Mendelssohn is only esoteric in his studied avoidance of esotericism.

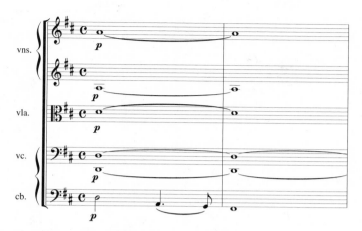

Example 17. Mendelssohn, *Calm Sea and Prosperous Voyage,*
opening on primary motive.

The Adagio begins with a perfect image of embryonic motion as
solo basses state the primary motive under the veil of a static D-major
chord (mm. 1–2, Example 17). The motive can be divided into a sig-
nature rhythm, ♩♩.♪ | 𝅝, and a signature melody, a lightly embellished
descending triad. These signatures, separately or in combination,
form the kernel of virtually every melodic gesture in the overture. In
saying this, however, I am explicitly *not* saying that the signatures are
a source of unity or serve an ideal of unity. Rather the opposite: the
signatures are the means by which the overture can diversify itself
prolifically but intelligibly within the almost inescapable unity imposed by Classical tonic-dominant harmony. The diversification may
not be exactly disseminal, but it does nothing—one might say actively
does nothing—to curb or contain dissemination.

Before that diversification can take place, however, the primary
motive must establish itself as the vehicle of an originary impulse, the
dynamic core of all motion to follow. This it does by exfoliating across
the otherwise neutral texture, detaching itself for solo statements, at
successively higher pitch levels, on clarinet, cellos, violas, and first
violins (mm. 10–26). The opening image then undergoes an expan-
sion that is also a mirror reversal (mm. 29–37). The first and second
violins start an upper pedal that becomes the longest in the Adagio
while the lower strings trace wave patterns in quarter notes. The incipient dynamism proves decisive, and even as the lower strings fail to

Example 18. Mendelssohn, *Calm Sea and Prosperous Voyage*, (Adagio), upper pedal and primary motive.

sustain it the first violins renew it by resolving the pedal into the primary motive (Example 18). A moment later, the opening image returns in its original form but enhanced by a strong feeling of liminality, of something, as they say, in the wind.

Very much in the wind. The signal for the beginning of the Allegro is a vivid tone picture of a fluttering breeze: a dipping and rising phrase on the solo flute sounded and repeated *perdendosi* over a dominant pedal. The phrase, however, also marks an important moment of indirect reflection. It sounds something like a bird call. And the call of a bird over tranquil waters has allusive resonance: it could suggest the stirring of the mythical halcyon, ready to release the seas from enchantment and depart from its floating nest; or, more remotely, the dove lofted over Noah's ark; or, more broadly, a displaced acoustic image of pastoral pleasure, borne, so to speak, on the impending breeze. Or the phrase might not mimic a bird call at all. In sum, without actually committing the listener to a reflective interpretation, Mendelssohn makes a range of such interpretations tacitly available within the process of listening.

The Allegro that follows carries out the prolific, multifaceted *Steigerung* of the primary motive. The signature rhythm animates the first and third Allegro themes and generates a great abundance of subsidiary figures. The signature melody fills wide registral spaces with diatonic energy, extending itself through multiple triadic descents in the first and second themes and continually varying the number and position of its embellishing notes. The work of both signatures is selectively illustrated in Example 19.

This flourishing foreground dynamism also extends to the next highest level of melodic structure. The cardinal element here is the third Allegro theme, the only one subjected to any sonata-style development. The theme is a narrow-gauge version of the primary motive; it repeats the signature rhythm but contracts the triadic motion of the signature melody to the descent of a third. In its defining statements, however, the theme unfolds through a three-part sequence in which the missing triadic motion is structurally articulated in ascending form (Example 20). This triadic articulation is missing from the developmental episodes based on the third theme (mm. 271–83, 335–75), and its absence sets up a diffuse structural tension that is resolved when the theme makes its last appearance (mm. 379–96). The resolution is many sided. As last heard, the third theme not only restores the extended triad but also replaces the extended dominant triad of its first version with a tonic triad and, for good measure, articulates that tonic triad as a sixth chord, the form it takes in the primary motive (Example 20; the ascending form of the extended chord releases

Example 19. Mendelssohn, *Calm Sea and Prosperous Voyage,* primary motive and selected derivatives.

Subsidiary idea (mm. 239-246)

Subsidiary idea (mm. 255-259)

Subsidiary idea (mm. 457-460)

Example 19. (*continued*)

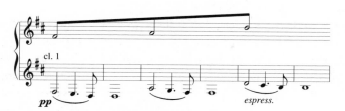

Example 20. Mendelssohn, *Calm Sea and Prosperous Voyage*, final statement of third Allegro theme, mm. 379–84.

the potential energy locked in the descending motive). For yet a further measure, the instrument that does all this is the solo clarinet, enhancing—this is pure *Steigerung*—the work of the solo clarinet in the Adagio which gives the primary motive its first separate, unveiled statement and impels its ascent through the string choir.

The Maestoso epilogue is introduced by a timpani crescendo that efficiently upstages the rest of the orchestra and evolves into an unaccompanied solo (starting *fortissimo* and getting louder) on one note. The drumbeats concretize the prolific musical energy of the Al-

legro in a material form, felt as much as heard, a form directly linked
to bodily vigor and pleasure. The one-note passage, on the tonic
rather than the dominant, is fulfilling, not expectant. The timpanist
should regard the whole episode as a written-out cadenza—better
still, a solo break before its time—and play every note to the hilt. The
idea is to jubilate.

The Maestoso proper begins by building up a tutti as various
groups of instruments join in successively with the timpani. A last an-
tiphonal flurry of wind-and-wave motion then ushers in an invitation
to festivity: a fanfare for three unaccompanied trumpets. First joined
by the timpani in gala trumpet-and-drum style, the fanfare becomes
the core of another tutti built up from successive blocks of sound, this
one animated by the signature rhythm. Moving at its Allegro pace, but
at half the tempo, the rhythmic motive is now expansive rather than
propulsive. Enhancing its rise to prominence in the Adagio, it fans out
confidently throughout the entire orchestral texture: here proclaiming
itself in one instrumental group, there overlapping from one group to
another, and finally abbreviating itself to parade to a close through the
tones of the tonic triad.

"The seas all cross'd, weather'd the capes, the voyage done."[13] But
where have we been and gone? *Calm Sea and Prosperous Voyage*
casts its tripartite form as the supplement of a familiar modernist narrative of progress, the passage from a lack in nature to the plenitude
of civil society. Invoking this narrative runs the obvious ideological
risk of glamorizing the dominant social order. Hegel, whom Mendelssohn knew as both man and thinker, notoriously did just that when he
anointed the modern (Prussian) state as the goal of history.[14] But
Mendelssohn's music, although grazed by this ideological shadow, has
other ideas. Like the Mozart string trio considered in chapter 1, it
refigures the ideal of civil society in the process of reaffirming it.

To this end, the overture submits its *geistig-organisches* form to a
principled discontinuity. Although narratively linear, the tripartite
form is semiotically a frame structure; the outer sections, alike in being primarily representational, frame the middle section, alone in being primarily constructive. As the primary motive traverses the whole,
therefore, it gets caught up in an oscillation between unlike modes of
signification, or even between signification and the lack thereof. The
same motive is syntactical in the middle section and rhetorical in the

frame, abstract here and pictorial there. The "marking" of these differences (together with their occasional erasure) highlights the music's self-conscious mimicry of unself-consciousness, the artifice by which it construes the "sentimental" as the naive. The felicitous result is to limit the overture's chances of summoning a listening subject whom it can simply interpellate.

The dialogue of figurative and constructive modes becomes particularly suggestive at the point of transition between the Allegro and the Maestoso. The timpani conjure away the orchestra piecemeal by ebulliently striking the tones of the tonic and dominant. Only when the drumbeats are all alone do they hone in on the tonic, one on one, and play (with) it until the orchestra chimes in to start work on the grand ceremonial climax. A formal segue thus becomes a kind of theatrical transformation scene; a moment of structural emphasis turns into a pictorial device; and individual energy, in its most basic material form, emerges from and remerges with a social energy that both absorbs and magnifies it. Central to this process is its placement at a moment of festivity. As in *The First Walpurgisnight,* to which we will turn shortly, festivity here symbolizes the social totality that governs it. The totality thus appears as the outcome of a dynamic principle rather than as a static, omnipresent, rationalized state of affairs.

The festive hullabaloo of this epilogue also offers several new objects for indirect reflection. As portrayed by the Allegro, the prosperous voyage of the overture fully retains the mythic-heroic aura that belongs to it by tradition. The public celebration of the Maestoso, however, adds a connotation not usually thought of as auratic, namely the idea of mercantile adventure, the modern (that is, capitalist) heroism of voyaging for wealth. The suggestion is heightened by the deliberate archaism of the epilogue, the atmosphere of which is more suggestive of a Renaissance city-state (easy to idealize) than of a nineteenth-century harbor (impossible to idealize). By appropriating both the heroic-mythic and the heroic-mercantile, and appropriating them with willed naivete, Mendelssohn offers the listener a chance to celebrate the historical power of Enlightenment-style bourgeois idealism, with its cross-cultivation of cultural, social, and economic productivity.

Potentially disenchanting, this offer is not made to disenchant. The three final measures, which Donald Tovey called "a poetic surprise of a high order," seem specifically designed to sustain the possibility of enchantment.[15] The surprise is a grateful reminiscence of the calm sea of the opening: a sudden decrescendo into a simple plagal cadence. There could be no clearer suggestion that the dynamic process traced by the overture is cyclical and self-renewing, that the multiple forms of dynamism represented in the overture are interconvertible. If there is also a hint of rest after labor, a touch of Sabbath feeling underlined by the plagal progression, so much the better.

.   .   .   .   .

The cantata (or ballad) *The First Walpurgisnight* involves a Sabbath of another sort. Not a more dynamic piece than *Calm Sea and Prosperous Voyage,* it is certainly a more rambunctious one. Its text traces the origin of the Walpurgisnight, the mythical witches' Sabbath celebrated on the Brocken over May eve, to a raucous masquerade staged by a group of medieval pagans to frighten off their Christian oppressors. (The trick worked.) Goethe, who had long wanted his treatment of this subject set to music, greeted Mendelssohn's plan for a cantata with warm encouragement—and interpretive advice:

In a true sense the poem is highly symbolic in intention. For in world-history it must continually be repeated that something old, established, proven, reassuring is pressed, shifted, displaced by emerging innovations, and, where not wiped out, nonetheless penned up in the narrowest space. The medieval era, where hatred still can and may produce countereffects, is here impressively enough represented, and a joyous indestructible enthusiasm blazes up once more in radiance and clarity.[16]

Mendelssohn placed this statement at the head of the score that he published at 1843. Clearly, he was sympathetic to Goethe's sketch of a historical process that counters blind hostility with dialectical subversion and answers destructive hatred with creative mockery.

In representing that process, Mendelssohn's *The First Walpurgisnight* nominates the premodern social energy of Goethe's pagans as an ideal for the modern age. The pagans have not yet separated the terms—self and society, nature and culture, secular pleasure and spiritual elevation—that the civilization of modern Europe is famous for wanting to reunite. Unbeset by internal divisions, the pagans can even embrace Saturnalian extremes without fetishizing the frenzy of antagonism. As Mendelssohn stages it, working from mere hints in

Goethe's text, the witches' Sabbath embraces more than just the *Schadenfreude* enjoyed by the pagans as they triumphantly flyte the Christians. Irradiated by its closeness to traditional festive practices, the Sabbath evolves into a vehicle of pleasure and self-renewal for both its imaginary celebrants and its real audience. Without ever losing its aggressive edge, it becomes above all an interlude of uninhibited collective play in which social and bodily energies merge and circulate.

The music imparts this character to the revelry in the most straightforward of ways. The Sabbath begins with *moderato* march rhythms as a male chorus summons the people and the orchestra gradually catches fire. The march, however, is only a prelude to the revelry itself, which begins as the orchestra ups the tempo drastically and whirls forth in $\frac{6}{8}$ triplets. What follows is like a wild song-and-dance routine. In form, it is something like a gigantic *stretto;* in feeling, it is something like a fertility rite. The male chorus takes an extended turn to start things off, the women's chorus answers in kind, and then the two unite. Thereafter this pattern is repeated irregularly with ever-increasing animation. The interplay of choruses is condensed into a hurly-burly of short phrases, bursts of antiphony imploding into massed singing that reexplodes to renew the antiphony. The male and female voices seem to hurl the music back and forth before rushing together, a process that ends, like a ritualized consummation, when the choirs enter successively, basses to sopranos, to build up a final outburst for full chorus.

The most prominent choral device in this Mendelssohnian *Les noces* is the conclusion of a rising soprano phrase on a high note, sometimes a sustained high note. The striking effect, heightened by the fast tempo and busy texture, is to combine a cry of pleasure with a cry of triumph—both of them predominantly feminine. This treatment of the sopranos does more than merely give the pagans' infernal din its cutting edge. Or, rather, in doing that it reveals something about patriarchal cutting edges; it argues for sexual difference with a difference.

Like Goethe's text, Mendelssohn's cantata stages a conflict between two patriarchal cultures, one repressive, the other humane. The pagans' organization of sexual difference is familiarly hierarchical, but it seems to occupy two historical moments at once, with felicitous results. One moment is modern, "enlightened," bourgeois; its women are the functionaries of an idealized domesticity, daughters and mothers who lament the Christians' slaughter of fathers and children. The other moment is archaic; its women—the same women—are independent agents endowed with a precultural (re)creative energy that precedes and envelops domestic life.

The modern moment is definitely Mendelssohn's, not Goethe's. The latter's original text assigns the familial lament to an unspecified man of the people who cries, "Ach, sie schlachten auf dem Walle / Unsre Weiber, unsre Kinder" [Ah, on the ramparts they slaughter / Our wives, our children];[17] Mendelssohn transfers the lament to an old woman of the people and changes "Weiber" [wives] to "Väter" [fathers]. When the cantata's Christians destroy families, they do not emasculate pagan men but brutalize pagan women. Mendelssohn's setting of the old woman's verse, and the subsequent women's chorus, is notably dignified, pointedly unhysterical.

The archaic moment is more unruly. After an orchestral prelude, the sourly agitated "Bad Weather," has spent itself and softened, the cantata announces the coming of spring in terms that identify resurgent vitality with feminine pleasure. A solo tenor intones "Es lacht der Mai" [May is laughing] with slightly incongruous solemnity and quickly finds himself silenced by a women's chorus. The women rush forth exuberantly to celebrate the season, repeating and expanding the tenor's text, their voices backed by fleet, percussive woodwinds in dialogue with the strings, a sunburst of musical energy.

This passage finds its heroic, "higher," complement in the male chorus that subsequently marches the pagans into the central hullabaloo. But the hullabaloo itself revives the irrepressible force of the women's voices, enhanced by dissemination, in the continual witchy war whoops of the sopranos. These whoops are resonant in more ways than one. In association with the phrase "Kauz und Eule" [screech- and night-owl], they allude to the warrior-goddess Athena, to whom the owl is sacred. In self-reflexive association with the words "heul'" [howl] and "Rundgeheule" [howling round], especially as protracted notes or melismas, the whoops transvalue a time-honored object of masculine revulsion: the "hysterical" female "screeching" that segues into the sound of the castrated voice. The pagans thus rout the Christians mainly by showing them a musical Medusa's head, but one that sounds less like Perseus' Medusa than Hélène Cixous's: "Wouldn't the worst [for oppressive patriarchy] be . . . that [you] only have to stop listening to the Sirens (for the Sirens were men) for history to change its meaning? You only have to look at the Medusa straight on to see her. And she's not deadly. She's beautiful and she's laughing."[18] Mendelssohn, of course, is no Cixous. But what his Walpurgisnight shows is that the power of patriarchy is inextricable from the nightmare image of its other. And what his Walpurgisnight claims, with genuine critical force in its historical moment, is that patriarchy can humanize itself by recasting that nightmare as a midsummer night's dream.[19]

Like *Calm Sea and Prosperous Voyage, The First Walpurgisnight* seeks to be simultaneously many sided, spontaneous, and lucid. Drawing on multiple dynamisms, it interrelates them in ways that, though uninhibited, never become alienated from normal quotidian rationality. Many of Mendelssohn's contemporaries admired this in the work. Berlioz, most famously, praised the score for achieving "impeccable clarity" despite its textural complexity. "Voices and instruments," he wrote, "are completely integrated, and interwoven with an apparent confusion which is the perfection of art. . . . One does not know what to praise most [in the pagans' 'howling-round'] . . . the orchestral or the choral writing or the whirling momentum and sweep of the whole."[20] The compliment is the more telling because Berlioz's own Saturnalian movements, the witches' Sabbath from the *Symphonie fantastique* and the Brigands' orgy from *Harold in Italy*, neither have nor, perhaps, seek such clarity; they are more orthodox in their Romantic unorthodoxy.

The mention of orthodoxy starts a related issue that deserves more attention than I can give it here. It is odd to find the devout Mendelssohn writing an anti-Christian piece, even if the Christians in question are safely Catholic—*dumpfen Pfaffenchristen*, as the text calls them. Not that the music is seriously anti-Catholic; it is just pro-pagan. The oddity diminishes when we recognize that the music of Mendelssohn's Druids is distinctly Christian in its rhetoric, especially the concluding C-major hymn to light, with its prominent ecclesiastical trombones. The pagans actually seem to personify a certain type of progressive bourgeois Christian, bred of the Enlightenment; this suggestion is heightened by another rhetorical affinity of the concluding hymn, which is reminiscent of Sarastro's ceremonial music in *The Magic*

Flute. So the object of Mendelssohn's carnivalesque flyting is, not (of course) Christianity, but Phariseeism, the narrow, dogmatic, anticosmopolitan cast of mind that Robert Schumann identified with the Philistines.

Perhaps the issue of cosmopolitanism should take pride of place here. Mendelssohn uses the bass drum and cymbal to punctuate the witches' Sabbath and even adds a transitional postlude that strikes a clear-cut Janissary note. His pagans would seem to have ties to the non-Christian east, ties that not only intimate the long history of European conflict with the Islamic world but that may also intimate something closer to (Mendelssohn's) home. Anti-Semitic rhetoric in the early nineteenth century tirelessly insisted that the Jews were aliens in Europe, "oriental" figures, figures from the east.[21] In a work protesting the oppression of a minority by Christians, the stylish use of Turkish music would form a conveniently indirect way to bite back at anti-Semitism. Mendelssohn, it is true, was normally a tight-lipped assimilationist, but that fact does not necessarily betoken indifference. Perhaps the voice of the pagans in *The First Walpurgisnight* is the voice of the Mendelssohn who refused, defying his father, to call himself Bartholdy, and who, in the flush of triumph, exclaimed to his collaborator in the revival of the *St. Matthew Passion,* the actor Edward Devrient: "To think that it should be an actor and a Jew that gave back to the people of Europe the greatest of Christian works!"[22]

If the large Goethe-based pieces are any index (and the composer himself thought of them as milestones), then Mendelssohn's music demands a thoroughgoing rethinking that cuts through encrusted habits of reception and takes seriously the far-from-extramusical factors of cosmopolitanism, literacy, and sociability. The familiar music needs to be defamiliarized, so that my local classical-music radio station stops making aural wallpaper of the *Italian* Symphony an average of once a week; the less familiar works need to become familiar; criticism must stop making neo-Wagnerian noises about Mendelssohn's unadventurous harmony and start paying attention to how his music behaves; and (with apologies to the biographers) the gentle genius, whose song without words rises on wings of song, can decently retire to the attic.

Six

The Lied as Cultural Practice

Tutelage, Gender, and Desire
in Mendelssohn's Goethe Songs

If there is an archetypal Lied text, Goethe's little poem "Erster Verlust" [First Loss] may be it. Set by Zelter, Schubert, Mendelssohn,
Wolf, and many other nineteenth-century composers, the poem begins by speaking of what need not be spoken:

Ach, wer bringt die schönen Tage,   [Ah, who can bring the beautiful
jene Tage der ersten Liebe,   days, those days of first love, ah, who
ach, wer bringt nur eine Stunde   can bring back but a single hour of
jener holden Zeit zurück?   that lovely time?]

Nothing is said of the beautiful days, that lovely time, because their
character goes without saying. The poem causes this not-saying to appear as a positive plenitude in the intricate phonetic music that plays
among key words and brims over into phrasal repetitions. The addition of real music raises this process to a higher power. To set this
poem, to sing it no matter what the music, is to make sonorously present the verbally absent imagery of a whole fictional world: a Lied-
world of birds and blossoms, sighs and tears, *Heimweh* and *Heimkehr,*
the turns of all natural cycles.

The world of the nineteenth-century Lied is above all a mosaic of
such generalized images, a scene of love and death removed from
history. It consists, as Roland Barthes once suggested, of "little
scenes . . . [each] the starting point of a wound, of a nostalgia, of a
felicity . . . [scenes] intense and mobile, uncertainly located . . . [al-

ways] out of date."[1] The Lied-world has the weightlessness of the typical, which it takes for the universal. In this respect it forms a striking antithesis (perhaps no accidental one) to the densely material, history-heavy world evoked by the nineteenth-century camera—like the piano a machine in the parlor. Unlike a collection of photographs, a collection of Lieder forms no archive. The world it depicts is always, to borrow Barthes's term for the songs of Schubert and Schumann, *inactuel:* nonpresent in both space and time.

Criticism of the Lied traditionally recognizes, but only because it also misrecognizes, this generalized character as basic to the genre. In Carl Dahlhaus's formulation, the music of the Lied projects a broad "lyric tone," readily identifiable in itself, that serves to "reflect the outer and inner form of the underlying poem."[2] On this account, the Lied works by abstracting from an abstraction: treating the poem as a transparent form, a rhythmic (outer) nexus of typical (inner) images, the music distills it into an attitude, mirrors it at a distance. And since most criticism of the Lied has followed a similar account, it has tended to reproduce rather than to identify and interpret the dehistoricized generality of the Lied itself.

The generality—and the ideology. The loss of specificity in understanding the Lied is also a loss of sociality, a loss that this chapter will try to begin recouping. Like the purloined letter, the Lied has been hiding in plain sight. Its origins as a popular middle-class form have been obscured by its later status as art music, which is to say, in the aesthetic era, as music that transcends its origins. But its ideological force is virtually an open secret: the images that make up the Lied-world advance the authority of the modern nuclear family by representing its psychosexual rites of passage as universal. Like most song genres, whether popular or cultivated, the Lied is a convivial means of positioning listeners as subjects within a certain social order, a certain symbolic economy.

From the modernist critical perspective represented by Dahlhaus, still ruled by the formulas of the aesthetic era, the Lied can only be disenchanted by the recognition of its sociality.[3] From a postmodernist perspective, the same recognition may be a way to save the Lied from disenchantment, not to mention oblivion, as the Lied-world loses the little that remains of its grounding in social reality. A postmodernist criticism might conceive of the Lied dynamically, not as a

dehistoricized ideological product, but as a locus of the dehistoriciz-
ing process. A given Lied could enact that process, not only with ideological blindness, but also with varying degrees of critical, transformative, or problematizing insight.

. . . . .

To get at this dynamism critically, we need to begin with what is most
distinctive about the Lied, its status as an art of *accompanied images*.
Whatever else it may do, a Lied becomes expressive by representing
its music as the fulfillment, the otherwise impalpable plenitude, of
cardinal images from the Lied-world. If music, as we saw in chapter 4, is the supplement of narrative, it is also the imaginary of the
image. This representation cuts across all declamatory styles and is
independent of the tightness or looseness with which a Lied follows
the discourse of its text. As "Erster Verlust" indicates, the text need
not even specify the images in question. Such images, to theorize further, circulate both implicitly and explicitly, visually and verbally,
within the cultural field. What constitutes the image as such is not its
literal or material visibility but its status as a discrete part of an imaginary scene in the Lacanian sense of "imaginary."

In this expressive modality, the Lied is surprisingly cinematic. Or
not so surprisingly, despite the anachronism: film, too, has coupled
images and music (live, mechanical, or recorded) from its very beginnings. Granting the differences specific to the media—the verbal versus the visual image, the Lied's foregrounding of music versus the
film's foregrounding of the image—the coupling in each case signifies
the presence (or disavows the absence) of plenitude. And when film
music, during the sort of lyric climax referred to in chapter 4, goes
beyond the supplementation of voice to suffuse and envelop the image, the film is transposing into its own technology the basic expressive process of the Lied. As an art of accompanied images, the Lied,
and song in general, has more in common with movies than with
opera.[4]

What makes this analogy important is the dynamic relationship between the film image and the spectator, something that has a likely
counterpart in the relationship between the Lied image and the listener. Drawing concurrently on feminism, psychoanalysis, and semiotics, and with the usual dissensus on detail, film theory has argued

that the film image is above all a means of constructing subjectivities. The image allows, or coaxes, or impels the spectator to adopt positions of identification with the person looked at on screen, or the person looking, or the "person" who presides over these looks from without, the virtual author whose eye is the camera. These subject positions neither require nor reject identification with a fictional character or virtual author as such. Rather, they represent points within the hierarchies of knowledge and desire that connect one subject to another within the narrativity of the film. Such positions model the coalescence of psychological and cultural identity, with particular emphasis on the interrelations of sexuality, gender differentiation, and discursive authority.[5]

The significance of the image-spectator nexus has proved to hinge on what might be called the disciplining of the image. This topic is far too complex for convenient summary. Suffice it to say that, as Christian Metz was the first to argue, film unreels in the realm of the Lacanian imaginary, the preoedipal register of images and identifications, but it addresses a (normatively masculine) subject who watches from within the symbolic order, the Oedipal register of law and language.[6] From this recognition, questions proliferate. To what degree is the subordination of the imaginary to the symbolic—typically represented, in film as in culture generally, by the subordination of the feminine as object to the masculine as subject—reenacted by films and film genres? To what degree am I the normative subject of the film and what are the consequences if I am not? How far does the film succeed in determining the content and regulating the meaning of my imaginary through acts of visual and narrative structuring? How far does it persuade me that its ideologically invested images should be, or, better, already are and could only have been, my psychologically invested images? Or, to broach the topic from the other side, how far does the film's founding, desire-laden embrace of the imaginary empower me to find new subject positions that resist, escape, or transform the symbolic order?

What I propose here is that song in general, and the Lied in particular, raises this same set of questions. Like film, the Lied constructs subjectivities by setting up positions of identification in and around the coupling of image and music. The listener may identify (in the relational sense described earlier) with the speaker, as personified by the singing voice, with the subject addressed by the speaker, or with a presiding, virtual-author subject who observes from without. A song will typically seek to manage the interplay of text, voice, and musical technique in order to privilege one of the available positions.

Not that this effort always succeeds. Nor is it always meant to. In song as in film, the identificatory positions do not form a stable order; they can shift over time, vary in hierarchical value, displace or subsume one another, and be occupied simultaneously. The degree of mobility probably depends most on the status of the external, virtual-author position. In both song and film, as Metz observes of the latter, the "person" of this position never engages in first-person enunciation; he (the normative he) never says "I."[7] This elision of the first person can equally well give an impression of transcendental unity (hence authority and control) and of decentered fluidity (hence an appealing or unsettling dispersal of authority and control). Criticism of the Lied, and indeed of classical music as a whole, has generally, one might almost say preemptively, treated the first possibility as the only one, as if to repress its deconstruction by the second. One aim of what I call postmodernist music criticism is to keep, as the music does, both possibilities continually in play.[8]

In the most general terms, the identificatory process in the Lied turns on the register—meaning the register of signification, but with a pun on musical register—in which the composer, listener, or performer grounds the singing voice. As Guy Rosolato has suggested, the imaginary voice is a medium or envelope of identification, in the first instance with the mother; it is the voice heard in the "acoustic mirror" formed when the child hears the sound of his own voice and mingles it, neither inside nor outside, with the sound of the (m)other's voice.[9] The imaginary voice, however, is constructed after the fact, like the Kristevan semiotic; in a sense, no one ever hears it but the subject of the symbolic order. And for that subject, the imaginary voice may, as Kaja Silverman suggests, be either cherished as a plenitude that can make good all lack, dreaded for the power to rupture that plenitude, or despised as the representative of everything the symbolic order has transcended.[10] This division of value is reduplicated in the division of the imaginary voice from its symbolic counterpart, the latter tethered to the ideal of discursive mastery and to the structuring, regulatory, interdictory qualities of language.

"Music," Rosolato suggests, "finds its roots and its nostalgia" in the "atmosphere" of the imaginary voice, the "murmuring" of which he provocatively likens to the music of the spheres.[11] For all its considerable appeal, however, this suggestion, like Kristeva's that music is purely semiotic, forgets its own presupposition that what is anterior to the symbolic is itself a fiction of the symbolic. Music may well have the capacity to "voice" the nostalgia Rosolato hears in it, but the capacity is only one of many, and not always in play. With song in particular, the varying relationship of voice to text, as it ranges between the possible extremes of vocalise and secco recitative, may be taken to enact a negotiation between the imaginary and the symbolic voices. Concurrent with this negotiation, and basic to its value and meaning, is the interplay between the singing voice and the independent, always compelling, sometimes authoritative musical voice constituted by the accompaniment. Song may approach the effect of the imaginary voice with unrivalled explicitness, but it also makes explicit the multiplicity of positions involved in all constructions of subjectivity.

▪   ▪   ▪   ▪   ▪

In order to test out the theory rehearsed here, I turn not only to the interpretation of selected Lieder but also to the solving of a riddle—a small one, but intriguing. Despite his close personal and artistic ties to Goethe, some of which we considered in the previous chapter, Mendelssohn wrote very few Goethe Lieder. He attempted six, finished five, and published four, as follows. (The scores of "Die Liebende schreibt" and "Suleika" 1 and 2 appear in full in the appendix.)

Gretchen ("Meine Ruh' is hin"), WOO (inc.)

Die Liebende schreibt (1831), op. 86, no. 3

Lied einer Freundin (1837) ("Zarter Blumen leicht Gewinde"), WOO

Suleika 1 (1837) ("Was bedeutet die Bewegung"), op. 57, no. 3

Suleika 2 (1837) ("Ach, um deinen feuchten Schwingen"), op. 34, no. 4

Erster Verlust (1841), op. 99, no. 1

These songs show continuities strange and strong enough to require explanation. Except for "Erster Verlust," all are for female voice and all set texts expressing specifically feminine desires. Of the completed songs, "Die Liebende schreibt," "Suleika 1," and "Suleika 2" are impassioned addresses by women to their far-off beloveds, from whom they demand a gift of knowledge in the form (named explicitly in "Die Liebende schreibt") of a sign. "Zarter Blumen leicht Gewinde" is a more restrained address of the same type. "Erster Verlust," for a singer of either sex, develops related themes of alienation and desire in the form of a meditative soliloquy. In the process, as we have already seen, it tacitly encapsulates the imaginary world of the other songs and of others like them.

So much thematic consistency in so little a corpus can scarcely be mere coincidence. In each case but the last, Mendelssohn requires an explicitly feminine position in order to write Goethe Lieder. He composes Goethe only for a woman. This is true, not just for the obvious reason that the songs are for female voice, but because the texts cause this voice to reflect continually on its own femininity. For a man to sing these songs would make little sense. It is as if the figure of Goethe as author somehow mandated a feminine complement.

More important, Mendelssohn goes beyond simply providing this complement. In a recurrent act (both deed and performance) of vocal cross-dressing, he identifies with it. He composes Goethe only *as* a woman. The first indices of this identification are the texts of the songs of 1831 and 1837, in which the activity of the speaker mirrors the activity of the composer. These texts center, not on the woman's feelings per se, but on the problem of her expressing them: of her moving, like the poet or composer of a Lied, from feeling to the signifiers of feeling. "Die Liebende schreibt" approaches the matter literally; the poem, as its title announces, is about a woman writing. The same is true of "Zarter Blumen," a text preoccupied with the conditions of its own possibility. The "Suleika" poems, both textually and musically composed as a pair, depend on a metaphoric chain in which the wind equals a messenger equals a text. (Text, not voice: the wind's messages require interpretation.) In "Suleika 1" the speaker reads the text of the east wind; in "Suleika 2" she writes her answer on the west. These two poems focus with such intensity on a woman's place in the circuit of discourse that a woman might have written them—and did: although published under Goethe's name in the *West-Ostlicher Divan*, they were written by "Suleika" herself, Marianne von Willemer. ("Zarter Blumen" is also by von Willemer, published without attribution as part of an epistolary exchange with Goethe.) The reason for this vicarious authorship is not that the poems' expression of impassioned devotion would violate the era's standards of feminine modesty (it carefully does not) but because, as we will see, such devotion was supposed to do the cultural work of supporting and subsuming itself under masculine authorship. Von Willemer was not writing behind Goethe, but for him: as, perhaps, Fanny Mendelssohn was composing for Felix when she published songs under his name.[12] Finally, to complete the textual overview, even "Erster Verlust" turns on the failure of the speaker's continually renewed laments ("stets erneuter Klage") to provide a cathartic release from the sense of loss.

Looked at chronologically, the completed songs suggest a phantom cycle, a narrative that Mendelssohn traced out intermittently but finally disavowed. In 1831 "Die Liebende schreibt" frames the terms of identification: Mendelssohn sets Goethe by imagining the way a young woman seeks love and knowledge from her far-off beloved. In 1837 the paired "Suleika" songs repeat these terms and eroticize them; Mendelssohn responds after the fact with apparent discomfiture and publishes the songs, their sequence reversed, in separate collections. The cognate "Zarter Blumen" remains unpublished. In 1841 "Erster Verlust" cancels the terms, and with them Mendelssohn's setting of texts by Goethe; the song replaces absence with loss and an exclusively feminine with a possibly masculine subject.

But what is at stake in this unwritten narrative? Why do just these terms of identification and representation, with all their potential ambivalence, move into play? What weaves the articulations of gender difference, sexual desire, and the gift of the sign into a single network?

.   .   .   .   .

One answer may lodge in the social and discursive construction of what might be called relations of tutelage in early nineteenth-century Germany. I take the term *tutelage* from the famous opening of Kant's essay "What Is Enlightenment?":

Enlightenment is man's release from his self-incurred tutelage. Tutelage is man's inability to make use of his understanding without direction from another. Self-incurred is this tutelage when its cause lies not in lack of reason but in lack of resolution and courage to use it without direction from another. *Sapere aude!* "Have courage to use your own reason!"—that is the motto of enlightenment.[13]

In Mendelssohn's Germany, the normative subject of culture was a man who had freed himself from tutelage through a process of self-development, call it *Bildung* or, with Kant, coming of age. As Friedrich Kittler has shown, the various means to this freedom were explicitly recognized and grounded, at home and school, in concrete practices of reading and writing.[14] They included, first, the organization of tutelage in terms of gender difference and, conversely, of gender difference in terms of tutelage; second, the constitution of tutelage as an amatory relationship; and, third, the appropriation of Goethe himself to personify an enlightened tutelage that ends by enfranchising its disciples, transmitting cultural authority through the gift of a sign.

What Kittler emblematically calls the "discourse network of 1800" depends on a sexual division of labor that puts women in charge of reading, men of writing. The woman's role, based on an ideal of motherhood, is complexly reproductive. Taking over a function previously reserved for fathers, the mother of "1800" teaches her children not only how to talk but also how to read, using newly developed systems of phonetic instruction. The child learns reading directly from the mother's mouth: the daughter so that she can repeat this instruction to her own children, the son so that he can translate it to the medium of published writing once he comes of age. In school, the children encounter curricula geared to their future specialities: the girls learn "the reading, recitation, reception, and enjoyment" of German literature, especially the poetry of Goethe; the boys prepare incrementally, largely through "free-time reading in German, encouraged and guided by newly-founded school libraries," to write a graduation exercise, the German essay, demonstrating, in the words of Friedrich Schleiermacher, "the development [both] of the understanding and of the powers of fantasy."[15]

At the end of this process, the boys, now men, mark their freedom from tutelage by enrolling in a discursive relay system: men read each other in order to write. The girls, however, now women, enroll in a system of pure consumption: they reproduce the maternal role of mirroring for the subject his mastery of language. The authors of tutelage in children, women remain in tutelage to the authors among men. It is in this context that women denied their identity as writers even when they published. When Mendelssohn's aunt, Dorothea Veit, later Schlegel, published a novel, the author was not identified but the title was *Florentin: A Novel Published by Friedrich Schlegel.* If this is a product of feminine masochism, it is what counted for normal; as Therese Huber wrote of her similar practice, "My name was never published, and I guarded against its occurrence, for this silence was the last vestige of the pure, feminine relationship to writing that remained to me."[16]

Both Dorothea Schlegel and Therese Huber, writing for their beloveds, show how easily discursive and amatory relationships could intertwine. But the ideal of *Bildung* did not limit amatory ties to cross-sex partners. The era that Kittler names "1800" witnessed the rise of philology, along with philosophy, as a master discipline in German universities. Largely following Johann Joachim Winckelmann, who ascribed the cultural achievement of classical Greece to a cult of ideal manhood and promoted both the cult and the culture as models for modern Germany, the philologists began to interpret Greek pederasty as a model for modern learning.[17] It is unclear to what extent this "boy-love" [*Knabenliebe*] originally registered as homosexuality in something like the modern sense, as it had irrevocably begun to do by the time Thomas Mann wrote "Death in Venice" in 1911. The philologists disagreed over the admixture of "lower sensuality" in an ideal love intended "to make physical beauty into a purified psychic beauty,"[18] an issue that Mann treats with studied ambiguity. What is clear, however, is that praise for *pederastia* as a source of noble virility, "closely associated with liberty, manly sports, severe studies, self-sacrifice, self-control, and deeds of daring,"[19] substantially influenced both pedagogy and nationalist politics in Germany for more than a century.

Two vignettes, one cruel, one comical, can serve to illustrate. In 1806, the philologist Friedrich Creuzer once again refuses the pleas of his beloved, the poet Karoline Günderrode, to live in the same city he does, even though he wishes "to be *one* with [her] in my spirit and in my work (where that is possible)." Günderrode, to whom Creuzer regularly gives masculine names, would destroy his "calm presence of mind," making it impossible for him to accomplish his "life's work, [which] is to open up the *silent* temple of antiquity to a number of boys." As Friedrich Kittler, recounting this anecdote (which ends with Günderrode's suicide), remarks:

the philosophic interpretation of antiquity has as little room for women's bodies as it does for their names. Any noise of the lips, whether it be speaking or kissing, disturbs the hermeneutic of the silent temples. Only as long as women do not set foot in Heidelberg and remain instead the distant source of all philosophizing can the initiation ritual of the university be successful.[20]

Socrates must save himself for Phaedrus.

Similarly, in 1911 Robert Musil imagines a dream for the schoolboy hero of his novel, *Die Verwirrungen des Zöglings Törless* [Young Törless]. Two tiny figures, Törless's parents, flit across a "great circular plain" to be replaced by two more, apparently larger, Törless's mathematics master and an unknown figure bearing a heavy book. Boylike, the master seems to be solving theorems in a "squeaky little voice":

As he spoke they were stooping over the book . . . making the pages fly. After a while they straightened up, and the other stroked the master's cheek five or six times. Then once more they went on a few paces, and after that Törless yet again heard the voice, just as if it were unraveling the long skein of some theorem . . . and this went on until the other again stroked the master's cheek.[21]

Törless wakes and stretches "luxuriously" at just the moment that he recognizes the caressing figure as none other than Immanuel Kant! The luxury and the caress both belong to the genealogy of tutelage. The speaking figure advances from his master, Kant, toward his disciple, Törless, encouraged in each new step by the master's love. Cultural authority passes along a chain of tender bodies, as if to verify the philologist Friedrich Welcker's claim of 1816 that *pederastia* "assumed part of the character of fatherly love [note the presence of Törless' parents in the dream] and took over the pedagogical role."[22]

Mendelssohn's account of his final visit with Goethe in May 1830 strongly suggests the playing out of an amatory master-disciple relationship just at or below the threshold of acknowledgment. In particular, the visit organized itself around the production of amatory signifiers, the purpose of which was to draw out a modest courtesy call into a ten days' idyll. Mendelssohn started the process, apparently unawares, by "begging" Goethe to address him with the intimate "Du."[23] Goethe responded, shaking off a long spell of lethargy or depression, with a virtuoso courtship mediated through his daughter-in-law, Ottilie, and her sister Ulrike, to both of whom Mendelssohn was attracted. Goethe, indeed, showed himself an expert in what would now be called homosociality, drawing Mendelssohn close by playing on the latter's attraction to women. On several occasions, the "Weimar beauties" were asked to the house, "an extremely rare thing" in Goethe's old age. "When I go up to him on such occasions," Mendelssohn wrote, "he says, 'My young friend, you must join the ladies, and make yourself agreeable to them'" (25 May).

Mendelssohn at first found Goethe's overtures as much disconcerting as dazzling. His pleasure in tutelage conflicted with his own desire to be a "man of determination," which eventually led him to speak of leaving Weimar. Goethe responded by drawing Ottilie into a window bay and saying, "See to it that he stays here"; with Ulrike's help, and some extra stage managing from Goethe, she succeeded. Given such persuasion, Mendelssohn admits, "I no longer wished to be a man of determination, and stayed" (6 June; translation modified). He did not regret the decision. In retrospect, he found the idyll in Weimar "unforgettable," a gift, as he told Goethe by letter, that had made him inexpressibly happy (16 June). He was even more emphatic in a letter to C. F. Zelter, describing how "every hour [had] brought nothing but elation, joy and pride" (22 June).

The focal point of this happiness was the process of tutelage itself, which Goethe ritually enacted, haloed with warmth, and then, whether on impulse or by design, symbolically dissolved. For an hour every morning, the disciple would play the piano for the master like a latter-day David before Saul;[24] for an hour after dinner, the master would discourse to the disciple, his "marvelously pleasant" words flowing nonstop (25 May; 6 June). When Mendelssohn thanked him for one particularly scintillating talk, Goethe replied, "It is mere chance, it all comes to light incidentally, called forth by your welcome presence" (6 June). Gradually, both master and disciple recognize that they are enacting a rite of passage, the end of which is Mendelssohn's release from the tutelage that had begun in the same house nearly a decade before. When Mendelssohn does at last depart, Goethe marks his "graduation" threefold: with a kiss, a gift, and a privilege. The kiss uncannily prefigures Kant's caress in the dream of young Törless. The gift is a precious sign of cultural authority, a manuscript page of *Faust* inscribed "To my dear young friend F. M. B., powerfully tender master of the piano—a friendly souvenir of happy May days in 1830. J. W. von Goethe" (6 June). The privilege, confirming the inscription's tacit salute to a "young master," is that of being Goethe's correspondent, of taking as a reader the man whom all men read. When Mendelssohn leaves Weimar, he does so as a man of determination, after all.

Neither Mendelssohn nor those around him could doubt the status Goethe had conferred. In the discourse network of 1800, Goethe is the ultimate master in all scenarios of tutelage, the equivalent, as Kittler remarks, of the Name-of-the-Father in Lacan's symbolic order.[25] Novalis calls Goethe "the true custodian of the poetic spirit on earth"; Clemens Brentano advises his sister Bettina to "read some history, but otherwise mostly Goethe and always Goethe"; Dorothea Schlegel writes after her first meeting with Goethe, "To know that this god was so visible, in human form, near to me, and was directly concerned with me, that was a great, everlasting moment!"; and, lest Dorothea's half pun on "Gott" and "Goethe" seem prescribed for feminine disciples alone, her brother-in-law August goes her one better:

Not to know Goethe is to be a Goth. . . .

Goethe, you who by the mercy of the gods came
To us, an angel from the stars; we are not loth
To call you godly in form, look, heart, and name.[26]

Goethe is the angel of culture, the mediator between the *Goth* and the *Götter*. No wonder, then, that in 1810, the Bavarian minister of education Immanuel Niethammer asked Goethe to compile a "National Book," a secondary-school reader of New High German classics that would replace the Bible as "a unifying point for the education of all classes."[27] The project fell through when Goethe, unlike Clemens

Brentano, failed to prescribe mostly Goethe and always Goethe—at which point the school authorities stepped in and did it for him.[28]

When Mendelssohn turned to composing "Die Liebende schreibt" in 1831, his memories of the "happy May days in 1830" might still have been fresh. In any case, and consciously or not, he chose a text that recycles all the culturally numinous features of the Weimar visit. Six years later, he would repeat this choice with the "Suleika" poems. All three texts center on the experience of tutelage, representing it as amatory, as mediated through the feminine, and as idyllic. All three texts close by anticipating the loving gift of a sign, something that all three songs project through a climactic vocal elaboration on the word that designates the sign. And all three texts invest the pleasures of tutelage with the idealizing pathos of distance, as Mendelssohn did retrospectively in his follow-up letters to Goethe and Zelter.

These connections belong to a kind of cultural unconscious that, like the more famous Freudian unconscious that perhaps only personifies it, can weave even the simple act of composing a few songs into a dense tapestry of meanings. As expressions of character and situation, Mendelssohn's Goethe Lieder model the work of the discourse network in which feminine tutelage supports masculine *Bildung*. They address a female listener presumed to belong to that network; they invite her to identify with the abject, effectively masochistic position of the singer-protagonist; and they repay her imaginary compliance by (con)fusing it with rapture. The songs, however, make the same, yet not quite the same, invitation to the male listener. They urge him as well to identify, cross-vocally so to speak, with the singer-protagonist. If he does, he will find tutelage modeled for him in its masculine version, which ends with the disciple acquiring the cultural authority to which he submits.

The songs suggest this outcome in the way they call for the gift of the sign. The climactic invocations are moments, not of feminine receptivity (Therese Huber's pure feminine relationship to writing), but of masculine appropriation, moments in which the agency of the disciple exceeds what the text requires or even allows. At this point the origin of the sign figuratively shifts from the master to the music, which the singing disciple rather than the silent master controls. Even the later, semipalinodic "Erster Verlust" culminates with this shift.

Male cross-vocal identification is an unstable process that raises important questions about the interrelations of gender and sexuality. I will defer discussion of these, however, until the individual Goethe Lieder have come into focus.

.   .   .   .   .

Goethe's "Die Liebende schreibt" ["The Loving Woman Writes"] is a study in feminine psychology, as grounded in the sort of self-abnegating adoration exemplified by Dorothea Schlegel and Therese Huber. These real-life women suggest that while Goethe certainly performs an ideological service when he represents abject dependency as normative pleasure, there is still some historical truth to the representation. Goethe, indeed, was celebrated for understanding women so deeply that, as the educator Betty Gleim remarked, it was "as if the whole sex . . . had brought their confessions to him."[29] Nonetheless, "Die Liebende schreibt" cannot help deconstructing itself a little when it figures love in the rhetoric of knowledge:

Ein Blick von deinen Augen in die meinen,
Ein Kuß von deinen Mund auf meine Munde,
Wer davon hat, wie ich, gewisse Kunde,
Mag dem was anders wohl erfreulich scheinen?

Entfernt von dir, entfremdet von den Meinen,
Führ' ich nur die Gedanken in die Runde,
Und immer treffen sie auf jene Stunde,
Die einzige; da fang' ich an zu weinen.

Die Thräne trocknet wieder unversehens;
Er liebt ja, denk' ich, her in diese Stille,
Und solltest du nicht in die Ferne reichen?

Vernimm das Lispeln dieses Liebewehens;
Mein einzig Glück auf Erde is dein Wille,
Dein freundlicher zu mir; gieb mir ein Zeichen![30]

[A look from your eyes into mine, a kiss from your mouth on my mouth, whoever has, as I do, certain knowledge of/by these, what else could seem enjoyable to her? Distant from you, estranged from my family, I only lead my thoughts in a circle, and they always strike on that hour, that single one; then I start to weep. The tears dry again unawares; he loves, I think, even here in this stillness, and should you not reach into the distance? Hear the whisper of this breath of love; my only happiness on earth is your will, your kindliness to me; give me a sign!]

The woman writer interprets looks and kisses as sources of "certain knowledge" [gewisse Kunde], the certainty of which she figures rhetorically in the phonetic coupling of "Mund" and "Munde," mouth and mouth. Apparently, it is possession of this knowledge that allows her to break the circle of her obsessive thoughts and address her beloved in writing. But the address itself calls, indeed pleads, for a sign the writer is not supposed to need, a sign that will give her what she is already supposed to have: certain knowledge of the beloved's love. Contrary to her claim, this love is not present with her in the stillness. Knowledge of it has only been signified, not sacramentally transmitted, by looks and kisses that were no less acts of rhetoric than the writer's phonetic coupling of "Mund" and "Munde." Certain knowledge *of* (*davon*) the looks and kisses does not mean certain knowledge *by* them (again: *davon*). That knowledge can come only from the *next* sign—and the next and the next, assuming that the called-for sign is given at all.

Mendelssohn's song intervenes at precisely this point, transforming the call for the sign from a moment of pathos and dependency into a moment of self-enfranchisement. The song treats the call as both its goal and its climax, three times repeating the phrase "gieb mir ein Zeichen" [give me a sign] to conclude a setting that otherwise, in all feminine modesty, avoids expressive repetition. This triple articulation also has a climactic shape of its own (Example 21). The first and third statements of "gieb mir ein Zeichen" occur *piano,* in declamation, in the singer's lower register; the second statement occurs *forte,* in melisma, in the upper register. Reached by crescendo and left by diminuendo, the second statement forms the kind of singular climax, at once disruptive and synthesizing, that feminist theory has persuasively found to link the normative rhythms of narrativity and male sexual pleasure.[31]

We can hear this climax, and especially its climax-within-a-climax, as crowning a self-possession that Mendelssohn's singer slowly but steadily gathers to herself. It is important to remember, though, as the echo of male orgasm reconfirms, that the primary subject of this self-possession is masculine, not feminine. For the male listener, the singer may be literally female, but her position is only figuratively feminine. Only in the space of this difference, which denies entry to

Example 21. Mendelssohn, "Die Liebende schreibt," the call for the sign.

women, can the listener take full advantage of the music's impulse to end the singer's tutelage. The era "1800" requires the female listener to find her pleasure in being constrained by the framing statements of the call for the sign, but it offers the male listener the pleasure of being released by the central statement. For the feminine subject of "1800," even the singer's strongest utterance is significant only in relation to the awaited reply of the beloved, the reply of the symbolic. For the masculine subject, the same utterance is (or seems) significant in its own right; it crystallizes into the acoustic mirror of his dawning autonomy.

The song encapsulates the rising curve of self-possession in the difference between its settings of the first "ich" and last "mir" of the text. The "ich" comes on a short note that must virtually be swallowed, an awkwardness—presumably deliberate in an otherwise smooth vocal part—that undercuts the claim to certain knowledge that immediately follows (m. 6). The "mir" evolves out of the triple call for the sign, in the course of which the agogic emphasis shifts from "Zeichen" in the first two statements to "mir" in the last (Example 21). "Give me a *sign*" becomes "give *me* a sign."

The process framed by this "ich-mir" contrast unfolds primarily in the relationship between the singer and the accompaniment and in a group of formal discontinuities that mark the call for the sign. The accompaniment in "Die Liebende schreibt" acts as a source of dynamism; it constantly moves one step ahead of the singer, charting her emotional course and enhancing the energies at her command. Changes in note motion bear the main expressive burden. For most of the first two verses, the accompaniment consists of a near-continuous throbbing in eighth notes, an icon of the excessive emotional susceptibility ascribed to women. But the throbbing gradually transforms itself into a confident mobility. Just as the singer refers to her fits of weeping, the piano jump-cuts to a lively rocking figure that continues through the pathetic, perhaps deliberately banal melisma on "weinen" [weep] (Example 22). Sixteenths on the upswing, eighths on the down, this figure proves to be the accompaniment for the singer's statement that her tears dry up unawares. It recurs almost continuously until the start of the last verse but yields briefly in mid-course for an arpeggiolike episode in pure sixteenth notes (mm. 26–28²).

Example 22. Mendelssohn, "Die Liebende schreibt," emergence of the rocking figure.

Example 23. Mendelssohn, "Die Liebende schreibt," vocal recapitulation.

Example 23. (*continued*)

And this is another proleptic gesture, for motion in arpeggiolike six-teenth notes turns out to be the accompaniment for the last verse and its proliferation into the triple call for the sign. Each advance in motion precipitates an advance in power.

This dynamism not only multiplies the call for the sign but also becomes part of it. Without disrupting its structural role as the means of closure, the call breaks both with the formal processes that frame it and, in so doing, with the order of tutelage that frames the singer. The initial break problematizes the form of the song. Although the evolution of its accompaniment is continuous, "Die Liebende schreibt" suggests a ternary form when its vocal setting of the last verse (mm. 32–34) begins by recapitulating the opening (mm. 1–4³) (Example 23). The recapitulation, however, soon comes to grief on an emphatic chromatic alteration (m. 35, downbeat), after which it quickly disintegrates (mm. 35–36). The call for the sign follows at once to go its own way.

The remaining breaks occur during the climactic second statement of the call, which they work to estrange from its surroundings. The second statement evolves out of a short passage for solo piano (mm. 39–40¹) that rises melodically from the first to the fifth degree of the tonic scale but with the framing degrees set askew, raised by a semi-tone. (The voice enters [m. 40] by doubling the piano's raised fifth degree.) And more than just this is askew. The first and third statements form a half cadence and answering full cadence, both appro-priately "feminine." The second statement stands apart from this cad-ential order, beginning with marked dissonance and ending with an internal, pointedly "masculine," cadence on the subdominant. Similarly, the first and third statements together project a descending line in the middle register, corresponding to the descent of the Schenkerian fundamental line, in overlapping steps: $\hat{3}$ to $\hat{2}$ (g^1 to f^1) in the first statement (m. 39), $\hat{2}$ to $\hat{1}$ (f^1 to e^{b1}) in the third (m. 44). The second statement interrupts this process with a false completion that reaches the first scale degree an octave too high. It even includes a triplet figure that encapsulates the entire $\hat{3}$-$\hat{2}$-$\hat{1}$ descent an octave too high. In sum, the second statement voices the call for the sign, and voices it eloquently and ecstatically, from outside the sphere of authority that is supposed to answer it. Uttered from the masculine subject position, the feminine singer's call for the sign *is* the sign. The call answers itself.

Its answer even finds an acoustic image in a brief strain of instrumental melody. First sounded in abbreviated form under the rocking figure (mm. 23, 25), this strain introduces the first statement of the call and recurs as a postlude to the last (Example 24). Played *espressivo* deep in the bass, the strain seems to adumbrate the lyrical singing of a male voice. The female listener may be supposed to hear this voice as the beloved's, already answering her call from the distance. But the male listener knows that the voice is his own.

Mendelssohn's treatment of the call for the sign contrasts instructively with its counterpart in Schubert's setting of "Die Liebende schreibt" (1819). Schubert reiterates textual fragments from the final verse, even skirting the edge of nonsense, in order to abstract and highlight the link between the beloved's will and the singer's only happiness (mm. 49–61). This carries the equation between dependency and bliss to extremes even by the standards of the poem. The result is a call for the sign, voiced as a closing cadential descent through the tonic triad, that blandly idealizes feminine self-abnegation. Mendelssohn's song may do otherwise primarily on behalf of the male listener, but at least the singer-protagonist is dignified and intelligent; Schubert makes her a giddy goose.

.   .   .   .   .

The first of Marianne von Willemer's "Suleika" poems begins with striking abruptness: "Was bedeutet die Bewegung? / Bringt der Ost

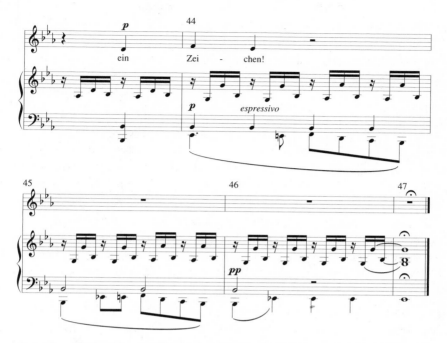

Example 24. Mendelssohn, "Die Liebende schreibt," bass "vocalization" and close.

mir frohe Kunde?" [What does this stirring mean? / Does the east wind bring me joyful news?] Seizing on the ambiguity between the stirring of the wind and the stirring of her feelings, the speaker poses a question of interpretation and thereby claims a place in the circuit of discourse. She goes on to read the stirring made legible by her question, producing a series of figures that equate idyllic nature, the feeling of being "moved," and joyful news of the beloved:

Und mir bringt sein leises Flüstern
Von dem Freunde tausend Grüße;
Eh noch diese Hügel düstern
Grüßen mich wohl tausend Küsse. (13–16)

[And the wind's light whisper brings me a thousand greetings from my friend; before these hills grow dusky a thousand kisses will surely greet me.]

These figures, however, do no more than *pre*figure the more authoritative discourse of the beloved himself:

Ach! die wahre Herzenskunde,
Liebeshauch, erfrischtes Leben
Wird mir nur aus seinem Munde,
Kann mir nur sein Atem geben. (21–24)

[Ah! the true knowledge of the heart, love's breath, renewed life, only from his mouth will come, only his breath can give it to me.]

The speaker, then, can reach fulfillment only in the beloved's masterful presence. But what she seeks from that presence is not an unreflective bliss, not a purely receptive tutelage, but the gift of the sign. Her goal is not the beloved's breath itself but the words for which the breath is a figure, and which she in turn will interpret as a figure for the true knowledge of the heart. Her network of figures contains no route to the literal; bliss depends on the indeterminacy of interpretation. The beloved controls the gift of the sign, but the speaker (already) controls its meaning.

This negotiation for discursive power is once more Mendelssohn's focal point. His first "Suleika" song recycles many of the expressive strategies found in "Die Liebende schreibt": the throbbing "feminine" accompaniment, the turning point that simultaneously redefines overall form and impels the call for the sign, the multiplication of the call itself. There is even a similar melisma for the climactic voicing of the call. Unlike "Die Liebende schreibt," however, "Suleika 1" never lets go of its inarticulate accompaniment, in the throbbing of which it mirrors the singer's bliss. This impulse toward disarticulation also extends to the text, which the song continually fragments and repeats. (The text salad may partly represent maladroit strophic writing, but its overexcited quality—"I hardly know what I'm saying!"—is clearly appropriate.) The result of this textual and instrumental chattering is to drive the singer toward the very position of unreflective fulfillment that von Willemer's speaker resists. Put in Kristevan terms: where the speaker claims symbolic agency, the singer is pressed to embody semiotic urgency, an urgency the symbolic order will take under its control when the singer thrills proleptically to the sound of the beloved's voice.

But the singer can resist, too, especially when she represents a male listener who identifies cross-vocally with her position. The strophic movement of "Suleika 1" divides into phases of stasis and dynamism,

A A followed by A' B. The dynamism seeks the same end reached in "Die Liebende schreibt": release from tutelage through the call for the sign. To further that end, the song three times joins the sustained throbbing of the accompaniment to strains of articulate instrumental melody: at the start of the A' strophe (mm. 20–22), during the climactic voicing of the call for the sign (mm. 34–35), and immediately thereafter (mm. 36–39). These passages, transient though they are, establish a bridge between receptive bliss and subjective agency. The last passage is virtually explicit on this point; it transfers to the piano the vocal melody for the first phrase of text, "Was bedeutet die Bewegung? Bringt der Ost, . . ." the hermeneutic question by which von Willemer's speaker gains an active discursive position (Example 25). The singer, having long since lost that position if she ever held it at all, (re)gains it at last through the piano at the very moment she affirms that only the beloved's breath can give her true knowledge.

This movement of recovery impels the entire B strophe, which gives the previously diffuse rewriting of the text a specific purpose and develops into the multiple, climax-centered call for the sign. The B strophe arises after the A' strophe reaches the end of the text but defers musical closure (mm. 29–30). Ostensibly meant to reprise the final stanza, the new strophe actually concentrates on, and concentrates, the final line. What ought to be the full reprise deletes the penultimate line, which refers to the beloved's mouth, and repeats the subsequent reference to the beloved's breath ("nur sein Atem") three times, all of them musically emphatic. The missing line follows, too little, too late; it is swept aside by a crescendo that climaxes on "Atem" and leads through yet another "Atem" to the final "geben" (Example 25). In short, the B strophe takes the words right out of the beloved's mouth. It transfers the origin of the sign from the mouth that forms it to the breath, or the figure of breath, that bears it. Repeating the breath word like a mantra, five times in all, and supported by the sound of her opening question on the piano, the singer appropriates this origin to herself. In her climactic voicing of the call (m. 34), the appropriation takes on the material form of the breath in her own body as she sustains the syllable "Ah" (the long A in "Atem") for just over a measure. The "Ah" sound is particularly suggestive here; as Kittler observes, the linguistic theories of "1800" regarded it as the

Example 25. Mendelssohn, "Suleika 1," transfer of vocal melody and climax on "Atem."

Example 25. (*continued*)

origin of pronunciation and hence of language: the primal sound of the human voice.[32]

. . . . .

Von Willemer's second "Suleika" poem parallels the first fairly closely but recasts it according to the difference between the subject positions of reader and writer. The marks of that difference are distinct but inseparable, like letters in cursive script: first, an enhanced discursive confidence for the writer, and, second, a definite sexualization of her aims:

Sag' ihm, [West], aber sag's bescheiden,
Seine Liebe sei mein Leben,
Freudiges Gefühl von beiden
Wird mir seine Nähe geben. (17–20)

[Say to him, [west wind], but say it modestly, his love is my life, a joyful feeling of both will his nearness give me.]

Where she first sought the beloved's breath to signify through speech, the writer now seeks his bodily nearness to signify through feeling. And her imperative to the wind, which is to say, to her own text, confronts forthrightly the need to convey both the strength of her desire and the modesty with which, as a woman, she is constrained to veil it.

Mendelssohn follows von Willemer's example in "Suleika 2" but with an agenda of his own. Where the poem treats the writer's sexuality and her enhanced authority as overlapping, the song takes the singer's authority as a premise and its overlap with her sexuality as a goal. Where the writer exceeds her tutelage only indirectly, through the phonetic virtuosity of her closing injunction to the wind, the singer enacts an ecstatic, almost orgasmic transition from tutelage to mastery through the proliferating call for the sign.

In what will prove to be the *Stollen* of its bar form, the song characterizes the singer as both impassioned and self-controlled.[33] Her vocal line is full of expressive emphasis, both dynamic and melismatic, but it strictly follows the letter of the text, refusing to muddy discourse with repetition. The accompaniment balances continual sixteenth-note figuration in the right hand, again suggesting the inarticulate agitations of feminine sensibility, with recurrent quarter-note phrases in the deep bass, again suggesting the articulateness of masculine subjectivity. (The song invites the female listener to ascribe this melodic bass to the guiding hand of the beloved, the male listener to masculinize his position with it.)

Yet the singer of the *Stollen* falls just short of full subjective agency. Her strophes end in paralysis, marked at the fraught words "Thränen" [tears] and "Schmerzen" [pain] by an interrupted cadence, dominant to diminished seventh (m. 17). Nothing could be more oppressive than the simple diminished chord, arpeggiated *pianissimo* and left hanging in the air by the pedal. It remains for the *Abgesang* to unlock the singer's powers. The turning point comes with her accession to the imperative voice ("Sag' ihm" [Say to him], m. 20), which coincides, first, with the start of the *Abgesang* itself; second, with the start of an accelerando from andante to vivace; and, third, with the start of a modal shift, minor to major, that reaches fruition, at the top of a crescendo, with the arrival of the new tempo (m. 24).

Supported by the lively tempo and major key, the singer launches the ensuing call for the sign by reversing her earlier relationship to the text. Rejecting control *by* discourse, she takes control *of* discourse, four times repeating, fragmenting, or expanding the line "Wird mir seine Nähe geben" [Will his nearness give me] so as to yield six repetitions of the cardinal words "seine Nähe." Both this emphasis and the expressive character of the vocal line indicate that the subject who controls discourse can also sexualize it, and vice versa: the reciprocity of sexual and discursive authority is the vehicle of mastery. For the singer, this means that the expression of desire may be a primary means of satisfying desire, the call for the sign that most fully answers itself. Her own call takes shape accordingly: four times it completes the phrase "seine Nähe geben" with a cadence, the second time emphatically so, but in each case except the last the cadence acts to *defer* closure. (In Schenkerian terms: the first three cadences defer the completion of the fundamental line by stalling it on 3̂.) The singer finds more pleasure in routing the cadential phrase along disseminal pathways than in letting it prefigure the nearness it names.

But the most remarkable feature of this *Abgesang* still awaits mention. Some melodic adjustments in the accompaniment aside, the climactic voicing of the call for the sign in "Suleika 2" is identical to that in "Suleika 1"; the singer's "seine Nähe" forms a perfect mirror image of her earlier "nur sein Atem." For the woman of "1800," this repetition grounds the singer's desires in the tutelary knowledge and power of the beloved. Nearness is contained by breath, the body by the authoritative word. For the man of "1800," however, the same repetition may shift the grounds of knowledge and power themselves from the regulatory agency of tutelage to the currents of discourse and desire that tutelage can never fully regulate. The cross-voiced call for nearness refers less to an anticipated sign than to the earlier call for breath; the two calls form a signifying loop around which their ecstatic, self-answering energy flows unimpeded. In this context, the substitution of "Nähe" for "Atem" suggests that the body of the beloved instructor and the body of knowledge are freely interchangeable. The masculine subject's desire for these bodies fulfills itself vicariously at the moment when the singer's voice becomes its own acoustic mirror. This is also the moment when her impulse (compulsion?) to repeat rends the integral fabric of the song: at what Roland Barthes calls "the site of a loss, the seam, the cut, the deflation, the *dissolve* which seizes the subject in the midst of bliss."[34] Tutelage promises to crest in bliss, but bliss comes instead in its rupture.

Schubert, it is worth noting in passing, also ends his setting of "Suleika 2" (1821) with a dissolve, but only in order to repeat the idealization of feminine abjection that he offers in "Die Liebende schreibt." The "Suleika" setting, rewriting von Willemer's text, closes with its singer's disintegration as a subject as her wind-borne words fade into the distance. Already prone to treat the imperative "Sag' ihm" as a *pianissimo* plea, the singer drops to *mezza voce* for a last repetition and settles on "Seine Liebe sei mein Leben" [His love is my life] as her chief message. She repeats the phrase twice in conjunction with a cluster of sinking motions: slackenings of tempo, decrescendos starting from *pianissimo,* and the registral descent of a leaping accompaniment figure. The erosion of the singer's musical energy proves the truth of her formula.

.   .   .   .   .

As I suggested earlier, "Erster Verlust" marks Mendelssohn's withdrawal from the allegory of tutelage to which Goethe's/von Willemer's lyrics drew him. The song does not require detailed commentary. Suffice it to remark here on the nostalgic richness of its accompaniment, on its continual reshuffling of the text to produce repetitions of "jener holden Zeit" [that lovely time], the phrase that names what is lost, and on its closing attenuation of the call for the sign into a pure and unavailing cry, a sustained high note yielding to a florid melisma, all on the loaded word "holden." The reasons for this leavetaking are not obvious, but it is suggestive that Mendelssohn composed "Erster Verlust" in the year before he turned to the revision of *The First Walpurgisnight.* The cantata is very much about resisting illegitimate tutelage by virile, aggressive means rather than negotiating the ambiguities of gender and sexuality posed by tutelage as an idyll. As we saw in the last chapter, the cantata offers male cross-vocal identification only with female voices whose whoops of pleasure are justified (or rationalized) by their use as weapons—as acoustic Medusa's heads. Being more diffuse, the identifications offered by the Goethe Lieder are also more risky; they make it too easy for both a susceptible male listener to slip into the feminine subject position, and a resistant female listener—or performer—to cross over into the masculine position. It may be, then, that by 1841 Mendelssohn had begun to retreat from the indeterminacies of desire and identity that his Goethe Lieder once embraced.

Certainly the most loaded of these indeterminacies concerns same-sex desire. To what extent does the male listener who identifies with the position of a woman in love identify with her desire for the beloved man? That would depend, runs one obvious answer, on whether the listener is straight or gay. But matters may not be so simple, especially for the 1830s, when the division between homo- and heterosexuality was still nascent.[35] As film theory has gradually recognized, it is sometimes possible to identify with the position of a gendered subject without necessarily identifying with the subject's gender.[36] By grounding himself in the discourse of tutelage, the male listener to Mendelssohn's Goethe Lieder, *any* male listener, can adopt the attitude of the female singer without necessarily adopting her (hetero)sexual desire for the masterful male beloved. The listener's desire can fasten, not on a man, but on a certain model of masculinity; the desire to *be* the master can represent itself as the desire to *have* him.[37] These two desires, however, are not easily separable, especially where an amatory relationship like tutelage is concerned; all cross-sex identification opens the possibility of same-sex desire. We might even speculate that Mendelssohn broke up his "Suleika" dyptich because its eroticism could be "borrowed" too easily by male same-sex desire. Tutelage could be amatory only by indirection; otherwise it might be confused with what one of the philologists called "the vice which it in . . . outward form so nearly resembles."[38] Desire, position, and gender most likely need to be retriangulated with each critical rehearing of songs like these. About the only things that should be ruled out in advance are Scylla and Charybdis: the presumption that criticism has an interest in protecting music from same-sex desire, and the crude claim that the cross-sex romance of the songs is a mere pretext for a same-sex counterpart.

Seven

Cultural Politics
and Musical Form

The Case of Charles Ives

According to Jean-François Lyotard, the postmodern originates as a recurrent moment within modernism. Its mark is

that which, in the modern, puts forward the unpresentable in presentation itself; that which denies itself the solace of good forms, the consensus of a taste which would make it possible to share collectively the nostalgia for the unattainable; that which searches for new presentations, not in order to enjoy them but in order to impart a stronger sense of the unpresentable.[1]

This account makes it tempting to anoint Charles Ives as a postmodernist composer. No one ever searched for "new presentations" more avidly or scorned good forms more cheerfully. Ives made heterogeneity the first principle of his music. His seemingly uninhibited mixing(-up) of structures, styles, and genres flouted the European aesthetic standards that ruled American musical life at the turn of the last century. Organic unity, sublime rhetoric, and the separation of high and low modes of expression all went by the boards. So, too, did the richly "presentable" sensuousness of fin-de-siècle sonority, as Ives searched for an alternative to what he saw as the debased modernisms of Debussy and Richard Strauss.

Ives's admirers have generally idealized his efforts, interpreting his formal procedures as musical projections of both democratic idealism and transcendentalist philosophy.[2] As if to anticipate the "Emersonian culture of creative democracy" that Cornel West calls prophetic pragmatism, Ives positions the unattainable as the object, not of nostalgia, but of utopian hope. Hence his plan for a *magnum opus*, the uncomposed and uncomposable *Universe* Symphony "to be played by at least two huge orchestras across from each other on mountaintops overlooking a valley." Or so the story goes.[3]

This chapter, however, has a different story to tell. Its aim is to undo the idealization of Ives—to unravel the eider quilt of his symbolic—by reexamining his music in relation to the cultural circumstances of post-Reconstruction America. Using interpretive strategies that put a deconstructive spin on Theodor Adorno's method of "immanent critique," I will rework Ives's own frame of reference in order to produce a revisionist reading of his work.[4] For better or worse, the results will not cast Ives as a "pre-postmodernist" but show him, instead, to be consumed by a "nostalgia for the unattainable."

Ives's modernism encompassed a defiant individualism, a principled indifference to traditional standards of musicianship, and a millenarian commitment to American democracy. The product of these forces was supposed to be both spiritually and materially emancipatory. But Ives's emancipatory ideal repeatedly proved to be a mystified form of populist-nativist ideology, an ideology foreign neither to the form of Ives's music nor its ethos. The sources of this slippage include the historical positioning Ives seeks through his music; his obsessive efforts, both overt and covert, to construct a "manly" aesthetic; and his reliance on culturally ascendant concepts of purity and social hierarchy. All too often, Ives is formally most advanced precisely where he is socially most retrograde.

I realize these claims do not sound very friendly. My purpose, however, is neither to praise Ives nor to bury him but to understand him—and in so doing to explore the interplay of critique and appreciation in an exemplary test case for politically informed musicology. If the communicative action of Ives's music is in some respects equivocal, even dismaying, then the music should surely be revalued. But it should not simply be *devalued,* or not devalued simply, any more than it should be dismissed because Ives's claims to originality, as Maynard Solomon has argued, may be exaggerated.[5] It is never enough to establish the brute fact of ideological complicity, especially with an easy target such as Ives. The full significance of any ideological formation depends on the "technologies" that maintain it, its package of discursive sources and strategies.[6] The same artwork that is ideologically mystified may illuminate and problematize the forces that mystify it. In "reading" Ives's music, therefore, even reading it against the grain, I will not willingly sacrifice nuance and complexity in order to paint Ives as the devil in disguise. Demonology, after all, is just hagiography turned inside out.

.   .   .   .   .

In two distinct senses, Ives's most characteristic music is spatial in conception. The first, and more limited, sense is supplied by formalist analysis and refers to a spatial form that seeks to "negate time as the primary mode of musical expression and experience" and to found continuity "largely on relationships that are simultaneous, reciprocal, and reflective in nature rather than successive, sequential, and unidirectional." This spatial form is a structural effect that arises from such typical Ivesian techniques as the superimposition (layering) of diverse musical styles and processes, the withholding of goal-directed harmonic motion, the fragmentation of material, and the drastic complication of texture.[7]

The second sense is supplied by hermeneutics. It understands musical space not only as an effect but also as an object of structure, and not at all as antithetical to temporal processes but as interlocked with them in historically specific ways.[8] In this sense, as we will see, the spatiality of Ives's music serves to model or prescribe the larger, socio-culturally constructed space in which the music is situated. Ives's efforts to map this space, moreover, form part of a larger mapping that has informed both the signifying and the material practices of American culture since the mid-nineteenth century.

This mapping is the topic of an important essay by Philip Fisher. Fisher observes that the problem of forming a national identity—a basic nineteenth-century preoccupation—could not be solved in America by European means. Especially as the country expanded, both internally through successive waves of immigration after 1820 and externally through transcontinental movement of the frontier, American diversity contradicted virtually all of the accepted conditions of nationhood. "Without a single *Volk*, without a single climate or environment, without a [common] culture, and without, in the deep Romantic sense, a language," America had to solve the problem of identity by "other, unprecedented means."[9]

Those means were found in an unprecedented form of space: a half-material and half-imaginary medium within which American life could be situated. This democratic social space, as Fisher calls it, is radically heterogeneous and radically nonhierarchical. Its basis is the unrestrained mobility and interchangeability of both persons and things. It is the material space of the mass production and distribution of consumer goods and the discursive space of mass advertising. It is a topographic space crossed by transportation systems in continuous development and the mythographic space of the open road. Finally, for the individual subject, it is a space that renders everyone equi-valent, implicates everyone in the identity of everyone else. Hence Walt Whitman:

I am of old and young, of the foolish as much as the wise,
Regardless of others, ever regardful of others,
Maternal as well as paternal, a child as well as a man,
Stuff'd with the stuff that is coarse and stuff'd with the stuff that
    is fine[. . .]
Of every hue and caste am I, of every rank and religion,
A farmer, mechanic, artist, gentleman, sailor, quaker,
Prisoner, fancy-man, rowdy, lawyer, physician, priest.
                              ("Song of Myself," section 16)

The bugle calls in the ball-room, the gentlemen run to their partners, the
    dancers bow to each other,
The young man lies awake in the cedar-roof'd garret and harks to the
    musical rain. . . .
The squaw wrapt in her yellow-hemm'd cloth is offering moccasins and
    bead-bags for sale,
The connoisseur peers along the exhibition-gallery with half-shut eyes bent
    sideways,
As the deck-hands make fast the steamboat the plank is thrown for the
    shoregoing passengers,
The young sister holds out the skein while the elder sister winds it off in a
    ball, and stops now and then for the knots[. . . .]
And such as it is to be these more or less am I,
And of these one and all I weave the song of myself.
                              ("Song of Myself," section 15)[10]

As these excerpts demonstrate, to inhabit democratic social space is to experience spatial positions as sites of identificatory possibility—in other words as subject positions—and to glide laterally from one position to another without any sense of progression. Individual identity is premised, not on one's separation from others, but on one's exchangeability with them. This exchangeability, in turn, crystallizes in a series of passing moments drawn at random from an enveloping simultaneity.

Once democratic social space has been conceptualized, its relationship to much of Ives's music becomes obvious. The material-imaginary collage of the social space is clearly both the model for and the object modeled by the stylistic collages of the musical space. In many movements by Ives, the projection of a spontaneous, quasi-random interplay among different types of music seems to override any projection of continuity. Consider, for example, the first movement of Ives's Second String Quartet (1911) as described by H. Wiley Hitchcock:

Alongside the most radical sort of jagged, wide-spanned, rhythmically disparate, chromatic melody is melody of the simplest stepwise diatonicism. Triadic harmony alternates with fourth- and fifth-chords, chromatic aggregates, and tone clusters. Canons without any harmonic underpinnings follow passages anchored to static harmonic-rhythmic ostinatos. "Athematic" writing is set side-by-side against passages quoting pre-existent melodies in almost cinematic collage.[11]

Like "Song of Myself," music of this kind models sequence without progression and structure without hierarchy. Sequence becomes an arbitrary sampling of simultaneous possibilities; structure becomes the principle of unrestrained mobility. Concomitantly, the diverse melodic materials of the music resist being ranked in value according to their social origin, as do Whitman's squaw and connoisseur. If Ives paraphrases "Columbia, the Gem of the Ocean," the tune does not sound banal, like a Ländler as parodied by Mahler, or sarcastic and embittered, like "Ach, du lieber Augustin" as quoted by Schoenberg in his Second String Quartet (1910). This social leveling of melody makes explicit the alliance between musical technique, democratic social space, and the American scenes that Ives's music so often seeks to picture.

A few disclaimers, however, need to be entered at this point. The first movement of Ives's Second String Quartet exemplifies heterogeneity at its most radical. The music is a melee, open to any and every combination, vertical or linear; it is not stratified into the distinct and consistent layers found in works such as *The Unanswered Question* or "The Housatonic at Stockbridge." As we will see, Ives writes such layered music, not to model democratic social space, but to defend against it: not to enfranchise heterogeneity, but, in every sense, to contain it. Furthermore, many of Ives's most heterogeneous pieces are radical only in part. Some combine a strongly heterogeneous texture with familiar techniques of musical continuity: motivic transformation in the "Emerson" movement of the *Concord* Sonata, continuous ostinato in *An Elegy to Our Forefathers* (the first movement of the Second Orchestral Set), cyclical structure in *Washington's Birthday*. Others, as Larry Starr has shown of songs such as "Ann Street," organize a succession of stylistically heterogeneous gestures to form a definite pattern, a kind of musical gestalt that, once again, serves to contain the mobility of texture.[12]

Ives's aesthetic ambivalence about radical heterogeneity meshes closely with his political ambivalence about democratic social space. In the next few pages, I will trace out the relevant political issues until they lead back full circle to Ives's music.

As our excerpts from "Song of Myself" demonstrate, to inhabit democratic social space is also to level differences in race, class, sexuality, and gender. Needless to say, not all Americans have embraced this prospect with Whitmanesque enthusiasm. It would be only a slight exaggeration to say that the social history of the United States has turned largely on the question of whether and how to structure the heterogeneity of its peoples. As Fisher observes, the actual conduct of American life has occurred within a "damaged" social space on which democratic social space is uneasily superimposed.[13] Social groups destabilized by the leveling effect have historically sought to "purify" social space by controlling both its material and imaginary organization. Privileged spaces were reserved for identities and traditions figured as truly American, American pure and simple. (This figure of authenticity could be realized in a kind of masquerade; in Connecticut Ives used to dress up like a farmer in bib overalls, an oversize hat, and heavy shoes.)[14] Purity discourse was a major means of social control in postbellum America, especially as circulated by the Social Purity movement, which flourished between the 1870s and the First World War. The unifying cause of this widespread crusade was the regulation of sexuality, which served as a fulcrum for the protection of what are now called "family values": the ideology of middle-class domesticity, which the Women's Christian Temperance Union tellingly (and perhaps unwittingly) labeled "The White Life" in 1885.[15]

At no time in American history has this mode of domination been more pervasive or more virulent than during the period between Ives's birth in 1874 and the end of his active career as a composer around 1921.[16] Tensions arose from multiple social upheavals, including the collapse of Reconstruction, the steady influx of new immigrants, and organized demands by women for voting and reproductive rights. The result was not only a predictable upsurge in racism, xenophobia, and misogyny but also an ideological discourse in which the various demonized others—the lusty black, the dirty foreigner, the castrating woman—became interchangeable through a common association with ideas of impurity, weakness, degeneracy, stupidity, and malevolence.

One measure of the power of this discourse is the enormous impact of D. W. Griffith's 1915 film *Birth of a Nation*. Generally acknowledged as both the formal and social prototype of modern narrative cinema, *Birth* is a racist Civil War epic that culminates with the defeat of a black rebellion by the Ku Klux Klan—in the words of a contemporary reviewer, "a vast grim host in white." North and South are reunited, and the modern nation "born," by the postbellum domination of all whites over all blacks. What is more, as Michael Rogin has shown, this domination also encodes the domination of men over women and of "Americans" over foreigners. The ultimate source of pollution in the film is the mulatto mistress of a vengeful Reconstructionist, a demonized figure who embodies both racist fears of miscegenation and misogynist fears of male disempowerment. Concomitantly, Griffith's ultimate aim for the film was to enlighten and Americanize the divergent, especially immigrant, members of an audience that cut across all lines of social demarcation. It should be added that Griffith succeeded all too well. Despite opposition from the NAACP and white liberals alike, *Birth* was widely acclaimed not only as great art but also as true history. "Go see it," exhorted Dorothy Dix, the Ann Landers of her day, "for it will make a better American of you."[17] The real Ku Klux Klan agreed and subsequently adopted the film as a recruiting device.

On the surface, Ives would seem to have nothing to do with these social pathologies. His music is anything but purist, and his politics are rudely populist, founded on an allegiance to the masses or majority and an antagonism to political and economic elites. He was certainly no racist by the standards of his day, and even more certainly no friend of the racist demagoguery typified by *Birth of a Nation*.[18] Nonetheless, Ives's evocations of small-town white America—protestant, patriotic, and patriarchal—encode in music the same nativist ideal that Griffith's do in film. The world fantasized on *Saturday Evening Post* covers by Norman Rockwell is not far off.

Much as Ives idealized "the people," he scorned the popular music composed by the urban Jewish immigrants who populated Tin Pan Alley.[19] His notorious aversion to the radio and phonograph seems linked to their role in creating a mass audience for that music at the expense of native musical vernaculars. And though Ives's polyglot style was open to black influence in the form of ragtime, it remained closed to the more plangent development of the blues.

More pointedly, Ives's musical collages virtually exclude black spirituals, which encroach uncomfortably on the privileged position of white gospel music.[20] To justify this exclusion, Ives claims that the spirituals represent no more than "exaggerations" of the characteristic gospel style and of "the fervor, conviction, and a real human something underneath, that the negroes heard in [it]." "I'm not trying to say," he continues, "that many of the spirituals, jubilees, etc. aren't in their own way natural, spontaneous, beautiful, and artistic—but some white Congregationalists or Methodists (drunk or sober) already had somepin' also natural, spontaneous, beautiful, and artistic—and that somepin' was to start the negro spirituals."[21] In a sense, Ives's music reproduces the social order as well as the sound of the nineteenth-century revival meetings so formative of its style and spirit. These events occurred in a "damaged" space that was socially integrated but musically segregated, blacks and whites crossing paths in the same campgrounds but attending separate services.[22]

Similarly, Ives's musical commemoration of the Fifty-fourth Massachusetts Infantry, the black regiment decimated at Fort Wagner, North Carolina, in 1863, unreflectively aligns a spiritual with a racial hierarchy. In his prefatory poem for this "Black March," the first movement of the First Orchestral Set, Ives gives dignity and pathos to the troops, "Marked by generations of pain," but Mosaic authority to the figure of the white officer who reincarnates the spirit of the Founding Fathers:

The man on horseback, carved from
A native quarry of the world Liberty
And from what your [the troops'] country was made.
You Images of a Divine Law.

The music does no less. Against a soft, somber, dissonant backdrop, phrases from two Civil War marching songs, "The Battle Cry of Freedom" and "Marching through Georgia," intertwine with themes from Stephen Foster's "Old Black Joe." Seeking a black voice in all good faith, the music finds only a white ventriloquist.

Even on the surface, moreover, Ives characteristically reproduces the violent logic of domination in the act of opposing it. His political program, elaborated in a long essay, "The Majority" (1919–20), aims to foster a democratic social space of "free and unrestricted intercourse in all transactions . . . [among] men," whether "commercial, industrial, racial, or religious, or [having to do] with the sciences, with art, or with any product of the labor of man's body, mind or soul." Yet the realization of this Whitmanesque ideal depends on a demonizing opposition between "the People" and the "Non-People," "the 'hog-mind' . . . of the minority" and "the Universal Mind, the Majority." The Majority values "Soul, Spirit, Christianity, Truth, Freedom"; the Minority values the "immediate over-obvious" more than the fundamental, commodity more than "perfect truths," the personal more than the universal. Ives proposes government by referendum as a means of ensuring the triumph of the Majority. The Minority, the perennial losing side, would be left in much the same situation as Griffith's blacks:

The Minority man can do as all good losers do: (1) abide by the winner's terms, live up to the Majority law like a man . . . or (2) [he] can go to some other country whose laws are more congenial to him; or (3) he can begin to shriek, get nasty, hysterical, and begin to throw things around—and then the Majority will strangle him—and treat him like a farmer treats a skunk who loses his self-respect.[23]

Turning to Ives's aesthetics, we find the domination of the Majority over the Minority recast as the domination of the masculine over the feminine. Ives's misogyny is legendary by now, but most commentators have tended to play it down and above all to protect the music from it. Even Frank Rossiter, whose biography effectively demystifies Ives without debunking him, half-excuses Ives's obsessive degradation of the feminine as a realistic rather than a fantasmatic response to the social conditions surrounding concert music in the late nineteenth century.[24]

Ives's particular brand of misogyny conforms to what classical psychoanalysis calls the masculine protest. This is an obsessive need to be "manly"—autonomous, combative, rugged, dominating—in all things. Its basis is a dread of being feminized in relation, not to women, but to other men. The object of its mingled fascination and loathing is not so much femininity as effeminacy, and it is therefore also cognate with a common form of homophobia. Freud, who is more often recognized for his complicity with masculine pathologies than for his critique of them, described this one in terms that fit Ives very well. As he ruefully observes, some men are almost impossible to convince "that a passive attitude towards another man does not always mean castration and that in many situations in life it is indispensable."[25]

The logic of Ives's aesthetic is, at least too often, the "logic" of the masculine protest. What Ives loathes in the music of others and fears in his own is an emotional sensitivity that might "sissify" him, make him a "mollycoddle," give him (a remarkably erotic image, this) "soft ears." This is not to suggest that his antagonism to such things as bland conventionality, facile beauty, and empty virtuosity can be written off as mere castration anxiety. It is to suggest, though, that the innovative energy of his music is fringed by defensive panic, a panic made audible in the arbitrary harshness and discontinuity on which Ives so candidly prided himself.

No wonder, then, that the Second String Quartet, which shows Ives at his most heterogeneous, should also show him at his most misogynistic—and homophobic. He does not mince words on the matter:

It used to come over me . . . that music had been, and still was, too much of an emasculated art . . . [with] Sybaritic apron-strings, keeping [it] too much tied to the old ladies. [Especially] string quartet music got more and more weak, trite, and effeminate. . . . [So] I started a string quartet score, half mad, half in fun, and half to try out, practice, and have some fun with making those men fiddlers get up and do something like men.[26]

Ives has the most fun near the start of the quartet's second movement, where the second violin famously impersonates an effeminate character dubbed "Rollo." Marked Andante emasculata and Largo sweetota, Rollo's "pretty" music is violently hooted down by the rest of the ensemble. Granted, it's all just a joke, but this joke is a clear instance of what Freud called tendentious wit: it aims to hurt. And though the movement quickly moves on to the vigorous "Arguments" named in its title, the Rollo episode cannot simply be shrugged off as if one were naive to take it too seriously. Ives, at least, is unapologetic: he chooses to man his aesthetic guns where femininity has been cast out by a time-honored symbolic means: gay-bashing.[27]

Ives's misogyny undoubtedly has personal roots, but its exclusionary logic is part of a broader field of cultural practices that bear closely on the problems of heterogeneity and democratic social space. The aesthetic of the Second String Quartet is meant to be New World and populist, but it might just as well be Old World and reactionary. Many of Ives's European contemporaries shared his defensive preoccupation with the decadent style of a Rollo—or a Wagner, or an Oscar Wilde. Popular works of social philosophy, notably Max Nordau's *Degeneration* of 1892 and Otto Weininger's *Sex and Character* of 1903, promoted the idea that the modern age, with its polymorphous mass culture, was caught in the throes of an evolutionary regression, one symptom of which was a rampaging effeminacy.[28] Ives defines his aesthetic as a redemptive opposition to this feminizing/homosexualizing trend in music. He faults his chief modernist rivals, Debussy and Strauss, for failing to do likewise; in the long run, neither is quite man enough:

[Emerson] has not Debussy's fondness for trying to blow a sensuous atmosphere through his own voluptuous cheeks. . . . Debussy's content would have been worthier his manner if he had hoed corn or sold newspapers for a living.

[Strauss's] magnifying the dull into the colossal produces a kind of "comfort"—the comfort of a woman who takes more pleasure in the fit of fashionable clothes than in a healthy body.

Turning to lesser lights, Ives castigates musicians who pose "all dolled up in their purple-dressing-gowns, in their twofold wealth of golden hair, in their cissy-like postures over the piano keys."[29] Playing on traditional associations of femininity with seductive false display, he rejects both composers and performers who appeal to the "lady-part (both male and female)" of their audiences by subordinating the "over-value" of "substance" or spirit to the "under-value" of "manner" or technique.[30]

But the resonance of Ives's misogyny does not stop with his immediate historical moment. As we noted in chapter 2, the polarity masculine/feminine is an especially hardworking member of a long series of self-other polarities including sameness/difference, culture/nature, spirit/matter, light/darkness, reason/emotion, and Ives's own substance/manner.[31] Because the very construction of these polarities idealizes their "over-values" at the expense of their "under-values," partisans of the latter are always at a loss. No simple reversal is possible; the language of idealization does not transfer unproblematically from one set of values to another. The under-values may be affirmed, but only from an alienated or transgressive position. Ives's dilemma is that he is deeply attracted by such a position but finds it impossible to occupy. His aesthetic ideology juxtaposes the love of heterogeneity, an under-value, with a need for idealization that only an over-value can satisfy. His affirmation of the artistic and national energy that he finds in heterogeneity can be unambiguous only if heterogeneity itself can ultimately be subordinated to a higher, "transcendental" unity. The misogynistic side of Ives's music, its aggressive, anti-sensuous, rebarbative side, represents an overzealous effort to supply the virile energy on which that subordination classically depends.

Ives's dilemma is neatly encapsulated by the song "Majority" (1915), a tribute to the masses (and a calculated affront to the "old

Ladies") that he chose to head his collection *114 Songs* (1921). The
song begins with a piano prelude in which various melodic lines are
posed against crashing forearm clusters. Obviously meant to suggest
the raw power of the masses, these clusters impel the musical action.
The poem (by Ives himself) consists of six verses, each one set differ-
ently; each setting reconfigures the sheer noise of the clusters as a
more structured dissonant sonority that supports a (temporarily)
stable texture. Fourth chords, for example, dominate the setting of the
second verse, and mixed thirds stacked into quasi-thirteenth chords
dominate the setting of the fifth. The music is thus prolific and dynamic, like the masses as they travel through democratic social space.

In its last setting, however, the song becomes regressive. Para-
phrasing Robert Browning—"God's in his heaven, / All will be well
with the world!"—the setting takes the form of a musical collage in
which a perfect F-major cadence is "pasted up" with divergent material. In fourfold repetition, the outlines of the cadence are first enveloped by lower- and upper-register tone clusters to form a complex
but perspicuous texture (Example 26, cadential material circled). A
briefer closing passage then interweaves a precadential IV-V progression in F major with an analogue in F-sharp major (Example 26). The
effect is quasi-cinematic, in the first case suggesting montage, in the
second a cross-cutting between simultaneous planes of action. For
once, it seems, idealism will not be compelled to revoke heterogeneity, despite the blatancy of the text, already a cliche by 1915. And
yet the ending does revoke heterogeneity, and affirm unity and totality, by the most "compulsory" of means. That means is nothing
other than the F-major cadence, which, extracted from its earlier envelope of clusters, is presented in isolation as the tonal and spiritual
essence of the collage. Like the text, and sharing its impetus, the music closes with a slogan. The sublimation of a formula has shaded into
the reproduction of one.[32]

"Majority" realizes in microcosm the design of Ives's most ambi-
tious multimovement works, where, in effect, the role of the F-major
cadence is played by the stratification of texture. The *Concord* Sonata,
Second String Quartet, First and Second Orchestral Sets, and Fourth
Symphony all conform, though in different ways, to the same underlying structural rhythm: a movement *away* from a primary, radical

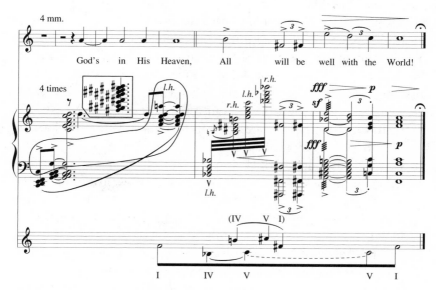

Example 26. Ives, "Majority," conclusion.

heterogeneity. This Ivesian masterplot consists of three phases—call them phases of interplay, excess, and hierarchy—that proceed in a fixed order, one phase per movement, as follows.

Interplay. The first movements, in slow to moderate tempo, pursue the linear and vertical freedom through which music can project the experience of democratic social space. This projection is somewhat foreshortened, more embryonic than otherwise, in the Fourth Symphony and Second Orchestral Set, where the first movements are preludial. The remaining pieces develop their radicalism to the full, in each case with strong programmatic support: the crisscrossing perspectives of independent characters in the Second String Quartet; Emerson's transcendentalism in the *Concord* Sonata, a "search for the unknowable, unlimited in any way or by anything[,] . . . [as revealed] in any phenomena of Man, Nature, or God"; [33] the "drumbeat of the common heart" in the First Orchestral Set, sounding above Augustus Saint-Gaudens's bas-relief of Colonel Robert Gould Shaw and the Massachusetts Fifty-fourth. All five first movements model a possible interpenetration of idealism and heterogeneity. This possibility, however, is put into question by the very fact of first-movement position:

the position, in large-scale works after Beethoven, of arrested but un-resolved conflict, committed but uncompleted quest. Ives treats his first movements in precisely these terms. "Emerson," for example, dissolves at the close into tonal and motivic inconclusiveness;[34] "Dis-cussions," the first movement of the Second String Quartet, ends with the solitary droning of a pedal point on the cello, exposed when a return to the opening measures abruptly breaks off; the Prelude to the Fourth Symphony invokes the hymn "Watchman, Tell Us of the Night" and traces its gradual disintegration in order to pose "the searching questions of What? and Why? which the spirit of man asks of life."[35]

Excess. Ives's up-tempo second movements are essentially scherzos in which heterogeneous cross-cutting is wildly accelerated and inten-sified. The effect of this excess is to express an ambivalence so funda-mental to Ives that his aesthetic can be said to hinge on it. On the one hand, the scherzos gleefully flout conventionality and release a flood of exuberant, antinomian musical energy. Ives, as one would expect, identifies this energy as masculine and often associates it with memo-ries of his boyhood, as he does in "Putnam's Camp," the second move-ment of the First Orchestral Set. On the other hand, the hectic piling up of diverse and fragmentary materials verges on chaos: argumenta-tive violence in the Second String Quartet, "the Fourth of July in Con-cord—brass bands, drum corps, etc." in the Fourth Symphony, the "wilder, fantastical" workings of Hawthorne's imagination, "dripping wet with the supernatural, the phantasmal, the mystical" in the *Con-cord* Sonata.[36] Ambivalent or not, this kind of movement appealed deeply to Ives, and many of his single-movement works—*Central Park in the Dark, Washington's Birthday, Decoration Day, The Fourth of July*—conform to the type. All but *The Fourth of July,* however, seek to contain their excessively democratic energy by framing it with soft, static music that intimates a higher reality. For that matter, even *The Fourth of July* begins in a slow-moving mist of muted strings.

Hierarchy. The slow final movements, to borrow from Ives's pro-gram for the Fourth Symphony, seek "an apotheosis of the preced-ing content in terms that have something to do with the reality of existence and its religious experience." (The four-movement works precede this phase with a false resolution: a fugue in the Fourth Sym-phony, representing "the reaction of life into formalism and ritualism," and a scene of domestic—in other words, feminine—tranquility in the *Concord* Sonata.)[37] The movements identify their search for apotheosis with the projection of a containing gestalt of the sort described by Larry Starr. The apotheosis itself arises as a stratified texture in which one layer acts as first among equals: that is, as a distinctly if not sharply delineated figure to which the other layers stand as ground.[38]

The privileged layer consists of an ideologically fraught melody: a gospel hymn in the Second String Quartet, Fourth Symphony, and Second Orchestral Set; an original melody representing distant gospel singing, heard across the Housatonic River, in the First Orchestral Set; a "transcendental tune" representing the sound of Thoreau's flute over Walden Pond in the *Concord* Sonata. In each case, the privileged layer emerges late within the final movement as a climactic event, the fulfillment of intimations heard earlier in the movement or the work; in "The Housatonic at Stockbridge," the climax (as we will see in a moment) is significantly doubled. In several cases, the climactic melodies are supplemented by ostinatos: as a continuous background in the Fourth Symphony; as an intermittent background that becomes a textural element in the *Concord* Sonata; as the climactic texture itself, repeated along with the melody to evoke a sense of timeless revelation, in the Second String Quartet (Example 27). In all cases, the purpose of the climax is to transform an equi-valent spatial order into a hierarchical order of value. In all cases, too, the value accorded hegemonic status affirms a social order that is rural, white Protestant, patriarchal, and premodern. Formal and ideological unity is achieved through the exclusion of radical heterogeneity.

This exclusionary effect is particularly clear in the finales of the two Orchestral Sets. In the first set's "The Housatonic at Stockbridge," two privileged layers emerge in immediate succession. The first serenely translates into hymnody the string sonorities associated with the fluid, enveloping riverside idyll, as if the realms of nature and spirit were interfusing. The second, with something like revulsion, violently opposes hymnody on brass to a turbulence that wells up suddenly in the rest of the orchestra. It is as if the preceding fusion had prompted or revived an urgent need for separation. As I observed in chapter 2, the closing reappearance of pure string sonority is a moment of reversion exceptional in Ives, despite his frequent use of similar effects as postludes—for instance in the Finale of the Second Orchestral Set.

Example 27. Ives, Second String Quartet (Finale), hymn-tune "apotheosis"/
ostinato.

That Finale, "From Hanover Square North, at the End of a Tragic
Day, the Voice of the People Again Arose," commemorates an event
Ives witnessed in May 1915 after the sinking of the liner *Lusitania* by
German U-boats. Waiting for an elevated train near his New York of-
fice, Ives heard

a hand-organ or hurdy-gurdy . . . playing in the street below. Some workmen
sitting on the side of the tracks began to whistle the tune. . . . A workman
with a shovel over his shoulder came on the platform and joined in the chorus, and the next man, a Wall Street banker with white spats and a cane,
joined in it, and finally it seemed to me that everybody was singing this

tune. . . . There was a feeling of dignity all through this. The hand-organ man seemed to sense this and wheeled the organ nearer the platform and kept it up fortissimo.[39]

This description would not be out of place in "Song of Myself"; although moved by a single impulse, the crowd retains all its diversity down to the homely detail of shovels and spats. No crowd of Whitman's, however, excludes women the way this one does, and neither do the sidewalks of New York. Ives's Third Avenue "El" station would not only have housed laboring men and businessmen but also a heterogeneous mix of women just come from work or shopping. The entry of women into the public sphere—including, as a contemporary photograph shows, the insurance firm of Ives and Myrick—was one of the notable events of the era, and at a peak in 1915.[40] Ives is blind to these women: or, more exactly, deaf to them. Needing an aura of masculine solidarity, a homosocial warmth, in which to ground his musical image of "people . . . going through the same deep experience, together," Ives hears a figurative male chorus that proliferates beyond the boundaries of Hanover Square "as though every man in New York must be joining in it."[41]

Furthermore, Ives's subsequent description of the charismatic tune scorns as other the musical culture of the urban crowd:

Now what was this tune? It wasn't a Broadway hit, it wasn't a musical comedy air, it wasn't a waltz tune or a dance tune or an opera tune or a classical tune, or a tune that all of them probably knew. It was (only) the refrain of an old Gospel hymn that had stirred many people of past generations. It was nothing but—*In the Sweet Bye and Bye.*[42]

The redemptory quality of the old Gospel hymn is marked precisely by the urban crowd's probable ignorance of it. Most of the music opposed to the hymn exemplifies what Michael Rogin calls "the melting pot sound"; the entertainment music of a "polyglot metropolis," it is openly at war with the social and racial hierarchies of "Protestant, genteel culture."[43] The foreign pedigree of classical and operatic music stirs them, too, into the melting pot, where they insinuate (or enhance) the danger of effeminacy.

Ives's "Hanover Square" music takes the Gospel hymn as a latent presence and a latent goal, as if the hymn were an archetype lodged in a kind of nativist collective unconscious. The music proceeds by constructing the space of the crowd, adding layer on layer of sound in a long crescendo to form a texture of extraordinary complexity. As the crescendo mounts, intimations of the Gospel hymn crisscross the texture with growing clarity and frequency. This process culminates abruptly with a brass chorus on "In the Sweet Bye and Bye" that reduces the rest of the texture to a generalized turbulence, the chaotic ground to which the hymn stands as transcendental figure. The burly brass chorus relegates the cultural other to a "feminine" position, passivizing the collective virility of the crowd. More broadly, the down-home chorus, a transcription of the hurdy-gurdy's *fortissimo* for a transcendental town band, appropriates the crowd's polymorphic social energy and renders it monolithic. *Pace* H. Wiley Hitchcock, the "atmosphere of timelessness and universality"[44] that Ives hears in this climax wishfully encodes the triumph of old-time, rural, Protestant America over the irreducible diversity of modern urban life.

The outcome of that triumph is a condition, both musical and social, of abstract purity. When the brass chorus ends, the complex texture associated with the crowd precipitously breaks down. The urban scene vaporizes, leaving only quiet echoes of the hymn tune behind to fade into one of the static, "distant" textures by which Ives typically signifies the presence of ultimate mysteries. At the (rhetorical) site of transcendence, the other disappears.

The Finale of the Fourth Symphony, perhaps Ives's closest approximation to a "definitive" spiritual statement, takes the same transcendental rhetoric as its goal. The consummatory hymn tune, "Bethany," is intoned by a wordless chorus, initially a women's chorus, against a densely layered background. The texture is reminiscent of Debussy's "Sirènes," but Ives is not recycling the traditional trope by which women personify (but perhaps falsely) the truth sought by men. The hymning women's chorus represents a collective possibility of religious epiphany within a difficult workaday world. Evidently, Ives's musical relationship to femininity is not always as monochromatic as his bellicose pronouncements would suggest. Nonetheless, the actual realization of epiphanic possibility is a job for men. Beginning with a powerful pedal tone, tenor voices join in to imbue the texture with the traditionally virile qualities of fullness, strength, authority (Example 28).

Example 28. Ives, Fourth Symphony (Finale, voices only), hymn-tune "apotheosis."

There are to be no basses. Instead, the all-tenor sonority, light and comfortable in register but solid in its close three-part spacing, projects a manly etheriality that is meant to raise the spiritual aura of the women's chorus to a higher plane. (Presumably, we will forbear to hear this gesture deconstructively as a kind of vocal cross-dressing.) The tenors' entry also exalts the hymn tune, which proceeds at once to its apotheosis, transforming itself from "Bethany" proper into a kind of primordial hymn sound, an Ur-hymn. This "higher" hymn fades gradually into the orchestral texture, which in turn deletes layer on layer of sound until only the underlying ostinato remains.

Scored for an unpitched percussion battery, the ostinato consists of nothing but an independent cyclical polyrhythm. Once again, the site of transcendence is marked by an image of abstract purity which is also ideologically fraught. The ostinato pares music down to a sublimated marching rhythm, at once parade music for the rugged Yankee individualism that advances out of step to the beat of Thoreau's different drummer, and processional music for a fraternal transcendentalist church militant. Once again, at the site of transcendence, the other disappears.

That same disappearance crowns the Finale of the *Concord* Sonata, where Ives tries to invest it with a cultural authority and resonance of explicitly mythic proportions. Here the site of transcendence is archetypally localized as Walden Pond and the American self is personified in Thoreau, whom Ives prefers even to Emerson as an icon of manly spirituality.

Like the Fourth Symphony and Second Orchestral Set, the sonata ends with a double gesture: a climactic musical image, in which the stratification of texture becomes closural, and an "open," speculative afterimage. The closural image evokes the sound of Thoreau's flute, which consummates a day's meditation in the woods by lofting its "transcendental tune of Concord" over the pond. The sound is a real one, materialized in an obbligato flute layered over the solo piano.[45] The afterimage, for piano alone, suggests the dissolution of the epiphany borne on the flute but still preserves a "glimpse" of the "shadow-thought" that had first prompted Thoreau to meditate amid "the morning's mist and haze."[46] Musically, the afterimage marks this persistence of vision by returning to the hazy arpeggio with which the "Thoreau" movement begins.

In structural terms, the purpose of Thoreau's flute tune is to unite fragments of melody that have recurred throughout the sonata but have so far failed to cohere. Two melodic strains combine to form a period, yield to a contrasting middle section, and combine again. If we like, we can hear this A B A sequence as a miniature sonata-form skeleton: two-theme exposition, development, recapitulation. The "recapitulation," indeed, operates on several levels; it coincides with the piano's recapitulation of the ostinato bass that has figured importantly in the movement, and it marks a double moment of large-scale harmonic integration. The flute tune can be harmonized either in B-flat major, Ives's choice in the preceding movement, or the relative minor, G, but its melodic line emphasizes the filling-in of the interval G–D. During the recapitulation, this emphasis closely conjoins the tune and the ostinato. As the ostinato resolves to a dominant-ninth chord of D major, the tune both intimates a subdominant (G minor) and rises to sound the tonic note repeatedly above the dominant chord (Example 29). This resolution is not only the focal point of "Thoreau" but also a reply to the unanswered question that closes the first movement, "Emerson." The flute tune thus forms a multiple apotheosis; it is at once a privileged textural layer, the closed symmetrical structure that totalizes fragmentary melody, and the explicit long-term goal of the sonata.[47]

It is also, however, a repression of femininity: a double for the subsumption or appropriation of the feminine enacted by the tenor choir in the Finale of the Fourth Symphony. In the sonata's penultimate movement, "The Alcotts," the two strains of the flute tune combine several times, but without ever forming a perspicuous structure. According to Ives's program, this staged failure occurs in the American *ne plus ultra* of feminized domestic spaces, the parlor in the "home of the Marches" from Louisa May Alcott's *Little Women*. More exactly, the scene is set in the original of the Marches' parlor, the parlor at the Alcott's Orchard House where Beth Alcott is said to have "played at" Beethoven's Fifth Symphony on a "little old spinet piano" given by Sophia Thoreau, Henry's sister.[48] (The music imitates the sounds of

Example 29. Ives, *Concord* Sonata ("Thoreau"), "recapitulation" of flute tune.

Example 29. (*continued*)

both the spinet and the "played-at" symphony.) The successful flute tune of the Finale replaces the sociable sister with the self-reliant brother, the cozy parlor with the rugged woods, and effeminate "accomplishment" with virile structure.

Ives's Thoreau is a cultural ideal precisely because he is a masculine ideal or, more exactly, a densely compacted cluster of masculine ideals. He is a Romantic solitary, half Wordsworth, half Natty Bumpo, who can decode the "vibratory hum" of the "universal lyre."[49] He is an Arcadian shepherd turned post-Cartesian philosopher by virtue of westward migration, his contemplative detachment figured in the sweet-sad pastoral melancholy of his flute as it sounds over the hushed agitations of the piano and charms them into the tonally clarified version of a bell-like ostinato.[50] He is a New World Pan, his flute the phallic remainder of the metamorphosed Syrinx, a personage hinted at distantly in Ives's program through allusion to the transfiguring effect of "notes sung by a wood nymph." He is an American Tamino, playing a magic flute to master the elements—but this Tamino has left Pamina to tend the chores and lit out for the territories.

.   .   .   .   .

Where, then, do we stand with Ives? His nativist posturing and masculinist swagger are so blatant that well-meaning critics might be tempted to write them off as quirks in order to concentrate on what really matters, his music. But we can do that in good conscience only if we take the extreme formalist position that art, personality, and ideology are separate spheres, so that only what we can posit as purely artistic—here purely musical—values really matter. I am not willing to take that position, and neither, not for a minute, was Ives himself.

Ives's music rudely calls on us to acknowledge that its heterogeneity taps robust social energies and unsettles unthinking norms, and the claim is hard to deny. We can go even further and acknowledge that the musical image of a fully democratic social space is available to us only in and through the damaged spaces projected by Ives's major works. And the transcendental rhetoric of Ives's hierarchical finales is arguably compelling in its meditative dignity in spite of its ideological freight.

Still, the freight is there, and it alters, or should alter, our use and understanding of the music and the cultural status we are willing to grant it. As I noted earlier with reference to Walt Whitman, democratic social space imparts a fluidity to the sense of self, creating an individuality that is not premised on one's separation from others but on one's exchangeability with them. Ives anxiously resists this fluidity. When his musical innovations lead toward it, he intervenes to arrest it with signs of mastery, signs that confound innovation with belligerent masculinity and America with its antebellum past. Not to hear this in the music would be not to hear the music at all.

When we do hear it, moreover, we hear more than what I earlier called the brute fact of domination, important though that is. We hear modes of identity playing out their conflicted history, nostalgia being invented in the service of cultural purity, formal closure seeking both to subsume musical tradition (the long echo, say, of Beethoven's Fifth and Ninth Symphonies) and to distance itself from social upheaval.

We hear, too, a series of exemplary signifying "technologies," forms of communicative action by which (in this case) subjective mobility and its leveling effects are contained or appropriated. These involve a continual overlapping of terms for gender, sociality, and knowledge. "From Hanover Square North" equates the native with a true virility that returns the city to its rural roots and envelops every man with—should it be paternal or maternal?—comfort in the face of tragedy. The Finale of the Fourth Symphony combines manly ethereality, the virile appropriation of an initially feminine position, with a sublimated image of spiritual militancy (but ultimately, perhaps, the militancy of the Union during the Civil War). The *Concord* Sonata identifies the American self with the "concord" between Old World musical heroism, embedded in the Beethoven Fifth, and New World transcendental reflection, a concord perfected at the site where Thoreau literally takes possession of part of the original New World. At the grand ostinato-climax of the Second String Quartet, where four men settle their differences by viewing the firmament from a mountaintop, the cello's deep, descending line traces out a foundational virility under the stratospheric surging of the first violin, the other instruments filling the space between; the effect is to identify transcendental reflection with the homosocial amity of a band of brothers, joined in a kind of sublime barbershop quartet. In this context, "The Housatonic at Stockbridge" emerges as a dangerous piece for Ives. Here the projection of a "murmuring maternal nature" (as I called it in chapter 2) threatens to go too far, to blur the transcendental figure into the enveloping natural ground. The violent second climax can be heard as a projection of Ives's horror at such blurring onto maternal nature itself. In sum, Ives's music, as it prepares for and realizes all these acoustic images, becomes an image of the communicative economy at work—although at work under stress, both resisting and yielding to the constraints of the symbolic order.

So where we stand with Ives, and with virtually any other artist of consequence, is at the juncture of the aesthetic and the real, a site at which all sorts of valuations, but no idealization, may arise. Traditionally, criticism of the arts has fostered an equation between appreciation or advocacy of an artist's work and a rhetorical identification, by the critic, with the artist's point of view. During the 1980s, literary critics led the way in abandoning this critical rhetoric for one less dependent on myths of authorship and its authority. Perhaps it is time for music criticism to take the same direction and to find works of art compelling, not because their truth or beauty immunizes them from critique—there is no such immunity—but because they engage vital issues in terms that are folly to ignore.

Eight

Consuming the Exotic

Ravel's *Daphnis and Chloe*

Maurice Ravel composed his ballet *Daphnis and Chloe* between 1909 and 1911; Sergei Diaghilev's Ballets Russes premiered it in 1912. The story of the ballet, which also serves as a program for the music in concert performance, derives from a third-century Greek pastoral romance by Longus. The place is Arcadia; the time is the antiquity of myth. Daphnis and Chloe, a shepherd and shepherdess, fall passionately in love at a religious festival. Some pirates seize Chloe and carry her off to their brigand's orgy, but the god Pan rescues her and reunites her with Daphnis at dawn on the following day. The lovers express their gratitude by dancing out the story of Pan and Syrinx, of which their own story forms the imaginary reversal. The youth of Arcadia soon join them in a wild Bacchic dance of celebration.

Igor Stravinsky called *Daphnis and Chloe* "not only one of Ravel's best works but one of the most beautiful products of French music."[1] Ravel's friend and pupil Roland-Manuel agreed; to illustrate "the secret power which gives the calculated graces of [Ravel's] art an angelic charm which is at its freest in the world of the supernatural," he turns to the nocturne and daybreak episodes of the ballet. "Here," he writes of the latter, "at the very limit of effort and calculation, [Ravel] attains . . . that pure beauty which is at one with the apparent simplicity of nature."[2] These remarks should be understood, not only as an index of Ravel's aesthetic success, but also as a description of his expressive intentions. Although he adhered to an artisanal ideal—

really, as we will see, a faux-artisanal ideal—of beautiful workmanship, Ravel by no means always chose to write beautiful music, as
pieces such as *La valse*, "Le gibet" and "Scarbo" from *Gaspard de
la nuit*, and "Méfiez-vous des blancs!" from *Chansons madécasses*
clearly attest. *Daphnis and Chloe* is beautiful because its beauty has a
job to do.

The job can be done because the beauty is of a determinate historical type. It is a beauty sensuous, urgent, and hypnotic but at the
same time lucid and artificial. It is a type of beauty much sought after
by French artists and writers during the second half of the nineteenth
century: the beauty of Symbolist poetry and of art nouveau. It is at
once ornamental and organic, part frozen urban artifice, part meta-
morphic natural growth:

[A] tide of white assumed wings, hurried off and lost itself, like a flight of
swans. And the white hung from the arches, a fall of down, a snowy sheet of
large flakes; white counterpanes, white coverlets floated about in the air, sus-
pended like banners in a church; long jets of Maltese lace hung across, seeming to suspend swarms of butterflies; other lace fluttered on all sides, floating
like fleecy clouds in a summer sky, filling the air with their clear breath. And
the marvel, the altar of this religion of white was, above the silk counter, in
the great hall, a tent formed of white curtains, which fell from the glazed
roof. . . . It made one think of a broad white bed, awaiting in its virginal
immensity the white princess, as in the legend, she who was to come one
day, all powerful, with the bride's white veil.[3]

Although it may read like a Symbolist prose poem, with its combination of sensual religiosity, the feminine image of a veiled ideal, and the
Mallarméan swans, this passage is a description of a giant white sale
at the fictional department store The Ladies' Paradise, from Émile
Zola's novel of the same name. Yet Zola's artificial paradise is neither
a joke nor (only) a fantasy, and neither is its superimposition of the
commercial and the aesthetic as modes of the beautiful. Ravel's Arcadian paradise is, so to speak, cut from the same cloth as Zola's, and
the rhythm of Zola's prose, with its reiterated "white" motives in a long
undulating line, feels uncannily like the ebb and flow of Ravel's music.

Ravel uses an ornamental-organic beauty to embody both of the
contrary forces that determine the form of *Daphnis and Chloe:* the
archaism of a narrative set in Arcadian Greece and the modernism of

a musical technique born of fin-de-siècle Paris. In relation to the narrative, the beauty of the music is immediate and natural; in relation to the musical technique, the same beauty is reflective and artificial. Similarly, this Janus-faced beauty also becomes the medium in which the contrary forces that determine the ballet's content—eroticism and violence, the sacred and the profane—continually intermix.

The beauty of *Daphnis and Chloe* is what interests me in this chapter: beauty as a deliberate, purposeful effect, not as the praiseworthy quality we like to ascribe to the art that we like. I want to explore the character and purpose of this beauty: to understand it not as a self-sufficient or self-explanatory aesthetic end but as a means to several different ends that are no less cultural and political than they are aesthetic. My approach will thus be to shuttle interpretively between the cultural circumstances of Ravel's score and the musical imagery by which the score produces and conveys its beauty.

· · · · ·

Edward Downes described the special quality of *Daphnis and Chloe* very well in a New York Philharmonic program note: "With all its brilliant orchestration, intoxicating color, sensuous harmonies, and orgiastic rhythms, *Daphnis and Chloe* is an essentially patrician score. Ravel was a spiritual aristocrat who knew the elemental drives and could appear to give them full reign without once relaxing his mastery of form and precise craftsmanship."[4] This statement says more than it knows. On Downes's account the elemental drives, the impulses of the body in desire and the mind in fantasy, are both released and confined by their artistic representation in Ravel's score. In Kristevan terms, the music is a seamlessly symbolic representation of the semiotic, an artifice that frames and tames the energies of elemental drives. In other, more Freudian terms, Ravel's score is an exercise in sublimation. But this is sublimation of a special kind: one that, like the late nineteenth-century style of leisure-class consumption described by Thorstein Veblen, is meaningful only when it is observed.[5] The drives appear to be free only the better to serve the display of mastery and craftsmanship. This is *conspicuous* sublimation.

To understand the beauty of *Daphnis and Chloe*, therefore, we first have to understand it as the product of conspicuous sublimation. We

then have to ask what values and ideals might have prompted Ravel
to make conspicuous sublimation the expressive basis of the ballet.
The answer, which incidentally involves attitudes more bourgeois
than patrician, depends on the recognition that conspicuous sublimation is not merely *like* conspicuous consumption. It is actually a
translation of conspicuous consumption from the sphere of commerce
to the sphere of art. Conspicuous sublimation is a means of making
beauty consumable. Or, more exactly, it is a means for making precisely the kind of beauty epitomized by *Daphnis and Chloe,* the
beauty of sensuous artifice, consumable. That beauty, in turn, is precisely the kind that the culture of late nineteenth-century Europe associated with "elemental drives"—and in that capacity associated,
above all, with the sights and sounds that Europeans had found, selectively, to be sure, in the world of their colonial empires. Conspicuous
sublimation was the basic technique by which the high arts partici-
pated in the cult of exoticism that flowered as a result of these
associations.

As we will see, this cult of exoticism had affiliations, not only with
the pleasures of empire, but also with the pleasures offered by the
increasing availability of affordable consumer goods and by the cultivation of the senses. The exotic became both the sign and the object
of triumphant consumption, explicitly in the marketplace and the
newly developing venues of mass entertainment, implicitly in the arts.

It should be added that recognizing these fields of affiliation does
not automatically commit us to a debunking critique, any more than
recognizing Ives's populism did in the last chapter. The issue of consumer culture is, in fact, an especially complex one. As Miriam Hansen has observed, consumerism since its inception has vacillated between "utopian" and "ideological" moments.[6] On the one hand, it
unsettles social hierarchies, normalizes abundance rather than scar-
city, and promotes the continuous exchange of work for pleasure. On
the other hand, it colonizes not only dependent nations and classes
but also the subjectivity of the consumer, which becomes identified
with the need for continual expenditure. Ravel's music is bound up
with similar ambiguities, not in unique ways, but in memorable, exemplary ones. The unsuspecting *Daphnis and Chloe* is not about to

be charged with blatant Eurocentrism, colonialism, imperialism, sexism, capitalism, racism, or any other -ism. It is, however, about to be situated with respect to important parts of its world: a world that, just like ours, is an imperfectly understood place all tangled up with international politics, sexual desire, and the exchange of goods and services. Acting on this recognition does, admittedly, sometimes require making moral judgments at odds with aesthetic appreciation. But it does not require sacrificing either for the other.

Besides, in Ravel's case the nexus of music, consumerism, and exoticism comes close to being a deliberate aesthetic program. A Baudelairean dandy in his youth, the composer who in maturity described himself as "artificial by nature" set out to modernize, by commodifying, the fin-de-siècle aestheticism that elevated exquisite artifice over vulgar reality. A proto-postmodernist, Ravel—who used to display a burned-out lightbulb as a globe of smoked glass—set copies over originals and the virtual over the real. "Falsehood," he wrote, "taken as the power of illusion, is the only superiority of man over the animals. . . . Isn't it better at least to be fully aware and acknowledge that art is the supreme imposture?"[7] From the faux-jazz of the Violin Sonata and G-Major Piano Concerto to the faux-Hispanism of *Alborada del graciosa* and *Rhapsodie espagnole* to the faux-Basque and faux-gamelan rhythms in the Piano Trio, Ravel's music is full of simulacra: popular-exotic borrowings of impeccable accuracy, undistanced by obvious marks of stylization.

Ravel says that he applies only "minute stylizations" to the originals of these musical images, thereby turning them into art.[8] What they turn into, however, might be more accurately described as reproducible *objets d'art*, like department-store curios. The music does to sonority what the middle-class country villa not far from Paris which Ravel bought in 1922 did to space. Ravel turned his home into both a model of modern kitchen and bathroom design and a kind of consumerist museum. Fond of showing off the little objects with which the house was filled—porcelains, doll furniture, glass-ball paperweights with flower centers, a blown-glass ship that could be rocked on painted waves, a mechanical nightingale in a gilded cage—he would reply to compliments on their exquisiteness by exclaiming, "Mais c'est de faux! Ça vient des grands magasins!" [But it's fakery! They come from the department stores!'] It is impossible to say whether his art was imitating his life or vice versa.[9]

·   ·   ·   ·   ·

With *Daphnis and Chloe,* Ravel aimed at artifice on a grander scale, a whole musical Bon Marché or Ladies' Paradise. He says he wanted to compose "a choreographic symphony . . . a vast musical fresco, less concerned with archaism than with faithfulness to the Greece of my dreams, which is similar to that imagined and depicted by French artists of the end of the eighteenth century." [10] As he informed us in "Le tombeau de Couperin," Ravel's love of simulacra sometimes expressed itself as a nostalgia for the lyrical artificiality of the ancien regime. But the Greece of, say, François Boucher, Mme de Pompadour's favorite painter, does not recognize elemental drives, even to sublimate them, and is, besides, entirely desacralized. Boucher's Greece is plush, and enervated by its plushness, where Ravel's imaginary Greece is ecstatic. What Ravel's nostalgic statement fails to observe, and may wittingly or unwittingly wish to obscure, is that in both subject matter and technique *Daphnis and Chloe* is an exemplary piece of nineteenth-century commercial exoticism, turned into art— and magically, too—by countless "minute stylizations."

Ravel's music, however, makes no secret of this fact. His score is brimful of exotic scales, colors, and melodic ornamentation, some adapted from the sound-worlds of orientalist operas such as Saint-Saëns's *Samson and Delilah,* Borodin's *Prince Igor,* and Strauss's *Salome,* some from the symphonic Arabian nights of Rimsky-Korsakov's *Scheherazade,* and some from the belly-dance music of Paris's "Oriental" cafés. Like these other works, not counting the belly-dance music, *Daphnis and Chloe* transfers the aura of nineteenth-century exoticism to its archaic narrative. This transfer reflects and enforces one of the primary qualities of the exotic, its supposed preservation of values that the advanced cultures of Europe had superseded. When Europeans consumed the cultures of distant places, they could glimpse the thrilling secrets of their own origins in distant times.[11]

This view of the exotic as a kind of living museum thrived in low and high culture alike. The international trade expositions popular in

Paris during the later nineteenth century featured cultural exhibits that were famous for their mishmash of times and places. One observer describes an exhibit representing Moorish Spain in which bowing and dancing camels stand in for Andalusian ponies, Oriental rugs hang on sale (priced as marked) amid hawkers selling beer, lemonade, and two-cent stereoscopic views of "licentious scenes," and a fourteenth-century courtyard, reproduced "with great fidelity and delicacy," discreetly displays the words *Menier Chocolate* in Gothic lettering.[12] A similar, if less colorful, casualness typified the period's ethnographic museum exhibits, which, reports Marianna Torgovnik, "resembled department stores during clearance sales."[13]

Conspicuously sublimated, this sort of jumble can be translated into an evocation of timeless beauty or menace, as in Walter Pater's famous description of the Mona Lisa:

She is older than the rocks among which she sits; like the vampire, she has been dead many times, and learned the secrets of the grave; and has been a diver in deep seas, and keeps their fallen day about her; and trafficked for strange webs with Eastern merchants; and, as Leda, was the mother of Helen of Troy, and, as Saint Anne, the mother of Mary; and all this has been to her but as the sound of lyres and flutes.[14]

Pater's equation of the exotic, the archaic, and the (feminine) other is exemplary, especially in its ambiguous invocation of "traffick," material and sexual, with Eastern merchants. The character and value of the exotic lie precisely in its embodiment of such "traffick" or commerce, the "strange web" of material exchanges across times, places, and bodies. Exemplary, as well, is the subject's passage through the secretive grave and the "deep seas," imaginarily both its own depths and those of past time; and exemplary, again, as chapter 2 would lead us to expect, is the condensation of all the equivalent terms of alterity into an imaginary music.

Daphnis and Chloe gives that music a material form. In its equally exemplary identification of the exotic and the archaic, the ballet continually evokes the sound of lyres (represented by harps) and flutes. A large battery of unpitched percussion adds a layer of "Eastern" color, sometimes suggesting an esoteric eroticism, more often a fierce, dervishistic energy. But the most exotic-archaic element of all is one that, for practical reasons grudgingly sanctioned by the composer, is missing from the popular concert suites by which the music of *Daphnis and Chloe* is best known. This is the prominent use of a chorus singing in a style as far removed as possible from that of the European choral tradition: a wordless chorus ecstatically vocalizing in short, fast-fading cries and long-drawn-out sighs and undulations.

The chorus reduces the human voice from a vehicle of agency and signification to a pure and mobile materiality. Voice in this form is meant to give the impression of "speaking" the semiotic from outside the symbolic. It mirrors a kind of subjectivity, sometimes called "ideodynamism," that preoccupied the *nouvelle psychologie* of late nineteenth-century France: an unconsciously determined flight of ideas (nervous excitations) associated variously with hypnotism, suggestion, and dreams. Popularly identified with the neuroses and sensory excesses of modern urban life, ideodynamism, as Debora Silverman has shown, could also find (or at least seek) a safe haven in highly ornamented private spaces, "interiors" of exotic and antique decor.[15] In the imaginary of Ravel's wordless chorus, ideodynamic reverie travels back to the mythical origins of such interiors. Unlike the roughly contemporaneous wordless choruses in Debussy's *Sirènes*, Ives's Fourth Symphony, and Holst's *The Planets*, Ravel's offers not a trace of ethereality or transcendental intuition. Sensuous without apology, it arises at the intersection of the fantasmatic and the bodily, offering itself as a souvenir of distant shores and remote, unheard-of pleasures.[16]

·   ·   ·   ·   ·

Why was the type of exoticism realized in *Daphnis and Chloe* so important from, roughly, the 1830s to the 1930s—important enough to command a certain nostalgia even today? The answer to this question is many sided. It derives from the cultural uses to which Europe put its colonial empires at the height of their economic exploitation and in an era when major technological advances in transportation and communication made the fruits of empire, both discursive and material, more available—and more marketable—than ever before.

By the late nineteenth century, the presence in European cities of exotic artifacts and images in museums, homes, and stores had come to signify at least three major aspects of modern European life. First, the exotic embodied the cultural supremacy that subsumed, classified, structured, and administered vast stretches of the non-European world. Second, the exotic symbolized the rising economic order of the mass production, distribution, and advertising of consumer goods, an order that offered the glow of well-being and, better, a sense of luxury to a growing number of middle-class Europeans, though not to far larger numbers of poor ones. The relationship between European culture and its colonial possessions is recapitulated in the relationship between the consumer and everyday life. Third, the exotic gave a degree of legitimacy to the pursuit of sensuous pleasure for its own sake. This legitimacy was achieved precisely by identifying such hedonism with the customs and environments thought to be typical of dominated peoples. Europeans could indulge themselves in the practice or fantasy of exotic pleasures because, in both a literal and a figurative sense, they owned them. The resulting "dream world of mass consumption," in Rosalind Williams's telling phrase, served to veil (and so to perpetuate) the regulation and deferral of pleasure on which most people's everyday life actually depended.

All of these meanings of the exotic are strikingly displayed on a turn-of-the-century postcard advertising the Grand Bazar de l'Hotel de Ville (Figure 1).[17] The card shows exotic peoples from every corner of the globe rubbing elbows with both whites and each other amid a traffic jam consisting of camels, elephants, a donkey, a rickshaw, and some automobiles, in a kind of genial pandemonium. Modern traffic policemen bring a dollop of order to the scene and at the same time suggest the way the European present controls and synthesizes the exotic record of the cultural past. Meanwhile, different races and castes mingle freely: a natty black African sports a tuxedo, a plump Frenchwoman rides in the rickshaw, an Indian driver stops his elephant for unloading by French workmen, one of whom stands on a ladder steadied by a black African in a loincloth.

Heterogeneous though it is, however, the scene is tightly controlled by European symbols and institutions. The cityscape is centered on the imposing facade of the Hotel de Ville, the center of which, in turn, is drawn as a barely concealed phallus atop which there perches a flag, presumably the tricolor of France. The entrance to the building at the base of this erection is the point of perspective from which the streets

Figure 1. Postcard: Grand Bazar de l'Hotel de Ville, ca. 1900. Reproduced by courtesy of Naomi Schor.

filled with the world's peoples radiate in a triangular pattern. And as if this were not enough, the scene is presided over by a jovial gendarme who stands at the viewer's left and chats benignly with a black man, who, holding a butterfly net, of all things, literally looks up to the gendarme with submission written all over his stereotypically negroid features.

Quite remarkably, this scene is not meant to sell the invidious racial and imperial stereotypes that are naively latent in it but merely to sell merchandise. The dream world of mass consumption is curiously democratic; it collapses the high bourgeois principles of social and racial exclusion, but only in order to transform everyone into a bourgeois subject. All these people, natives and Frenchmen alike, are on a shopping spree, and they can best gratify their urge to consume at the Grand Bazar de l'Hotel de Ville—a turn-of-the-century shopping mall in which, the postcard promises, goods of the highest quality abound in the greatest variety. Behind this imaginary scene there hover both the international trade expositions with their exotic bazaars and, closer to everyday life, a long line of exotic exhibits set up in Parisian department stores to attract and bedazzle customers. Even when the customer in such a store bought something with no exotic aura, surely the most common occurrence, the sheer number of goods to choose from, many of them of a kind that only the rich could buy before the advent of mass production, endowed the simple act of buying with the aura of colonial adventure.

Finally, this unusually revealing postcard shows us a scene of infectious pleasure. Such faces as we see are all smiles: the Arab in his mantle, the rickshaw lady, the black baby carried on the back of his Ubangi father, all are smiling; even the gendarme smiles. On the surface, the pleasure circulated here is simply a heightened version of the consumer's pleasure in ownership. This acquisitive pleasure is represented as self-sufficient, independent of what is consumed; all the purchases except the butterfly net are concealed by their trademark green wrapping. The imagery, however, as so often in advertising, also suggests sensual and erotic depths. The foreground is dominated by two couples walking with intimate closeness: the mantled Arab and his veiled wife, and the Ubangi parents. The Arab clutches his package as his wife clutches her chador, suggesting the hidden erotic value of both the package and the woman. The Ubangi father carries, not only a baby on his back, but also a small package on his tongue, suggesting a triple overlap of sensuous pleasure, consumption, and procreative power and pleasure. It is also suggestive that neither couple is European, as if the practice of sexualizing consumption and consuming sexuality were itself an exotic mystery.

. . . . .

Ravel's *Daphnis and Chloe* is cherishable in a hundred ways that this fascinating but ridiculous postcard is not, and yet the meanings we found in the postcard can be found in the music as well. We can go over them in sequence.

First, the music embodies the cultural supremacy by which Europe subsumes and organizes the non-European world. As I noted earlier, the form of the work depends on the combination of an exotic-archaic narrative or program with the most modern of European musical techniques. This technique is very much meant to be heard, to be on display over and above the scenes and feelings it evokes, to be a kind of sonic spectacle. To contain and express the exotic, the music re-

enacts the technical and administrative mastery that brought the exotic to Europe in the first place. Ravel thus composes a kind of master
class in orchestral technique. He makes virtuoso use of a large, richly
sonorous orchestra, employing the full range of auxiliary woodwinds,
an extra (fourth) trumpet, the wordless chorus, two harps, a wind machine, and twelve other percussion instruments not counting the
timpani.

From this state-of-the-art orchestral mechanism, Ravel produces a
dazzling array of textures, some fleeting, some sustained, from solo
turns to chamber-music passages to the most massive tuttis. What all
these textures share, even the most complex or abrupt, is a quality of
transparency, something especially significant in the tuttis. The orchestra always sounds as an ensemble, never as a mass, and the standard gradations of melody, countermelody, and accompaniment are
disenfranchised. Ravel assembles his sonorities out of distinct but not
contrastive shapes, the inlays of a musical mosaic. Musical materials—
themes, figures, colors, rhythms, ostinatos, pedal points—are superimposed, overlapped, and allowed to work out their energies both
individually and collectively. At their most exalted, in the opening evocation of pastoral Arcadia and the famous depiction of dawn that
blends into the reunion of Daphnis and Chloe, these mosaics in motion become incantatory, trancelike. As unmoving pedals and swiftly
moving figuration envelop the reiteration of a slow-moving melodic
phrase, the music effectively suspends the passage of time and simply
hangs, radiant, in the air (Example 30).

In its use of the most advanced musical techniques to evoke a world
of pretechnological wonders, Ravel's score bears a suggestive resemblance to the exhibits of "Distant Visions" [Visions lointaines] in turn-
of-the-century Paris, twenty-one of which could be found at the exposition of 1900. These immensely popular entertainments marketed
virtual reality with a panache worthy of Disney. They set their spec-
tacles (and sometimes their spectators) in motion, using revolving
panoramas and cinematography to create the illusion of traveling to
exotic lands. The illusion they produced, however, was consistent with
a reflective awareness of the illusionist mechanism, the higher exoticism, so to speak, of modern European technology. (Ravel's contemporaries routinely drew on exotic metaphors to describe technological

wonders.) In its own reflective illusionism, *Daphnis and Chloe* is the high-art equivalent of an exposition exhibit such as the "Mareorama," which, writes Rosalind Williams, "reproduced a sea voyage from France to Constantinople, complete with canvas panorama, the smell of salt air, a gentle swaying motion . . . and phonographic music 'which' [according to contemporary observer Michel Corday] 'takes on the color of the country at which the ship is calling: . . . [it] becomes Arabic in Africa and ends up Turkish after having been Venetian.'"[18] According to enthusiasts such as Corday, the combination of illusion and illusionism commodifies the whole world in the most benign of terms; the "Distant Visions" are "like liquors sparkling to the eyes, pleasing to the palate, which concentrate power and life in a small volume." *Daphnis and Chloe,* frankly cultivating beauty and pleasure with an abundance of high-modern means, transfers this kind of techno-fantasy from the arcade to the theater or concert hall.

What is true of the music's technique is also true of its structure. Ravel says that *Daphnis and Chloe* is "constructed symphonically according to a very strict tonal scheme by means of a few motifs; their development assures the work's symphonic homogeneity."[19] The term *homogeneity* in this statement is startling, because *Daphnis and Chloe* is a supremely *heterogeneous* score. Its heterogeneity, however, operates only at the level of color and texture, precisely where such heterogeneity is felt to be quintessentially exotic. But this heterogeneity is subsumed by a homogeneity of structure that is, contrariwise, felt to be quintessentially European, the structure of the symphonic ideal, with its principles of tonal hierarchy and thematic development. *Daphnis and Chloe* in particular evokes the conspicuously lucid ideal of a thematically integrated or "circular" symphonic pattern like that of Saint-Saëns's C-minor and (although Ravel was ambivalent about it) César Franck's D-minor symphonies. Once again, European order enjoys, by subsuming, non-European pleasures and energies. The music is like a sonic museum of exotic arts; it organizes the diverse expressions of the exotic, makes the exotic intelligible, by *curating* it.

Going on to the second field of meaning, *Daphnis and Chloe* embodies the new turn in European prosperity, the shift from a culture of production to a culture of consumption. Obviously, the size and sumptuousness of Ravel's orchestra has an economic as well as a tech-

Example 30. Ravel, *Daphnis and Chloe,* mosaic texture in opening evocation (simplified).

Les jeunes filles entourent les socles de guirlandes.

nical significance; Ravel himself thought the work could be performed authentically only in major metropolitan centers that could afford to hire a chorus as well as an orchestra. When Diaghilev tried to do the work in London using the version without chorus that Ravel had prepared for minor venues, the composer was furious.[20]

But the new value placed on consumption is present, not only in the means of performing the music, but also in the music itself. In his use of the symphonic ideal as a controlling vehicle of the exotic, Ravel emphasized the simple, sometimes lightly varied repetition of melodic ideas over their complex transformation. The movement of melody is governed, neither by Classical techniques of fragmentation and development, nor by Romantic techniques of continuous growth and change, but by techniques of reproduction, iteration, similitude— techniques, we might suggest, strikingly similar to those by which commodities are identified and distributed.[21] Neither static nor dynamic, the music expands to fill out what might be called the temporality of display. The department-store displays that Zola fictionalizes in *The Ladies' Paradise* also gain their sumptuousness by a kind of incessant microvariation that is also a repetition:

At first stood out the light satins and tender silks, the satins *à la Reine* and Renaissance, with the pearly tones of spring water; light silks, transparent as crystals—Nile-Green, Indian-Azure, May-Rose, and Danube-Blue. Then came the stronger fabrics: marvellous satins, duchess silks, warm tints, rolling in great waves; and right at the bottom, as in a fountain-basin, reposed the heavy stuffs, the figured silks, the damasks, brocades, and lovely silvered silks.[22]

Zola's association of this display process with figures of liquidity is also basic both to Ravel's score, which resounds with the "murmur of rivulets" filling the idyllic grotto of the nymphs, and more generally to fin-de-siècle representations of (initially sexual) desire.[23]

This type of repetition runs throughout *Daphnis and Chloe* at three distinct levels of organization, each with its own thematic and ideological aura. At the highest level, there is the cyclical recurrence of the famous main theme, its characteristic leaps of a fifth suggesting both distant visions and the ache of desire, in constantly changing colors and textures. This is supported by the similar recurrence of another figure heard at the outset, the undulation of a longer note with a shorter one a major second lower, suggesting the "murmur of rivulets" as a figure for receptivity to pleasure, perhaps even an "oceanic" receptivity that eludes all regulation. These two elements gently overlap and combine early in the opening evocation, the horns and winds taking the main theme, the voices the undulation (Example 31). Later, as the "Dawn" episode passes through successive climaxes, the voices return with their undulation in full cry and the main theme crowns the episode in full instrumental grandeur.

At the next level, there is the nearly continuous formation, recurrence, and reshuffling of short melodic ideas, the main theme and undulation included. *Daphnis and Chloe* abounds in these ideas, which are the silken stuffs of its display process. The piece essentially consists of their ever-renewed juxtaposition and combination. The ideas themselves are vivid and forthright (transparent as crystals— Nile-Green, Indian-Azure, May-Rose, and Danube-Blue). They range in scale from indivisible little gestures with characteristic or micro-varied sonorities to miniature episodes varied mostly by changes in texture and orchestration. Their repetitions are both full and fragmentary, both widely and closely spaced.

This process might be said to make expressive units function motivically, but it does not simulate the organicist logic of real motivic organization. It would be better to say that the reiterative process makes the music unfold cinematically; the mosaic-in-motion is a montage of sonorities. By 1913, when Paris could boast 160 venues for it, the cinema had established itself as the unrivaled heir of the department store and trade exposition as a purveyor of distant visions in what Williams calls the fantasy of consumption. By reiterating highly colored musical gestures that, like camera shots, are relatively brief, stable, and independent, Ravel invests them with an analogue to the peculiar doubleness that his contemporaries found in cinematic images: a combination of "photographic truth, luminous and trembling," with undisguised "artifice and . . . falsification."[24]

Finally, at the most local level of *Daphnis and Chloe*, there is considerable immediate repetition of melodic ideas, both simple and florid, in different tone colors. Richly textured and nonprogressive, this composition *à la Russe* offers the most obvious evocations of the exotic in the score.

At all three levels, the music acquires an exotic charm that the listener can possess, or consume, because each bit of the mosaic, each

Example 31. Ravel, *Daphnis and Chloe,* combination of motives in opening evocation.

item on display, is self-contained. What you hear is what you get. The surface of the melodic ideas conceals no depth; there is no pressure to integrate the succession of ideas into the perception of a complex, evolving unity. The melodic idea thus becomes an object, a dazzling and precious object, put on offer to the ear. This process reaches its

Example 31. (*continued*)

height amid the glittering textures of the great dawn episode, where the objectification of melody merges with the representation of both natural splendor and sexual love. Such a conjuncture of love, nature, and the precious object, the technique of quasi-fetishistic display also exemplified in Zola's rhapsody on silks, is a basic technique of modern advertising, already well established in the first years of the twentieth century. In saying this, I have no intention of belittling *Daphnis and Chloe*. Rather, the link between Ravel's musical imagery and the imagery of advertising should be understood as a sign of the importance that the fantasy of consumption holds in modern life in both high and popular culture. After all, the audience for *Daphnis and Chloe* derived from the very same population of middle-class consumers to which the Grand Bazar de l'Hotel de Ville directed its fabulous postcard.

Turning to the last field of meaning, *Daphnis and Chloe* is a celebration of material, sensuous, and erotic pleasure divorced from all moral and social concerns. This is perhaps the least debatable statement I have made so far, but its obviousness does not make its meanings equally obvious. As we've seen, Ravel uses the symphonic ideal as a means of both containing and consuming the exotic. But as we've also seen, his use of this ideal is deliberately simplified. It is this simplification that creates the effect of conspicuous sublimation. The musical values of the symphonic ideal are turned upside down: instead of color and texture serving as means to articulate structure, structure serves as a means to disseminate color and texture, providing a simple frame of reference within which these sensuous elements can luxuriate.

Ravel establishes this sensuous sound world at the very beginning of the work, which builds up a complex texture one layer at a time until the main theme emerges on solo horn. By shifting focus among the engaged layers of sonority, Ravel enables the texture of this passage and others like it to persist, fade, or swell, processes that recur throughout the score. The result is to render the orchestra a kind of artificial landscape, a space or atmosphere charged with a multitude of sensations.

Yet because they are structured so lucidly, sublimated so conspicuously, these are not *mere* sensations. They can not only be enjoyed, they can also be idealized, and, more importantly, they can be enjoyed *in being* idealized. Their promise of unrepresentable bliss, of *jouissance,* is not wholly sacrificed to the symbolic order; it persists as an aura around their sublimated form. When the wordless chorus suffuses the texture, it affirms the immanence—and imminence—of the semiotic and testifies to the proximity of bliss. The ballet ends with a veritable sunburst of that bliss—another kind of dawn—as the chorus engages in a varied series of broken gasps ending in a prolonged cry, altogether the most explicit representation of orgasm in all "classical" music (Example 32). Here is the culture of the exotic at its most uto-

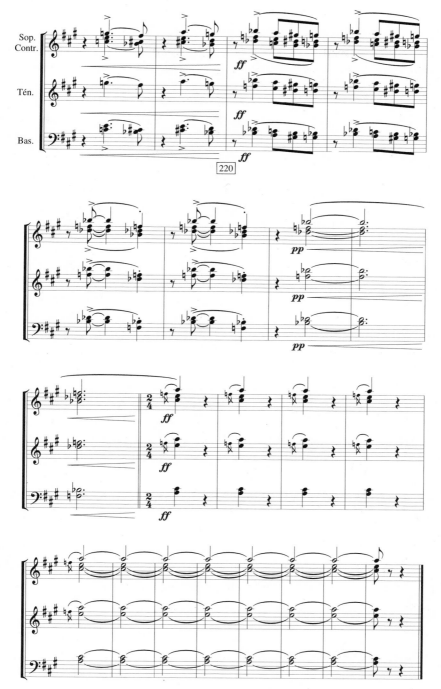

Example 32. Ravel, *Daphnis and Chloe* (Conclusion), choral representation of orgasm.

pian and subversive, ecstatically consumed by the pleasure it consumes. The force of the gesture is redoubled by a consistently high tessitura for all the voices, which "feminizes" the sound in a lyrical version of the war whoops in Mendelssohn's *First Walpurgisnight.* Closure is pleasure without an aftermath: sensuous, artificial, sexual, feminine. When Ravel let Diaghilev have a second-best version of the ballet omitting the chorus, he apparently did not foresee that this would become the norm for concert performance. It is plainly a norm that should be thrown out. The omission of the chorus amounts to an act of repression, both political and psychical, however practical it may be. One might even say that without the chorus the music risks being *merely* an exotic commodity.

Not that the risk is entirely missing even with the chorus present. The category of the exotic is so bound up with the appropriative energies of commerce (in the expanded sense of the term developed earlier) that no exotic pleasure can be entirely innocent. And any cultivation of pleasure in commodified form invites ideological critique, regardless of the prospects for utopian recuperation. The commonplace notion that Ravel's music in general is almost too appealing, that it has a glamorous surface but no real depth, is probably a reflection of this. Yet *Daphnis and Chloe* is remarkably effective in giving the impression—Ravel's "supreme imposture"—of utopian innocence. Perhaps this is largely because it seems free of the anxiety that surrounds the exotic elsewhere, the volatile mixture of fear and desire of the other that manifests itself in the violence of cognate works such as Stravinsky's *Rite of Spring* and Bartók's *The Miraculous Mandarin,* beside which the brigands' scenes in *Daphnis and Chloe* are tea parties.[25]

Unburdened by defensiveness, Ravel is able to figure the exotic in ways that are genuinely open to the energies of the other as well as appropriative of them. Those energies find their culminating expression in the "General Dance" celebrating the union of Daphnis and Chloe. By organizing its dithyrambic whirl with an irregular meter, 5/4, the dance becomes an orgy of "false steps" utterly alien to the European tradition of superenergetic finales. (Legend has it that the dancers of the Ballets Russes could not get the hang of the rhythm until they began counting to the mnenomic "Ser-gei Dia-ghi-lev, Sergei Dia-ghi-lev.")[26] H. H. Stuckenschmidt captures something of Ravel's attitude when he remarks on a general "Mediterranean" exoticism that "pays little attention to any difference between the eastern and western shores of that sea" and that in *Daphnis and Chloe* "does not hesitate to enliven ancient Greece with castanets and Basque drums."[27] Or, as Ravel himself would later observe, "It is not the developed artistic culture which fails to comprehend the significance of a culture and civilization different from itself. On the contrary, a developed artistic consciousness implies such appreciation."[28]

.   .   .   .   .

In sum, the material sound world of *Daphnis and Chloe* constitutes an ideal order—the order of the exotic—that is both utterly accessible, like a department-store display rich with "order and beauty," and utterly remote, like the artificial paradise in Baudelaire's "Invitation to the Voyage," from which the phrase "order and beauty" is lifted:

> Des meubles luissants,
>   Polis par les ans,
> Décoreraient notre chambre;
>   Les plus rares fleurs,
>   Mêlant leurs odeurs
> Aux vagues senteurs de l'ambre,
>   Les riches plafonds,
>   Les miroirs profonds,
> La splendeur orientale,
>   Tout y parlait
>   A l'âme en secret
> Sa douce langue natale.

La, tout n'est qu'ordre et beauté,
Lux, calme, et volupté.[29]

[The gleaming furniture, polished by the years, would decorate our room; the most rare flowers would mingle their odors with vague scents of amber; the rich ceilings, the profound mirrors, the oriental splendor, all there would secretly speak to the soul its sweet native tongue. There, there is nothing but order and beauty, luxury, calm, and delight.]

Or, to shift the terms of comparison, the Listener's Paradise of Ravel's "choreographic symphony" offers a wealth of innocent but passionate pleasures, the pleasures of a world where "to live is to sing and love," such as Paul Gauguin represented in his Tahitian paintings.[30] Like those paintings, the music of *Daphnis and Chloe* (re)locates the accessible-remote sensuous manifold of the exotic within the presence of the modern Western artwork.

In the process, the music, again like the paintings, suggests that ecstatic participation in this relocated manifold can assume values that would once have been adjudged spiritual or transcendental. And like those paintings, again, the music intimates that the cultural supremacy of modern Europe is both consummated and subverted by such participation. The pleasures on offer are acute, but they are also *de faux;* the masterly technique that displays them is also the sign of their absence, or more exactly of their presence as mere simulacra. As Gauguin observed, putting the best face on the problem, "By the combination of lines and colors under the pretext of some motif taken from nature, I create symphonies and harmonies which represent nothing absolutely real in the ordinary sense of the word but are intended to give rise to thoughts as music does."[31]

Gauguin's appeal to music intriguingly reverses Ravel's appeal to painting in describing the aims of *Daphnis and Chloe.* Symbolically, at least, each art can authenticate its fabrication of the exotic by figuring itself as the other. But the underlying problem remains, and at one climactic moment of the ballet Ravel unveils it with great poignancy. At the height of the dance commemorating Pan and Syrinx, Chloe, as the stage directions instruct, "in a mad whirling . . . falls into Daphnis's arms." At this point a rich orchestral sonority yields abruptly to a series of unaccompanied statements passing from piccolo to flute to alto flute. The effect is epiphanic, as if Pan's own pipes were sounding. Twice the alto flute, *très espressif,* plays the first part of the ballet's principal motive; twice the upper strings and a harp answer with an impulsive shudder. Then the string body takes over the motive in richly harmonized form. The strings repeat the alto flute's question, pause for a shudder (now on both harps), then supply a fuller answer themselves. Then the strings repeat the whole process, this time granting themselves an even fuller answer. The sound of the solo flute at once blossoms into and loses itself in the full, sensuous sound of the strings. The Eastern piping becomes a Western melody at once reflective, self-conscious, and imbued with an unmet yearning. The fantasy structure of "commerce" becomes audible as mimesis on the flute (replicating Pan) gives way to metaphor on the strings (sublimating Pan). With this gesture, Ravel encapsulates the contradiction at the exotic heart of consumer culture. Both the means and the end of the dream of mass consumption is the acquisition of pleasure in material form. But the pleasure acquired is dematerialized in the very process of acquisition. It is always, and of necessity, purely imaginary.

Epilogue à 4

Autonomy, Elvis, Cinders, Fingering Bach

As a skate's heel sweeps smooth on a bow-bend: the hurl
    and gliding
Rebuffed the big wind. My heart in hiding
Stirred for a bird,—the achieve of, the mastery of the
    thing!

Brute beauty and valour and act, oh, air, pride, plume, here
    Buckle!

—Gerard Manley Hopkins,
"The Windhover"

"One reason," writes Kofi Agawu in a recent essay, "why the notions of musical autonomy and transcendence have not yet been successfully resisted . . ."[1] Smooth on a bow-bend: the sheer panache of this pleases me in spite of myself. Surely those notions have been more than just resisted. Surely they have been taken apart so often, by so many, in recent years, that Humpty Dumpty is still in one piece by comparison. Agawu's statement is rhetorically shrewd, so offhanded in its assumption of what it seeks to prove that the reader almost misses the trick. But the shrewdness marks the site where a truth must be (dis)simulated. (Must be: this is mandatory, not a problem with Agawu's text as such.) Once upon a time the autonomous artwork could stand alone, no need for props. But time runs on; *hurry up please, it's time.* Persistent sightings notwithstanding, the Autonomous Artwork is dead as Elvis.

Unacknowledged Legislators. Autonomy: from the Greek *autos,* self, and *nomos,* law. To give oneself the law: it's a strange ideal for the artwork, an object supposedly defined by its capacity to give pleasure in being perceived. Pleasure and law are moral, if not mortal, antagonists. Unable to enjoin enjoyment, law allows, regulates, or forbids pleasure; it licenses some pleasures by burdening others with secrecy or guilt. Pleasure in relation to law shuttles between assent and transgression.

The concept of aesthetic autonomy implies that art is a means of overcoming these antagonisms. In traditional aesthetics, the artwork reconciles cardinal oppositions through its form, which addresses itself to the perception of a universalized subject. A postmodernist revision would hold that the artwork's form constitutes an appeal to be perceived from a historically situated subject position, often one meant to be misrecognized as universal. The appeal of the autonomous artwork arises amid the social transformations of modernity in the eighteenth and early nineteenth centuries. It addresses a subject that very much wants to be universal, to create its own symbolic traditions, to transfer numinous authority from the height of increasingly demystified central institutions to the depth of personal experience. Insofar as I answer the summons to personify (impersonate?) this subject, I both perceive the artwork's reconciliation of pleasure and law and, in perceiving it, seem also to perform it myself.[2]

So understood, this process necessitates a rewriting of the classical aesthetic-era formula for autonomy. Instead of the sundered Kantian spheres of subject and object, the artwork would address the intertwined Lacanian-Kristevan registers of subjectivity. Understood as the locus of aesthetic autonomy, art is what reconciles the imaginary/ semiotic, where pleasure rules law, and the symbolic, where law rules pleasure.

What general form would this reconciliation take? How would the artwork give pleasure in being perceived to give itself the law?

The ideal of autonomy focuses, not on the content of the law, but on its source, not on the rules that I give, but on the fact that I give them. For that very reason, autonomy is an ideal of assent, not of transgression: however heedless otherwise, I heed the law I give to myself. But in order to give oneself the law one must first have received a law from someone else. Everyone first learns to act lawfully from others; everyone first accepts the law at others' hands, from others' voices of guidance and admonition. In the first instance we heed our parents' law, symbolically figured as the father's, which according to Lacan is the way we become subjects.

The pleasure of the autonomous artwork would come from undoing this origin. It would be the pleasure—transgressive after all—of not heeding the law *as given by someone else.* Here again, the source of the law matters more than its content. The effect of autonomy does not depend on my giving myself any particular law, nor on whether I make or merely appropriate the law I give. There is autonomy enough, transgression enough, in giving the law in my own way, for my own reasons. The pleasure of autonomy would be happily guilty, the heady pleasure of taking the law into one's own hands careless of reproof. It is as if Prometheus could steal the fire without concern (well, with just a little) for the eagle and the rock. Beethoven suggested as much in the Finale of the *Eroica.* But in that case autonomy itself, once and forever, is a contested terrain; its name is a misnomer. In that case the pleasure of the autonomous artwork would be purely social.

The King Is Dead. Elvis just bewildered me at first. I was a bit too young to mark his mainstream arrival on the *Ed Sullivan Show* as a seismic event in popular culture or to recognize this famous bisected broadcast—the camera forbidden to gaze below the belt—as a latter-day revelation of how castration makes charismatic singers. A few years later, I could see and, better, could hear the charisma, but only at a distance; Elvis's aura fascinated but also repelled me. It seemed shot through with an indefinable falseness that no one else seemed to mind. At the time all I could do was call it "hokey"; a recent study by Marjorie Garber may suggest what prompted me: "From the beginning Elvis is produced and exhibited as parts of a body—detachable . . . parts that have an uncanny life and movement of their own, seemingly independent of their 'owner.' . . . [He] is a *marketable* body, exhibited and put on display, merchandised."[3] Elvis must have struck me as a prosthetic figure, somebody manufactured to satisfy a certain mass fantasy I couldn't identify—or identify with.

As an adult I thought I knew what the fantasy was. I thought of Elvis, alas, as an unwitting icon of American racism—more exactly of an unuprooted racist unconscious. We all know that Elvis became Elvis by "singing black"; above all he was a modern minstrel. But so easy to misrecognize, this minstrel at second remove, this southern white boy whose blackface was his voice. The minstrel Elvis offered his cleancut white body as the locus of white fantasies about the scary, limitless, resentfully envied desire(ability) of black men. The notorious silly slogan "Elvis the Pelvis" pointed, not just to any old displaced phallus, but to a big black phallus, pillar of yet another love that dare not speak its name lest somebody need lynching. The birth of a nation(al music) in reversible racial drag: Elvis blacking his voice as Bigger Thomas in whiteface. The bloated, drugged-out Elvis of the Las Vegas years is the castrated version of the same fantasy: both an atonement for it and its continuation by other means.

Vox Humana. "The words 'another voice,'" writes Derrida: "they 'call,' they 'ask for' another voice: 'another voice, again, yet another voice.' It is a desire, an order, a prayer or a promise, as you wish."[4] For me music has gradually become the labyrinth of another voice, threading those chambers of the ear that wind and unwind into every distance, that turn inside out to become the whorled spaces of the world, of other voices, another voice. Deaf to the autonomous artwork, I can finally hear the music. And when music "itself" solicits my deafness, asks me to hear it as the autonomous artwork, the sound only grates on me, gravels, scores the unwalled labyrinth with acoustic graffiti.

Hegelian Heavies. The autonomous artwork: not only a legislative ideal but also, and thereby, a gendered ideal. Strange, how well the privilege of giving oneself the law fits the atomized private subject of classical bourgeois fantasy, the one that used to (mis)take itself for civilized man. Strange how well it fits the dialectical opposite (*semblable* and *frère*) of this figure, the hairy murdering rapacious sex-crazed father of Freud's Primal Horde. It would be pretty to think that this dialectic is all gummed up by now, erased and discredited, just plain kaput. But the best we can say is that its star players are dead. (That will not, of course, necessarily keep them away.) The bourgeois monad succumbed to the twentieth century, having recognized himself one fine day as a Gorgon in drag. And the father of the Primal Horde was, *pace* Freud, dead from the start, always already dead, the better to be unkillable: another black phallus in a white-robed mind.

There Are Cinders There. In *Cinders,* part philosophical reverie, part prose poem, Derrida returns to his obsessive project of trying out, trying on, names for the unnameable. The Snark he hunts (but the Snark is a Boojum, you see) is the nonpresence—neither presence nor absence—without which no sign can come to presence: the internal divisibility that always accompanies, always precedes, the unison of signifier and signified in the sign: the trace of the Other within every order of the Same: that which lies in "the back room, in the shadows . . . prior to the oppositions between conscious and unconscious, freedom and constraint, voluntary and involuntary, speech and language." Derrida describes being haunted by one particular name for "this irreducible nonpresence of another now," a name not a word but disseminated across a recurrent phrase, "il y a là cendre": "cinders there are."[5]

Suffice it here to oversimplify by ignoring (as Derrida does not) the phonetic and rhetorical polyvalence of this essentially untranslatable phrase—untranslatable, you might say, even into French. Think only of cinders as metaphor, the figure of that which "remains without remaining," that which, "however slightly one touches it, it falls, it does not fall into cinders, it gets lost down to the cinder of its cinders."[6] Cinders burn but are not on fire; cinders are solid but have no substance; cinders are something but nothing, there but not there, a trace of what the fire has consumed and the trace that can be consumed by no fire.

Revenants. Do hundreds of sightings of Elvis constitute his resurrection *corpus delicti?* Haloed by the legend, the collective dream narrative, does a good—does a bad—Elvis impersonator become something like Elvis incarnate? Something like that: Elvis himself was a Little Richard impersonator. (He was even an Elvis impersonator.) So the autonomous artwork lives! Hundreds of sightings reported in the

New York Times! Dare I confess my own close encounter? Not a sighting, exactly, but certainly a sounding. *Full fathom five thy father lies.* I found the autonomous artwork lying disregarded in my living room. *Those are pearls that were his eyes.*

Not long ago I started playing the piano for pleasure again after a gap of many years. It's at the keyboard that I keep rehearing this. . . . The pleasure that springs from the interplay of my fingers, working and struggling to work to cull music from the jumble of notes, the syntactical rhythms of tension and release in harmony and counterpoint, the defamiliarized presence of a coherent, expressive totality held and shaped as if literally by my own hands: this pleasure makes its continually re-presented origin the autonomous artwork. The autonomy is a voice—an oracle's? a siren's? a *Leiermann's*?—in the fingers.

So the concept of music as autonomous artwork does not belong to the listener, and most especially not to the active listener for whom listening is a form of mutual inquiry, discovery, revelation. It belongs to the performer, and most especially to the amateur performer whose only motive in playing is pleasure. Admittedly, this does not get the autonomous artwork out of politics. The self-pleasuring performer is a social institution: a private identity even when playing with others, licensed in autohedonic behavior (even when playing with others), master or disciple but in any case owner of an instrument—heir, in my case, to the great signifier of nineteenth-century bourgeois autonomy, the piano (like the angel) in the house. Yet—and this is the amazing thing, uncanny as any *revenant*—the institution of the self-pleasuring performer utterly erases the signs of its social origins. At the keyboard I forget, I am licensed to forget, everything but the music. So the music becomes an "itself": I forget everything but the music itself. The autonomous artwork is the begetting of this forgetting; not memory, but its loss, is the mother of the muses. At the keyboard, the autonomous artwork is literally the handiwork of my forgetfulness.

But. The autonomous artwork appears only in cinders.

Revenants — Encore. Another lack speaks up: the autonomous artwork can never inhabit but only revisit the keyboard. The locus of autonomy is the gap in presence, the hyphen in re-presentation, a

perceptible-imperceptible fissure that can never be closed without a
seam, the irreducible nonpresence of another now, another's now. A
living Elvis can be seen but never sighted. As language can originate
only by harboring a "degradation at [its] interior,"[7] in the very embrace of signifier and signified, the autonomous artwork can arise only
by accreting around the mark of an abyss that consumes it. There are
cinders there.

One of the pieces I play is the Gavotte from J. S. Bach's Third "English" Suite. The movement of the hands here is particularly satisfying, a virtual reproduction of the dance in a continual play of mutual
approach and withdrawal, invigorated by pungent G-minor harmony
and by tonic pedal points that let the left hand stamp like a foot. The
music always seems on the verge of swapping its civilized manner for
a touch of its lost downhome matter, the earthy footing of the Alpine
hillbilly, the *gavot:* but in saying so I forget to forget and so dent the
autonomy of the artwork. Just call it a roughish dance with hands always coming and going. At the expressive high point of this dance, the
inception of the bearish climax, a trill stated earlier by the right hand
is reprised by the left (Example 33). For the right-handed player, such
left-handed trills are hard to master. Professionals, of course, master
them early and move on without fuss; amateurs like me never quite
lose their dread of them. Certainly the left-handed trill in the G-
minor Gavotte is the hardest thing in the piece; when I play this trill
(and I don't always) it never matches its right-handed dance partner

Example 33. J. S. Bach, Third "English" Suite (Gavotte), right- and left-hand trills.

in smoothness of sonority and integration with the melody in the other hand. This trill burns my fingers. It is a cinder.

Dal segno, now: in what sense is there a cinder there? The left-handed trill cuts in on the dance of fingers, forms, and feeling that constitutes the autonomous artwork. It is the locus of a resistance to the music within the music "itself," the music's "itself": a resistance, a self-divisibility, a "degradation in the interior of language" that plays itself out on the exterior of my body, on the awkward materiality of my maladroit fingers. In order for the music('s) "itself" to be re-presented, this resistance must be dissimulated. Someone must touch the cinders without burning a finger.

Vocalise. If Elvis were just another phallic icon, even one enhanced by racial crossover (even one enhanced by a prosthetic penis worn, so they say, in live performance), he would not have become the semi-sacred figure inscribed in the "mystical anagram" *Elvis lives.* There must be something extra in the mix. Garber thinks this extra is a femininity by which phallic display is always haunted: that Elvis's body, because it was culturally produced as an assemblage of detachable parts, was like woman's body. The parts, like woman's, circulated as fetishes: the pompadour, the pouting lips, the come-hither eyes rimmed by mascara, the swinging hips, the pelvis. Hence the cult of Elvis impersonation, the peculiar fact that "it is almost as if, in contemporary popular culture, the word "impersonator" may be modified by *either* "female" or "Elvis.""[8]

This femininity, however, is held in thrall—enthralled and checked—by Elvis's *other* phallus, the one thing that made him himself. This is the *musical* thing: the deep, resonant instrument that was Elvis's voice, whose power—in our culture fantasized as a virile power—was to replenish itself endlessly while mingling with the dangerous feminine charms of the body that housed it. The full scope of this mingling appears only when its racial elements are factored in. The voice, sexually pure but racially mixed, both upholds and transcends the body, racially pure but sexually mixed. The forbidden mixtures achieve their sublimated form as Elvis becomes the site of a redemptive double crossover, the rhetorical figure of chiasmus or a canon *per arsin et thesin* enacted between voice as presence and body as sign. The timbre of the voice rises above the body it invests as surely as the voice of Raphael, joining divine virility to the appearance of natural law, rises above chaos to begin the narrative of Haydn's *The Creation*. But Elvis's voice is a law unto itself. What it gives to his fans is a pleasure purely vocal, purely musical, the pleasure of being touched by absolute song: the transgressive pleasure of the autonomous artwork.

Bits and Pieces. Bach's trouble is that he writes masterpieces, most of which are too hard for me to play. My musical close encounters depend more on getting my hands on journeyman pieces by assorted *Kleinmeister* and throwaway pieces by the canonical *Meisterwerk* makers. That does the trick; it gives me a repertoire of autonomous artworks and a music box full of revisitational experiences neither over- nor underforgetful, neither too self-enclosed nor too self-subverting. The sounds, the voices, of this music need never be silenced, even when, professionally engaged in musical hermeneutics or composition, I treat the autonomous artwork as a phantasm, an ideological veil, a contingent effect, a nonentity. These voices, sounds, make an ambient stir that gives comfort and pleasure.

Only—and E. M. Forster's goblins would make this my trouble—I am not supposed to find the autonomous artwork where I do. In modernist theory, autonomy is a property of the masterpiece, the sign that the music itself has transcended all social utility and a sign into which the social as such disappears without a trace. But only a handful of minor masterpieces have that autonomy for me, namely the ones that I, though I can't play a left-hand trill, can play at the piano. Autonomy is an *accident* of the masterpiece—and of any piece. It is an imaginary nimbus around whatever pieces I can *almost* play without touching a cinder. If I find autonomy in Baroque keyboard music, it will be in a sarabande by Johann Jakob de Neufville, not in the "Goldberg" Variations.

> No wonder of it: sheer plod makes plow down sillion
> Shine, and blue-bleak embers . . .
> > "The Windhover"

The Sinister Touch. Evenhandedness is basic to Bach's keyboard style, which means that it is also basic to his pedagogy. (Agawu identifies pedagogy as a key factor in preserving musical autonomy: "the indisputable fact [is that] musical composition is recomposition . . . [something] simply inconceivable outside a specific pedagogical tradition."[9] Bach identifies pedagogy as the bridge between musical pleasure and musical workmanship. The Two- and Three-Part Inventions, reads the title page of the autograph over the signature *manqué Joh. Seb. Bach,* begin by teaching "lovers of the clavier, but especially those eager to learn [Lehrbegierigen]" to "play cleanly in two voices" and end by enabling the eager learners to get hold of [überkommen] "a strong foretaste of composition.")[10] The right and left hands must always be capable of acting as mutual mirror images; whatever one does, the other can do. For all which, this evenhandedness is not evenhanded in itself. The burden necessarily falls on the hand presumed to be the clumsier, the left. Ambidextrousness is a goal, not a gift; it must be mastered by practice and self-discipline, by repeated refusals to gratify the resistance of the hand. So it would be more accurate to say that the left hand must learn to act, when called on, as the mirror image of the right. Keyboard melody is essentially born right-handed. The left hand becomes musical only by complying with the law of the right. Not even the most perfect mirroring action can erase this originary difference.

And when the mirror cracks? Motion refracts, sparks fly over the keys. My left hand leaps down an octave, down a fifth more, up another octave and then, in three deliberate steps, mounts toward the trill. My touch tenses, the tension growing a notch with each successive step until the whole hand longs to rest rather than shake at the end of the ascent. Cinders there are in this longing. But also there is a contrary longing, a longing to pass this test: for a test is there, and this is a pedagogical moment. By submitting myself to the discipline of the trill I apprentice myself to Bach as music master. Giving myself his law, I invest his Gavotte with the autonomy of the autonomous artwork. Only insofar as I resist, granting my hand its comfort or wincing at its discomfort, only insofar as I compromise the quality of the trill or cheat by playing it as an upper mordent, do I lose or abrogate this autonomy.

And always I compromise. Often I cheat.

No doubt Bach's reproof would be severe, but I am playing for my pleasure, not my supper. And Bach, always fiery in his service to church and prince, would know a thing or two about the pleasure to be gained, not from giving myself the law, even a law of my own making, but of being, for a moment, willfully and defiantly and exquisitely lawless. This was a man who in 1705 drew his dagger and attacked a student who objected to being called a nannygoat-bassoonist [*Zippel-faggotist*]. In 1717 he was even—we don't recall this often enough—a jailbird.

The autonomous artwork appears only in cinders.

Return to Sender. We now know that Elvis is dead for sure because they put his face on a postage stamp; only the dead qualify. (Still, the post office could make a mistake. Does a letter always reach its destination?) Only it won't surprise anyone that the stamp issue became just another token of resurrection. The post office ran an election between portraits of the younger and older Elvis. When the younger won, people thronged the post office lobbies and snapped up sheets of stamps as if they were Warhol silkscreens to serve as sacred relics. It looks like the King will never die.

But why is his death not permitted? Why must there be sightings and jokes about sightings and pilgrimages to Graceland and tabloid photos of a jowly old Elvis settled down and married to a sweet young thing in Memphis? There are no posthumous sightings of John Lennon or Jim Morrison, let alone Joh. Seb. Bach.

Could dying in Las Vegas have anything to do with this? A throw of the dice will never abolish chance; Elvis couldn't have died, he must just have crapped out. Or is it the self-division in Elvis as a sign, only gradually revealed in the crumbling face of the older and confirmed only by his infirm, finally dead, body? The older was always the nonpresence in the younger, veiled by the sound of that blackface voice, the death knell of every fantasy entwined in the younger's performances. Couldn't, then, the younger also be the nonpresence in the older, the trace of proximity to Being that made the young Elvis the demotic incarnation of the autonomous artwork (and hence its undoing), the fleeting cindershape still warm from the heat of perfect bliss but ready to scatter like the ashes of the dead at the slightest breath?

So his fans hold their breath. The younger Elvis, when the older dies, returns to cinder. And, in short, the best stamp wins.

The Autonomous Artwork. "To treat the arts as autonomous"—so reads a text of my own about the extinguishing of fire as a paradigm for culture—"is to rob them of [their] power. . . . Art can afford to repress the real because the repressed always returns. The power of 'autonomous' art, indeed the effect of autonomy itself, comes precisely from the figure the artwork cuts against the ground supplied by the return of that repressed. What art *cannot* afford is a critical practice that represses not the real but art's repression of the real, that misrecognizes sublation as disavowal and fails to see the trace of the fire"—*cinders there are*—"in the shape of the water." [11]

B A C H. This much is famous. The final number in J. S. Bach's *The Art of Fugue* was left unfinished. A triple fugue, solemn, complicated, and vast, it was planned in four sections, the last of which has barely started when the page goes blank:

1. first subject: a variation of the motto theme that begins the collection's first fugue, but unlike cognate subjects or countersubjects in all the other fugues—a free, not a strict, variation [12]
2. second subject; combination of first and second subjects
3. third subject, the first four notes of which, in German nomenclature, spell B A C H
4. combination of the B A C H subject with the other two, perhaps leading up to a further combination of all three with the original motto theme, which, it just so happens, would fit perfectly into the contrapuntal matrix

The fugue breaks off scant seconds after its three subjects combine. Bach's son Carl Philipp Emanuel wrote on the autograph manuscript: "At the point in this fugue where the name B A C H is introduced as a countersubject, the author died" [Über dieser Fuge, wo der Name B A C H im Contrasubject angebracht worden, ist der Verfasser gestorben]. [13]

What fantasy emerges if we take Carl Philipp Emanuel exactly at his word? Bach dies in the fugue('s) itself, finally effaced by the autonomous artwork at the very moment when it reaffirms the inscription of his name. He dies at—dies of?—the sound of his own name. (Unlike Elvis, Bach is the signatory-auditory of his own death.) More exactly, he dies to the musical voicing of his name as it commingles with the sound of other, nameless voices. He dies, not when the fugue *states* his name, but when it takes his name into the consummating contrapuntal synthesis that both proclaims and establishes a purely musical unity. When *it* does this, the artwork, not *he:* the name B A C H arises in the passive voice, the name "is introduced," *angebracht,* brought on, by an unspecified agent. So Bach dies upon the musical sound of his name *being claimed by the autonomous artwork.*

What this (written) death reveals is the contradiction at the heart of that artwork whose own name is a misnomer. When I identify with aesthetic autonomy I lose my identity. When I give myself the law I escape from the lawgiver that makes me (a) subject. But I do this only by myself becoming that lawgiver. And the law that I give does not belong to me, or to anyone. It is the law. It gives itself through me, the lawgiver. In the autonomous artwork the law gives itself to itself.

But there are cinders there. The fugue can no more survive the name B A C H than the named Bach can survive the fugue. The name cuts into the artwork and ultimately cuts it off. A sign self-divided between language and music, designation and notation, writing and hearing, B A C H becomes a firebrand. Scored with, scor(ch)ed by this sign, the artwork situates its origin, not in the law, but in the ever-present nonpresence of the law. Singing but not singable, this name: that which, falling upon the music, makes Bach an Aschen-Bach.

Castration. Makes charismatic singers. The (male) signatory of the autonomous artwork is always a castrato. (The female signatory, should she exist, is also a castrato in this fantasmatic regime. This may yet change.) So much we learn from Bach's *Todesfuge,* among others. Joh. Seb. B A C H.

Laws.

1. The cadential six-four chord progresses to the dominant by step-wise motion of the upper voices.

2. The anagram of ELVIS shall be VEILS.

3. Women not to sing while menstruating.

4. The autonomous artwork appears only on condition of its own impossibility.

Enigma. Why is the name B A C H brought on climactically only as a countersubject—an inner voice, last heard of three? Is it a gesture of submissiveness, an acknowledgment that Bach the music master is also Bach the servant, subject to, subjected by, God and the prince? Does it protect the autonomous artwork by affirming that the fugue, even the death fugue, will give itself the right law? Or is it a gesture of self-authorization, the revelation of an interior counterauthority, the becoming-audible of an originary voice at the verge of its being silenced? Naming itself at the center, as the center, the voice appears only to disappear. Disappearing, it takes with it the autonomous artwork.

That Bach's life and work should end this way is a fate too good to be true. Could this be conceived (did Carl Philipp Emanuel conceive it) as an allegory? Could Bach, surmising he would not live to reach his destination, have let the death fugue end where it does on purpose?

Cen(t)otaph.

Er ruft streicht dunkler die Geigen dann steigt ihr als Rauch in die Luft

Quelle différence entre cendre et fumée: celle-ci apparemment se perd, et mieux, sans reste sensible, mais elle s'élève, elle prend de l'air, subtilise et sublime. La cendre—tombe, lasse, lâche, plus matérielle d'effriter son mot, elle est très divisible

dein goldenes Haar Marguerite

dein aschenes Haar Sulamith

In clenched cinders not yielding their abused

Bodies and bonds to those whom war's chance saves

Without the law: we grasp, roughly, the song.[14]

Analysis. Another Bach piece I play is the D-Minor Sarabande from the First "French" Suite. Bach often gave the stateliness proper to the sarabande a melancholy burden, and here, in this harried,

Example 34. J. S. Bach, First "French" Suite
(Sarabande, fingering added), end of first half (a);
end of piece (b).

mournful, implacable music, the burden is heavy indeed. The impulse
to drag, to invest the piece with an interiority in excess of Bachian
affect, is almost irresistible.[15]

It so happens that the first section of this sarabande ends with the
resolution of an extraordinary dissonance (Example 34a). The dissonant sonority emerges in the right hand in the form of an augmented
fourth stacked atop a perfect fourth. Such a "fourth chord" has a rec-
ognizable identity in the atonal style of Viennese expressionism. In
Bach's style it has no identity at all; it is just a nonharmonic dissonance, a by-product of the contrapuntal working. Yet it does not sound
that way. Bach, indeed, assigns the hands markedly different registers
in order to highlight the perceptual identity of the dissonance. This
chord smarts, burns, then crumbles; it is a cinder. ("I hear well,"
writes Derrida, "I hear it, for I still have an ear for the flame even if a
cinder is silent.")[16] When I play the chord, what I hear is, not something without identity, but a voice stricken through with nonidentity,
the not-itself in the music('s) itself.

Not that the chord is hard to play; I have never had the least trouble

with it. But it has a feel as well as a sound: the hand stretches to en-
compass it, splays out awkwardly, incurs an indelible discomfort. Nor
does the resolution bring relief; instead it enhances the discomfort by
widening the stretch, from which the hand must withdraw by execut-
ing a finger-twisting ornament. The undoing of the autonomous artwork is inscribed on the very actions of the hand that carries out its
mandate.

Relief, to be sure, is deferred here rather than flatly denied; it arrives in the parallel resolution that ends the Sarabande. It arrives,
though, only after the discomfort of the right hand has returned, typically (but nonetheless hauntingly, uncannily) in the left. Once em-
barked on the final cadence, the left hand must negotiate an awkward
stretch supporting a pungent (if no longer exotic) dissonance before
relaxing into the close (Example 34b). But something implacable lin-
gers. The cadence can never wholly contain the disseminal force of
the dissonance whose traces it incorporates for both the hand and
the ear.

Must the cinder be silent? Bach's fourth chord is not; it is the cinder as palpable cry, burning and burnt.

Envoi. The autonomous artwork appears always in cinders, burning
our fingers as blue-bleak embers, ah my dear, fall, gall themselves, and
gash gold-vermilion.

Mendelssohn

Three Goethe Songs

Mendelssohn, "Die Liebende schreibt,"
op. 86, no. 3

die ein — — — — — — zi — ge; da fang' ich an zu wei — —

— — — — — nen. Die Thrä—

— ne trock — net wie — — der un — ver — se — hens: er liebt ja, denk' ich,

her in die — se Stil — le, und soll — test du nicht in die Fer — — ne rei — chen?

Ver — nimm das Lis — — peln

die _ ses Lie _ be _ we _ hens; mein ein _ zig Glück auf Er _ den ist dein

Wil _ le, dein freund _ li _ cher zu mir; _____ gieb mir ein

Zei _ _ chen, gieb mir ein

Zei _ _ _ chen, _____ gieb mir ein

Zei _ chen!

Nº 3. Suleika.

Goethe.

Comp. 1837.

Mendelssohn, "Suleika 1," op. 57, no. 3

Un poco ritenuto.

3. Und so kannst du wei-ter zie-hen, die-ne Freun-den und Be-trüb-ten! Dort wo ho-he Mau-ern glü-hen, find' ich bald,___ ja find'___ ich bald den Viel-ge-lieb-ten.

Tempo I.

Ach, die wah-re Her-zens-kun-de, Lie-bes-hauch, er-frisch-tes Le-ben wird mir nur aus sei-nem Munde, kann mir nur sein A-them ge-ben. Ach, die wah-re Her-zens-

cresc. ritard. a tempo

M.B.146.

Nº 4. Suleika.

Goethe.

Comp. 1837.

M. B. 144.

Mendelssohn, "Suleika 2," op. 34, no. 4

cresc.

Bu _ sen stil _ les Seh _ nen; Blu _ men, Au _ gen, Wald und
sanft zu sei _ nem Her _ zen; doch ver _ meid', ihn zu be _

Hü _ gel steh'n bei dei _ nem Hauch in Thrä _ nen.
trü _ ben und ver _ birg ihm mei _ ne Schmer _ zen!

Sag ihm,

a _ ber sag's be _ schei _ den, sei _ ne Lie _ be sei mein

M. B. 144.

Un poco più vivace.

Le _ ben, freu _ di _ ges Ge_fühl von bei _ den wird mir

sei _ ne Nä _ he ge _ ben, wird mir sei _ ne Nä _ he, seine

Nä _ _ he, sei _ ne Nä _ he ge _

ben, wird mir sei _ ne Nä _ he ge _ ben, sei _ ne

Nä _ _ he ge _ ben.

M.B.144.

Notes

Preface

1. Donna Haraway, "The Actors Are Cyborg, Nature Is Coyote, and the Geography Is Elsewhere: Postscript to 'Cyborgs at Large,'" in Constance Penley and Andrew Ross, eds., *Technoculture* (Minneapolis, 1991), 22.

2. Wallace Stevens, "Anglais Mort à Florence," *Collected Poems* (New York, 1954), 148–49.

3. See Stephen Blum, "In Defense of Close Reading and Close Listening," *Current Musicology* 53 (1992): 41–54; Nicholas Cook, Review of Steven Paul Scher, ed., *Music and Text: Critical Inquiries*, in *Music and Letters* 74 (1993): 303–306; and Arnold Whittall, "Experience, Thought and Musicology," *The Musical Times* 134 (1993): 318–20.

Chapter 1

1. David Schiff, "The Bounds of Music," *The New Republic* 206 (3 Feb. 1992): 31–35. The books under review are Carolyn Abbate, *Unsung Voices: Opera and Musical Narrative in the Nineteenth Century* (Princeton, 1991); Lawrence Kramer, *Music as Cultural Practice, 1800–1900* (Berkeley, 1990); Susan McClary, *Feminine Endings: Music, Gender, and Sexuality* (Minneapolis, 1991); and Rose Rosengard Subotnik, *Developing Variations: Style and Ideology in Western Music* (Minneapolis, 1991). For other guideposts on the strange path, see Richard Leppert, *The Sight of Sound: Music, Representation, and the History of the Body* (Berkeley, 1993); Richard Leppert and Susan McClary, eds., *Music and Society: The Politics of Composition, Performance, and Reception* (Cambridge, 1987); Christopher Norris, ed., *Music and the Politics of Culture* (New York, 1989); Steven Paul Scher, ed., *Music and Text: Critical Inquiries* (Cambridge, 1992); and Ruth Solie,

ed., *Musicology and Difference: Gender and Sexuality in Music Scholarship* (Berkeley, 1993).

2. Theodor W. Adorno, "Music, Language, and Composition" (1965), trans. Susan Gillespie, *Musical Quarterly* 77 (1993): 402.

3. My rendering of "Wovon man nicht sprechen kann, daruber muß man schweigen," from Ludwig Wittgenstein, *Tractatus Logico-Philosophicus* (New York, 1961), 150.

4. See Simon Schaffer, "Self Evidence," *Critical Inquiry* 18 (1992): 327–62.

5. Willa Cather, *The Song of the Lark* (Boston, 1988), 407–8.

6. Ibid., 410. Cather also associates her heroine's triumph with the spirit of gilded-age capitalism—not critically enough, to be sure, but with perfect accuracy.

7. For an account of this development, see Leon Botstein, "Listening through Reading: Musical Literacy and the Concert Audience," *19th-Century Music* 16 (1993): 129–45.

8. Jean-François Lyotard, *The Postmodern Condition: A Report on Knowledge,* trans. Geoff Bennington and Brian Massumi (Minneapolis, 1984).

9. Entry for *"Encyclopédie,"* vol. 5 (1755); quoted in Denis Diderot, *Rameau's Nephew and Other Works*, trans. Jacques Barzun and Ralph H. Bowen (Indianapolis, 1964), 297.

10. Theodor Adorno and Max Horkheimer, *Dialectic of Enlightenment* (1947), trans. John Cumming (New York, 1972).

11. Donna Haraway, *Simians, Cyborgs, and Women: The Reinvention of Nature* (New York, 1991), 193, 196.

12. On the critical side, see Christopher Norris, *What's Wrong with Postmodernism: Critical Theory and the Ends of Philosophy* (Baltimore, 1990), esp. 1–48, 164–93; Terry Eagleton, *The Ideology of the Esthetic* (Oxford, 1990), 366–417; Fredric Jameson, *Postmodernism: Or, the Cultural Logic of Late Capitalism* (Durham, 1991), esp. 1–54; and Jürgen Habermas, *The Philosophical Discourse of Modernity: Twelve Lectures,* trans. Frederick Lawrence (Cambridge, 1987). The major skeptical texts include Richard Rorty, *Philosophy and the Mirror of Nature* (Princeton, 1980), and Jean Baudrillard, *Selected Writings,* ed. Mark Poster (Cambridge, 1988).

13. Haraway, *Simians, Cyborgs, and Women,* 187 (italics in original).

14. Norris, *What's Wrong with Postmodernism,* 100. Norris's remark belongs to his critique of the extreme skeptical position, which he identifies with postmodernism as such—a usage obviously different from my own.

15. Jacques Derrida, *Of Grammatology,* trans. Gayatri Chakravorty Spivak (Baltimore, 1976), 97–98.

16. See n. 12.

17. Jean-François Lyotard, "The Idea of History," in Derek Attridge, Geoff Bennington, and Robert Young, eds., *Poststructuralism and the Question of History* (Cambridge, 1987), 179; Donna Haraway, *Simians, Cyborgs, and Women,* 195.

18. See James Elkins, "On Visual Desperation and the Bodies of Protozoa," *Representations* 40 (1992): 33–56.

19. Michel Foucault, *The Order of Things: An Archaeology of the Human Sciences* (New York, 1970), 386; unattributed translation slightly modified. The gendered usage that identifies the modern subject as "man" is of course no accident.

20. Slavoj Žižek, "Grimaces of the Real, or When the Phallus Appears," *October* 58 (1992): 64. Žižek's conclusion, however, that the blank space outside symbolic tradition is the subject itself, seems unwarranted.

21. J. L. Austin, *How to Do Things with Words,* ed. J. O. Urmson and Marina Sbisa (Cambridge, Mass., 1962).

22. For a fuller account of this topic, with specific reference to music and including a consideration of the adaptations necessary to apply Austin's concepts to decentered subjects and phenomena other than speech, see my *Music as Cultural Practice,* 1–20.

23. On media independence, see W. J. T. Mitchell, "Ekphrasis and the Other," *South Atlantic Quarterly* 91 (1992): 695–720; on varied repetition ("iterability"), see Jacques Derrida, "Signature Event Context" in *Margins of Philosophy,* trans. Alan Bass (Chicago, 1982), 307–30; on the mandate of interpretation, see my *Music as Cultural Practice,* 5–17; on "transferences," see Cynthia Chase, "'Anecdote for Fathers': The Scene of Interpretation in Freud and Wordsworth," in Mary Ann Caws, ed., *Textual Analysis* (New York, 1986), 182–206.

24. Jacques Derrida, *Positions,* trans. Alan Bass (Chicago, 1981), 84, 85–86, 85; translation modified. The materials of this paragraph draw synoptically on pp. 44–47 and 84–87 of this text. The original of Derrida's "lapidary" statement is: "la dissémination figure ce qui *ne revient pas* au père." As Alan Bass observes (p. 113), *revenir à* means come back to, fall to (as an inheritance), and amount to. On the sexualizing of dissemination, Derrida observes that the resemblance between *seme* and *semen* is "purely fortuitous" but that "by means of this floating, purely exterior collusion, accident . . . sets something off" (pp. 45–46). Dissemination, as a concept, is itself disseminal.

25. See Derrida, *Positions,* 107–13. This paragraph and its successor draw largely on Jacques Lacan, *Ecrits: A Selection,* trans. Alan Sheridan (New York, 1977).

26. A quick note on the real. As Slavoj Žižek has recently been emphasizing, it is more than an inaccessible thing-in-itself. Although the real is unsignifiable, it can become manifest within signification. Although the relation of music to the real in a broad sense is the main theme of this book, the issue of the Lacanian real lies outside its scope. Suffice it to say that the locus of the Lacanian real in music is the intensity it exhibits or elicits, both pleasurably and otherwise. The topic deserves separate study. On the real, see Slavoj Žižek, *Looking Awry: An Introduction to Jacques Lacan through Popular Culture* (Cambridge, Mass., 1992).

27. Harold S. Powers, "Three Pragmatists in Search of a Theory," *Current Musicology* 53 (1992): 8.

28. Joseph Kerman, *Contemplating Music: Challenges to Musicology* (Cambridge, Mass., 1985).

29. Powers, "Three Pragmatists," 6.

30. Adorno, "Music, Language, and Composition," 404.

31. Ibid., 410–11. Adorno's use of an ocular metaphor for transcendental hearing is traditional; see pp. 88–89, this volume. It is also problematical, however, suggesting that the transcendental is precisely what cannot be heard.

32. Charles Seeger, *Studies in Musicology: 1935–75* (Berkeley, 1977), 16.

33. Powers once more supplies a touchstone: music "is like mathematics, in that, if you do want to talk about it, the language you have to use is esoteric" ("Three Pragmatists," 6).

34. Carl Dahlhaus, *Nineteenth-Century Music*, trans. J. Bradford Robinson (Berkeley, 1989), 94, 95.

35. Conceived in these terms, music criticism would not form a complement or opposite to music history, but consist, instead, of interwoven forms of hermeneutic and historiographical practice. For a challenge to this critical program, a reply, and a commentary, see Gary Tomlinson, "Musical Pasts and Postmodern Musicologies: A Response to Lawrence Kramer"; my "Music Criticism and the Postmodernist Turn: In Contrary Motion with Gary Tomlinson"; Tomlinson's further remarks; and Steven Blum, "In Defense of Close Reading and Close Listening," all in *Current Musicology* 53 (1993): 18–54.

36. "Structuring structures" is from Pierre Bourdieu, *Outline of a Theory of Practice*, trans. Richard Nice (Cambridge, 1977), 72. For the relevance of Bourdieu's concept of "systems of durable, transposable dispositions" to musical hermeneutics, see my *Music as Cultural Practice*, 10–13.

37. Lawrence Kramer, "Song and Story," *19th-Century Music* 15 (1992): 238.

38. Julia Kristeva, *Revolution in Poetic Language*, trans. Margaret Waller (New York, 1984), 21–30, 43–71.

39. Oliver Sacks, *Awakenings* (1973; rpt. New York, 1990), 60n; quotations from 282, 285.

40. Ibid., 60n–62n. My account tacitly relativizes Sacks's, which treats his patients' melodic and rhythmic preferences as universals.

41. On hermeneutic windows, see my *Music as Cultural Practice*, 5–11.

42. On this topic see Peter Rabinowitz, "Chord and Discourse: Listening through the Written Word," in Steven Paul Scher, ed., *Music and Text*, 38–56, and Botstein, "Listening through Reading."

43. For detailed studies of musical subject formation from the perspective of performance and (iconographic) reproduction, see Leppert, *The Sight of Sound*. My account, below, from the perspective of reception does not presuppose music as a "work" or "artwork"; it implicitly recognizes the musical work as a social fact, not a natural one. (For further discussion, see chapter 2.) It is a hallmark of classical music, however, to privilege the work, and musicology must follow suit, although it may—and should—problematize and deconstruct in the process; recognizing the contingent status of the work neither renders the concept ipso facto expendable nor settles the question of its value.

44. E. M. Forster, *Howards End* (1921; rpt. New York, n.d.), 33.

45. Richard Wagner, "On Conducting" (1869), in *Richard Wagner's Prose Works*, trans. William Ashton Ellis (London, 1912), 311.

46. Modernist forms of musical understanding can legitimately be criticized for idealizing, intentionally or not, the interpellative mode; for a critique consistent with this claim, see Rose Rosengard Subotnik, "Toward a Deconstruction of Structural Listening: A Critique of Schoenberg, Adorno, and Stravinsky," in Eugene Narmour and Ruth A. Solie, eds., *Explorations in Music, the Arts, and Ideas: Essays in Honor of Leonard B. Meyer* (Stuyvesant, N.Y., 1988), 87–122. On interpellation, see Louis Althusser, "Ideology and Ideological State Apparatuses," in *Lenin and Philosophy and Other Essays*, trans. Ben Brewster (New York, 1971), 127–86. On internally persuasive speech, see Mikhail Bakhtin, *The Dialogical Imagination: Four Essays*, trans. Caryl Emerson and Michael Holquist (Austin, 1981), 342–48; for the passage quoted, p. 345. Bakhtin's complementary concept of "authoritative discourse," also discussed in these pages, overlaps with the concept of interpellation.

47. Forster, *Howards End*, 33–34.

48. On music in relation to noise, see Jacques Attali, *Noise: The Political Economy of Music*, trans. Brian Massumi (Minneapolis, 1985).

49. Michel Foucault, *Discipline and Punish: The Birth of the Prison*, trans. Alan Sheridan (New York, 1979), 170–94.

50. Charles Rosen, *The Classical Style: Haydn, Mozart, Beethoven* (New York, 1972), 281.

51. Theodor W. Adorno, *In Search of Wagner*, trans. Rodney Livingstone (London, 1981), 82–84.

52. Norman Bryson, *Vision and Painting: The Logic of the Gaze* (New Haven, 1983), 159.

53. The homosocial is the general spectrum of same-sex affiliation and bonding. It continually mediates between work, pleasure, and affection and is easily sexualized; hence, according to Eve Kosofsky Sedgwick, there is a modern social imperative, incapable of realization, to mark a clear division between homosociality and homosexuality. See Sedgwick's *Between Men: English Literature and Male Homosocial Desire* (New York, 1985), 1–20.

54. It is important to remember that ornament, both stylistic and sartorial, does not become fully feminized until the mid-nineteenth century. In general, the gender of ornament should be considered highly mobile in a style such as Viennese Classicism, where ornament, so to speak, is of the essence.

55. See Jean-Jacques Rousseau, *The First and Second Discourses*, ed. Roger D. Masters, trans. Roger D. Masters and Judith Masters (New York, 1964), 101–16.

56. Sigmund Freud, *The Question of Lay Analysis*, trans. James Strachey (New York, 1969), 93–94.

Chapter 2

1. The "classical paradigm shift" is from Joseph Kerman, "American Musicology in the 1990s," *Journal of Musicology* 9 (1991): 131–44. Kerman supplies a representative bibliography, to which might be added mention of the journal *Repercussions*, founded in 1992 to promote "critical and alternative viewpoints on music."

2. On gender, see (e.g.) Sherry B. Ortner, "Is Female to Male as Nature Is to Culture?" in Michele Zimbalist Rosaldo and Louise Lamphere, eds., *Woman, Culture, and Society* (Stanford, 1974), 67–88; Hélène Cixous, "Sorties," from Hélène Cixous and Catherine Clement, *The Newly Born Woman*, trans. Betsey Wing (Minneapolis, 1975), 63–129; and, proverbially, Simone de Beauvoir, *The Second Sex* (1949), trans. H. M. Parshley (New York, 1974). On the primitive and evolved, see Marianna Torgovnick, *Gone Primitive: Savage Intellects, Modern Lives* (Chicago, 1990). On race and coloniality, see Edward Said, *Orientalism* (New York, 1979); Henry Louis Gates, Jr., ed., *"Race," Writing, and Difference*, special issue of *Critical Inquiry* 12 (1985): 1–299; Trin T. Minh-ha, *Women, Nature, Other: Writing Postcoloniality and Feminism* (Bloomington, Ind., 1989); and "Identities," special issue of *Critical Inquiry* 18 (1992): 625–884, ed. Henry Louis Gates, Jr., and Kwame Anthony Appiah. On class and cultural formation, see Peter Stallybrass and Allon White, *The Politics and Poetics of Transgression* (Ithaca, 1986). On the

nexus of gender, scientific knowledge, and postmodernity, see Donna Haraway, "A Cyborg Manifesto" and "Situated Knowledges," in her *Simians, Cyborgs, and Women: The Reinvention of Nature* (London, 1991), 149–82, 183–202, respectively.

3. I use the term *cultural trope* here as an equivalent to the term *structural trope* introduced in my *Music as Cultural Practice: 1800–1900* (Berkeley, 1990), 9–14. The alternative terminology reflects a shift in emphasis from the capacity of structures to act *as* tropes to the proclivity of cultures to act *through* tropes.

4. On historiography, see Leo Treitler, "The Politics of Reception: Tailoring the Present as Fulfillment of a Desired Past," *Journal of the Royal Musical Association* 116 (1991): 280–98; on tonality and sonata form, Susan McClary, *Feminine Endings: Music, Gender, and Sexuality* (Minneapolis, 1991), 12–17, 125–31; on genre, Jeffrey Kallberg, "The Harmony of the Tea Table: Gender and Ideology in the Piano Nocturne," *Representations* 39 (1992): 102–33; on signifying practices, Lawrence Kramer, "Liszt, Goethe, and the Discourse of Gender," in *Music as Cultural Practice*, 102–34; "Music and Cultural Hermeneutics: The Salome Complex," *Cambridge Opera Journal* 2 (1990): 269–94; and "Fin-de-Siècle Fantasies: *Elektra*, Degeneration, and Sexual Science," *Cambridge Opera Journal* 5 (1993): 141–66; on musicality, with a reading of what this chapter will call the "external" logic of alterity in relation to homosexuality, see Philip Brett, "Musicality, Essentialism, and the Closet," in Philip Brett, Elizabeth Wood, and Gary C. Thomas, eds., *Queering the Pitch: The New Gay and Lesbian Musicology* (New York, 1994), 9–26.

5. Treitler, "Politics of Reception," 287, 289.

6. McClary, *Feminine Endings*, 16, 15. McClary's argument is open to the objection that quasi-syntactic movement around a stable point of reference need not project a semantic or ideological othering. But it would be hard to deny that such movement *can* make that projection and very often has. McClary would be the first to acknowledge that many such projections are self-problematizing.

7. Ibid., 7.

8. Michel Foucault, *Discipline and Punish: The Birth of the Prison*, trans. Alan Sheridan (New York, 1979), 193.

9. On the question of inversion/transgression, see Jonathan Dollimore, *Sexual Dissidence: Augustine to Wilde, Freud to Foucault* (Oxford, 1991), esp. 21–35, 64–91.

10. On Wagner and Mendelssohn see Leon Botstein, "The Aesthetics of Assimilation and Affirmation: Reconstructing the Career of Felix Mendelssohn," in R. Larry Todd, ed., *Mendelssohn and His World* (Princeton, 1991),

5–42. For Schenker's cultural politics, see his "Rameau or Beethoven? Paralytic Standstill or Ingenious Life in Music?" trans. Sylvan Kalib, in *Thirteen Essays from the Three Yearbooks "Das Meisterwerk in der Musik,"* 3 vols. (Ann Arbor, 1972), 2:491–518. On Ives's virile ideal, see Frank Rossiter, *Charles Ives and His America* (New York, 1975), 126–44; Judith Tick, "Charles Ives and the 'Masculine' Ideal," in Ruth Solie, ed. *Musicology and Difference: Gender and Sexuality in Music Scholarship* (Berkeley, 1993), 83–106; and "Cultural Politics and Musical Form: The Case of Charles Ives," chapter 7 of this volume. On the Schubert controversy, see "Schubert: Sexuality, Identity, Culture," special issue of *19th-Century Music* 17, no. 1 (1993), ed. Lawrence Kramer; Susan McClary, "Constructions of Subjectivity in Schubert's Music," in Brett, Wood, and Thomas, eds., *Queering the Pitch*, 205–34; Edward Rothstein, "Was Schubert Gay? If So, So What?" *New York Times*, 16 Feb. 1992; Bernard Holland, "Tea for Two," *New York Times*, 17 Feb. 1992; and the letters to the *Times* (which did not publish them) by McClary, Brett, and Wood, *Newsletter of the American Musicological Society Gay and Lesbian Study Group* 2 (1992): 14–16.

11. D. N. Rodowick, "Reading the Figural," *Camera Obscura* 24 (1990): 11–46.

12. Donna Haraway, "Cyborg Manifesto," 161–65.

13. Matthew Arnold, "Preface to First Edition of *Poems* (1853)," in *Poetry and Criticism of Matthew Arnold,* ed. A. Dwight Culler (Boston, 1961), 213.

14. Friedrich Nietzsche, *The Case of Wagner,* in *"The Birth of Tragedy" and "The Case of Wagner,"* trans. Walter Kaufmann (New York, 1967), 172, 166.

15. See especially the essays "Tympan," "Différance," and "Signature Event Context" in Jacques Derrida, *Margins of Philosophy,* trans. Alan Bass (Chicago, 1982), ix–xxix, 1–28, 307–30, respectively; and Derrida's remarks in *Positions,* trans. Alan Bass (Chicago, 1981).

16. Michel Foucault, *Discipline and Punish,* and "The Subject and Power," part 2, trans. Leslie Sawyer, *Critical Inquiry* 8 (1982): 785–95.

17. Arnold, "Preface to First Edition," 209.

18. Sigmund Freud, *The Ego and the Id,* trans. Joan Riviere, rev. James Strachey (New York, 1960), 48.

19. Arnold, "Preface to First Edition," 213.

20. Nietzsche, *The Case of Wagner,* 186, 180, 185–86, 191, 182.

21. Friedrich Nietzsche, *The Gay Science,* trans. Walter Kaufmann (New York, 1974), 325–26.

22. Nietzsche, *The Case of Wagner,* 182.

23. Friedrich Nietzsche, *Ecce Homo,* in *"On the Genealogy of Morals"*

and "*Ecce Homo,*" trans. Walter Kaufmann (New York, 1967), 250–51, 247, 251.

24. Ibid., 250.

25. Nietzsche, *The Case of Wagner,* 159.

26. Friedrich Nietzsche, *Beyond Good and Evil,* trans. Marianne Cowan (Chicago, 1955), 194.

27. Botstein, "Aesthetics of Assimilation and Affirmation," 15.

28. Schenker, *Thirteen Essays from . . . "Das Meisterwerk in die Musik,"* 2:500.

29. Ibid., 2:220.

30. Ibid., 2:512.

31. Carl Dahlhaus, *Nineteenth-Century Music,* trans. J. Bradford Robinson (Berkeley, 1989), 1–8, 59, 102–3, 390–94. For a comprehensive overview of Dahlhaus's work and its traditions, see James Hepokoski, "The Dahlhaus Project and Its Extra-Musicological Sources," *19th-Century Music* 14 (1991): 221–46.

32. Phillip Gossett, "Up from Beethoven," *New York Review of Books,* 26 Oct. 1989, 21–26, and "Carl Dahlhaus and the Ideal Type," *19th-Century Music* 13 (1989): 49–56.

33. Dahlhaus, *Nineteenth-Century Music,* 1–15.

34. Ibid., 57–58.

35. Ibid., 9–11, 59, 64, 9.

36. Wilkie Collins, *The Woman in White* (1860; rpt. Harmondsworth, 1974), 250.

37. Dahlhaus, *Nineteenth-Century Music,* 64, 64, 86, 86.

38. For examples of the second alternatives, see respectively my "*Carnaval,* Cross-Dressing, and the Woman in the Mirror," in Ruth Solie, ed., *Musicology and Difference: Gender and Sexuality in Music Scholarship* (Berkeley, 1993), 305–25, and my *Music as Cultural Practice* (Berkeley, 1990), 176–214.

39. Donna Haraway, "Situated Knowledges," 198.

40. Dahlhaus, *Nineteenth-Century Music,* 63–64.

41. Joseph Kerman, *The Beethoven Quartets* (New York, 1966), 182. Beethoven underlines the resolution by taking F as the normative point of departure for the chromatic motive.

42. Elaine Showalter, *The Female Malady: Women, Madness, and English Culture, 1830–1890* (New York, 1985), 129–30.

43. Kim Ian Michasiw, "Nine Revisionist Theses on the Picturesque," *Representations* 38 (1992): 79.

44. Kevin Barry, *Language, Music and the Sign: A Study of Aesthetics, Poetics, and Poetic Practice from Collins to Coleridge* (Cambridge, 1987), 65,

104. My placement of the empty sign between concept and intuition is borrowed from Christopher Norris, *What's Wrong with Postmodernism: Critical Theory and the Ends of Philosophy* (Baltimore, 1990), 219; Norris, 208–21, routes the theories described by Barry through the Kantian sublime to the postmodernism of Lyotard.

45. Theories of specularity rely principally on the work of Jacques Lacan and Luce Irigaray; see "The Mirror Stage as Formative of the Function of the I" and "The Subversion of the Subject and the Dialectic of Desire in the Freudian Unconscious," in Lacan's *Écrits: A Selection*, trans. Alan Sheridan (New York, 1977), 1–7, 292–325, respectively, and Irigaray's *Speculum of the Other Woman*, trans. Gillian C. Gill (Ithaca, 1985), esp. 46–53, 133–227. (I should add here (1) that what Lacan calls the Other is an unconditional form of what this chapter calls the self. In general, the big Other is to the self as the self is to the other. (2) As its name suggests, specularity has been theorized around visual practices and metaphors, but it need not be literally visual; the specular is not the scopic. For a treatment of sonic and vocal specularity, see Kaja Silverman, *The Acoustic Mirror: The Feminine Voice in Psychoanalysis and Cinema* (Bloomington, Ind., 1988).

46. Georg Wilhelm Friedrich Hegel, *Aesthetics: Lectures on Fine Art*, trans. T. M. Knox (Oxford, 1975), 959–63, translation slightly modified. Hegel plays (dialectically, of course) on the difference between the vibrations produced by music within the subject (the vehicle of the subject's self-apprehension, ideal because removed from nature) and the materiality of musical sound, which places a limit on the subjectifying process. In his reading of the relevant passages from the *Aesthetics*, Derrida more or less represses the latter concern; see "The Pit and the Pyramid: Introduction to Hegelian Semiology," in his *Margins of Philosophy*, 88–94. Since Hegel's word for "sensuousness" is *das Sinnliche*, his use of *Sinnlichkeit* in relation to music is especially telling.

47. For a detailed study of this tradition and its ramifications, see Richard Leppert, *The Sight of Sound: Music, Representation, and the History of the Body* (Berkeley, 1992). Suzanne G. Cusick, "Gendering Modern Music: Thoughts on the Monteverdi-Artusi Controversy," *Journal of the American Musicological Society* 46 (1993): 1–25, traces the (re)activation of the tradition in an early-modern episode of particular importance.

48. See Ludmilla Jordanova, "Natural Facts: A Historical Perspective on Science and Sexuality," in Carol MacCormack and Marilyn Stathern, eds., *Nature, Culture, and Gender* (Cambridge, 1980), 42–69; Londa Schiebinger, *The Mind Has No Sex? Women in the Origins of Modern Science* (Cambridge, Mass., 1989), 214–44; and Friedrich Kittler, *Discourse Networks: 1800/1900* (Stanford, 1990), 3–173.

49. See Terry Castle, "The Female Thermometer," *Representations* 17 (1987): 1–27.

50. Jean-Sylvain Bailly, quoted in Simon Schaffer, "Self Evidence," *Critical Inquiry* 18 (1992): 357. Bailly's negative remark strangely prefigures Luce Irigaray's famous affirmation: "Women have sexual organs just about everywhere" (quoted from Irigaray's "This Sex Which Is Not One," trans. Claudia Reeder, in Elaine Marks and Isabelle de Courtivron, eds., *New French Feminisms* [New York, 1980], 103). From a certain masculine perspective, this putatively feminine mode of embodiment is the equivalent of psychosis. Thus the famous paranoic Daniel Paul Schreber reads his surplus of voluptuous pleasure as the sign of his transformation into a woman on the grounds that his "whole body is filled with nerves of voluptousness from the top of [the] head to the soles of [the] feet, such as is the case only in the adult female body" (quoted from Schreber, *Memoirs of My Nervous Illness* [1903], ed. and trans. Ida McAlpine and Richard A. Hunter [London, 1955], 204). Schreber and Bailly (and perhaps even Irigaray) draw on a common source, the Enlightenment neuroanatomy that traces "sensibility" to a mobility of nervous fibers especially characteristic of women. The result is a trope, the identification of woman with the music of vibrating strings, that is still going strong more than a century later:

> A woman drew her long black hair out tight
> And fiddled whisper music on those strings.
> —(T. S. Eliot, "The Waste Land,"
> ll. 378–79)

51. Antoine Lavoisier, quoted in Schaffer, "Self Evidence," 355.

52. Gustave Flaubert, *Sentimental Education,* trans. Robert Baldick (Harmondsworth, 1964), 149.

53. Marcel Proust, *Remembrance of Things Past,* 3 vols., trans. C. K. Scott Moncrieff and Terence Kilmartin (New York, 1982), 3:260.

54. Thomas Mann, foreword to *The Marquise of O. and Other Stories,* by Heinrich von Kleist, trans. Martin Greenberg (New York, 1960), xxii.

55. For a detailed development of this idea, see my *Music and Poetry: The Nineteenth Century and After* (Berkeley, 1984), 91–99. On transitional objects, see D. W. Winnicott, *Playing and Reality* (New York, 1971), 1–26.

56. T. S. Eliot, "The Dry Salvages," pt. 5, in *Collected Poems: 1909–1962* (New York, 1963).

57. Leo Tolstoy, "The Kreutzer Sonata," trans. Margaret Wettlin in *Short Masterpieces by Tolstoy* (New York, 1963), 349–50. For a detailed reading of this text in relation to musical articulations of nineteenth-century misogyny, see Leppert, *The Sight of Sound,* 153–88.

58. Oscar Wilde, *"The Picture of Dorian Gray" and Other Writings* (New York, 1982), 20.

59. Arthur Rimbaud, *Complete Works, Selected Letters*, trans. Wallace Fowlie (Chicago, 1966), 305.

60. For fuller discussion of this point, see my *Music and Poetry*, 130, 223–36, and Susan McClary's introduction to Catherine Clement, *Opera, or the Undoing of Women*, trans. Betsey Wing (Minneapolis, 1988), ix–xvii.

61. Walt Whitman, "Proud Music of the Storm," ll. 38–46, in *Leaves of Grass*, ed. Sculley Bradley and Harold W. Blodgett (New York, 1973).

62. Kate Chopin, *The Awakening*, ed. Margaret Culley (New York, 1976), 113, 64, respectively; Thomas Mann, *Stories of Three Decades*, trans. H. T. Lowe-Porter (New York, 1936), 164, ellipses in original.

63. Proust, *Remembrance of Things Past*, 3:668–69.

64. For a detailed account of the more transcendentalizing strain in Proust's "othering" of music, see Jean-Jacques Nattiez, *Proust as Musician*, trans. Derrick Puffett (Cambridge, 1989).

65. Julia Kristeva, *Powers of Horror: An Essay on Abjection*, trans. Leon S. Roudiez (New York, 1982), 1–89.

66. Nietzsche, *The Case of Wagner*, 174, 184.

67. Frank Walker, *Hugo Wolf: A Biography* (London, 1951), 156.

68. Mann, *Stories*, 423.

69. James Joyce, *Ulysses* (New York, 1961), 269, 274, 270, 271, respectively.

70. The multiple meanings are given by the OED. Other important modernist texts reflecting the "othering" of music include D. H. Lawrence's poem "Piano," in which the male listener is infantilized by the "insidious mastery of song," Joseph Conrad's *Victory*, with its account of the persecutory effect of the sounds produced by an all-female orchestra, and Willa Cather's "Paul's Case," with its quasi-homosexual protagonist whose antinomian spirit, compared to a genie in the *Arabian Nights*, is hysterically responsive to nineteenth-century art music.

71. Roland Barthes, "The Romantic Song," in *The Responsibility of Forms: Critical Essays on Music, Art, and Representation*, trans. Richard Howard (Berkeley, 1991), 287.

72. John Corbett, "Free, Single, and Disengaged: Listening Pleasure and the Popular Music Object," *October* 54 (1990): 79–101.

73. It is important to note that many jazz musicians (in contrast to fans and critics) resist the "othering" of improvisation, preferring to speak of craft, though this resistance may have a defensive side. Classical musicians, by contrast, enhance the othering of music in which improvisation is banned by routinely invoking its numinousness and ineffability.

74. Stallybrass and White, *Politics and Poetics of Transgression*, 5.

75. I take the metaphor of muteness from Edward Said's *Musical Elaborations* (New York, 1991), a text that is nonetheless chiefly concerned with the ideological uses of music.

76. Rose Rosengard Subotnik, "Toward a Deconstruction of Structural Listening: A Critique of Schoenberg, Adorno, and Stravinsky," in Eugene Narmour and Ruth A. Solie, eds., *Explorations in Music, the Arts, and Ideas: Essays in Honor of Leonard Meyer* (Stuyvesant, N.Y., 1988), 87–122.

77. For a defense of this state of affairs, see Nicholas Cook, *Music, Imagination, and Culture* (Oxford, 1990); for a critique, see my "The Politics and Poetics of Listening," a review-essay on Cook's volume in *Current Musicology* 50 (1992): 62–67.

78. Said, *Musical Elaborations*, 76; Carolyn Abbate, *Unsung Voices: Opera and Musical Narrative in the Nineteenth Century* (Princeton, 1991), 53. For an account of musical time that, though its terms are phenomenological and nonadversarial, posits a limited and variable absorptiveness, see my *Music and Poetry*, 8–11, 225–29.

79. Slavoj Žižek, *Looking Awry: An Introduction to Jacques Lacan through Popular Culture* (Cambridge, Mass., 1992), 38.

Chapter 3

1. "Substrate" is from Carl Dahlhaus, *Nineteenth-Century Music*, trans. J. Bradford Robinson (Berkeley, 1989), 87.

2. The disclaimer was appended to the symphony's title in the program of the first performance; an earlier version appears in one of Beethoven's sketchbooks.

3. Vernon Gotwals, *Joseph Haydn*, a translation of *Biographische Notizen über Joseph Haydn*, by Georg August Griesinger, and *Biographische Nachrichten von Joseph Haydn*, by Albert Christoph Dies (Madison, 1963), 200.

4. Nelson Goodman's critique of resemblance in *The Languages of Art* (Indianapolis, 1976) suggests the need for two subsidiary points. Unlike Goodman, I use the term *representation* to mean, not signification in general, but a certain type of signification. Hence Goodman's argument that denotation, not resemblance, is "the core of representation" (p. 4) has no bearing on my definition. Unlike Goodman, again, I assume that resemblance is always a relationship between significantly different terms. Peter Kivy's *Sound and Semblance: Reflections on Musical Representation* (Princeton, 1984) should also be cited here, although its taxonomic approach is far removed from the hermeneutic approach of this chapter.

5. On performatives, see J. L. Austin's *How to Do Things with Words*, ed. J. O. Urmson and Marina Sbisa (Cambridge, Mass., 1962). Austin addresses

the nexus of generality and situational contingency (in order to problematize his initial performative-constative distinction) on pp. 67–82; for a critique and deeper analysis, see Jacques Derrida, "Signature Event Context" in *Margins of Philosophy*, trans. Alan Bass (Chicago, 1982), 307–30; for a synoptic account of Austin and Derrida on this isssue, see my *Music as Cultural Practice: 1800–1900* (Berkeley, 1990), 6–9.

6. In some cases, adding up to a special type, one work of music actually imitates the performance of another; the party scene in Mozart's *Don Giovanni* is the most famous example. Peter Rabinowitz calls the result "fictional music"; for discussion, see his "Fictional Music: Toward a Theory of Listening," *Bucknell Review* 26 (1981): 193–208.

7. Mary Ann Caws, *The Eye in the Text: Essays on Perception, Mannerist to Modern* (Princeton, 1981), 9.

8. Jacques Derrida, "White Mythology: Metaphor in the Text of Philosophy," in *Margins of Philosophy*, trans. Alan Bass (Chicago, 1982), 214; see generally pp. 230–45. For a related account, but one that differs from Derrida's in maintaining that metaphor is "not the enigma [it poses] but the solution to the enigma," see Paul Ricoeur, "The Metaphorical Process as Cognition, Imagination, and Feeling," *Critical Inquiry* 5 (1978): 143–59, especially 142–52, which theorize the pictorial "work of resemblance."

9. I use the term *dialogue* in the sense developed by Mikhail Bakhtin: a process in which different modes of expression at once presuppose, question, and interpret each other. For discussion, see Bakhtin's *The Dialogical Imagination,* trans. Caryl Emerson and Michael Holquist (Austin, 1981), especially the essay "Discourse in the Novel."

10. Charles Altieri, "Can We Be Historical Ever? Some Hopes for a Dialectical Model of Historical Self-Consciousness," *Modern Language Quarterly* 54 (1993): 49.

11. Strictly speaking, Haydn's title for the instrumental movement is untranslatable. The term *Vorstellung,* appearing in the place of the more straightforward *Darstellung* [representation], combines the meanings of "conception" and (theatrical) "presentation." Haydn's choice of *Vorstellung,* I surmise, rests on a representational metaphor that is clearly pertinent to *The Creation* but beyond the scope of my discussion. This is the figure of *theatrum mundi*—of the world as a stage on which God watches (in some versions, manages) the drama of existence. For discussion see Ernst Robert Curtius, *European Literature and the Latin Middle Ages,* trans. Willard R. Trask (1953; rpt. Princeton, 1973), 138–44.

12. Heinrich Schenker, *Das Meisterwerk in der Musik,* 3 vols. (Munich, 1926), 2:163–68. For a detailed account of Schenker's interpretation of this music, and a reinterpretation in terms of Enlightenment science and ide-

ology, see my "Haydn's Chaos, Schenker's Order; or, Hermeneutics and Musical Analysis: Can They Mix?" *Nineteenth-Century Music* 16 (1992): 3–17.

13. Donald Francis Tovey, *Essays in Musical Analysis: Concertos and Choral Works* (1935–39; new ed., London, 1981), 349–53.

14. For full accounts, see John Hollander, *The Untuning of the Sky: Ideas of Music in English Poetry, 1500–1700* (New York, 1970), 3–51; and James Anderson Winn, *Unsuspected Eloquence: A History of the Relations between Poetry and Music* (New Haven, 1981), 30–73.

15. Isidore of Seville, *Etymologiarum sive originum libri*, quoted in E. M. W. Tillyard, *The Elizabethan World Picture* (1943; rpt. New York, 1961), 100. The full paragraph, "What Music Can Do," appears in a different translation in Oliver Strunk, ed., *Source Readings in Music History* (New York, 1950), 94.

16. Winn, *Unsuspected Eloquence*, 40.

17. Gabriela von Baumberg, quoted in Gotwals, *Joseph Haydn*, 258.

18. For a fuller account of Kepler's argument, see Hollander, *Untuning of the Sky*, 38–40.

19. Tovey, *Essays in Musical Analysis: Concertos and Choral Works*, 350.

20. Giuseppi Carpani, quoted in A. Peter Brown, *Performing Haydn's Creation* (Bloomington, Ind., 1986), 34.

21. Ibid., 34–35; Haydn also apparently used muted horns, but the horns do not play in the *Urklang*.

22. Haydn all but explicitly associates this motive with the striving of formlessness after form. As H. C. Robbins Landon observes, the motive is later cited after the phrase "Und die Erde war ohne Form und leer" (m. 69). H. C. Robbins Landon, *Haydn: Chronicle and Works*, vol. 4, *The Years of "The Creation," 1796–1800* (Bloomington, Ind., 1977), 414–15.

23. William Kerrigan, "Atoms Again: The Deaths of Individualism," in Joseph H. Smith and William Kerrigan, eds., *Taking Chances: Derrida, Psychoanalysis, and Literature* (Baltimore, 1984), 87–98.

24. All quotations from Milton are from *Complete Poems and Major Prose*, ed. Merritt Y. Hughes (New York, 1957). *Paradise Lost (PL)* is, of course, the ultimate source of the text of *The Creation*.

25. "On the wat'ry calm / His brooding wings the Spirit of God outspread, / And vital virtue infus'd, and vital warmth" (*PL* 7, 234–36). The image ultimately derives from the Gospel accounts of Christ's baptism.

26. The connection between Beethoven's Benedictus and elevation music is made by Warren Kirkendale, "New Roads to Old Ideas in Beethoven's *Missa Solemnis*," in Paul Henry Lang, ed., *The Creative World of Beethoven* (New York, 1971), 163–99.

27. Landon, *The Years of "The Creation*,*"* 414; Brown, *Performing*

Haydn's Creation, 72; Charles Rosen, *The Classical Style: Haydn, Mozart, Beethoven* (New York, 1972), 370. Brown develops the ricercar idea fully in his essay "Haydn's Chaos: Genesis and Genre," *Musical Quarterly* 73 (1989): 18–59.

28. On chaos and the *Mischmasch*, see Brown, "Haydn's Chaos," 59.

29. When Rosen rationalizes the pedal, he seems to forget his own un-equivocal claim that second-group material is not resolved until it is heard in the tonic (Charles Rosen, *Sonata Forms* [New York, 1980], 275). His remarks occur in an article that takes my interpretation to task, both because some other Haydn recapitulations also contain dominant pedals and because "as far as [Rosen] knows, Kramer is the only one who has ever worried about this detail of 'Chaos'" ("Music à la Mode," *New York Review of Books*, June 23, 1994, 56). My interpretation, however, does not claim that dominant pedals never occur after the beginnings of Classical recapitulations, only that when they do the effect may be considerable. What matters is not whether something is unique but how it is used. Haydn's "Chaos" uses the pedal, for representational reasons, in a way that subverts the recapitulatory function.

As to Rosen's second point, I doubt that critical precedent is needed to justify taking an emphatic, obviously climactic passage like the recapitulating pedal as a hermeneutic window (not that marginal passages may not also be candidates for the same treatment!). It is worth noting, though, that for Tovey the pedal sounds "as if it represented some actual knowledge perma-nently gained" (*Essays in Musical Analysis: Concertos and Choral Works*, 353). The gain may be questionable, at least in the positive sense Tovey in-tends, but to raise the issue of knowledge in this connection is right on target.

Rosen's article reveals with particular clarity some of the limitations of modernist musicology; on this subject, see my reply, *New York Review of Books*, September 22, 1994, 74–75.

30. Brown, "Haydn's Chaos," 18–19.

31. Blake's poem also raises many of the same issues:

> When the stars threw down their spears
> And water'd heaven with their tears:
> Did he smile his work to see?
> Did he who made the Lamb make thee?
>
> Tyger, Tyger, burning bright,
> In the forests of the night:
> What immortal hand or eye,
> Dare frame thy fearful symmetry? (ll. 17–24)
>   —Text from *The Poetry and Prose
> of William Blake*, ed. David V. Erdman
> (New York, 1965).

32. Immanuel Kant, *Critique of Judgment* (1790), trans. J. C. Meredith (New York, 1973), 91–92.

33. Kerrigan, "Atoms Again," 96.

34. Mladen Dolar, "'I Shall Be with You on Your Wedding Night': Lacan and the Uncanny," *October* 58 (1992): 7.

35. Slavoj Žižek, "Grimaces of the Real, or When the Phallus Appears," *October* 58 (1992): 64–68; the quotation, in italics in the original, is from p. 66. Mladen Dolar's argument in "Lacan and the Uncanny" strongly parallels Žižek's.

36. The formulations here are from Francis Bacon, *The Advancement of Learning*, cited in Merritt Hughes's note to *PL* 7, 176, in John Milton, *Complete Poems and Major Prose*, new. ed. (Indianapolis, 1962). Both Lucretius and Ovid (drawing on Epicurus) can also be said to present creation as a reformation, specifically a sorting out of confused elements. The Christianized version of this idea is exemplified in Dryden's "A Song for St. Cecilia's Day" (1687), which describes how "cold, and hot, and moist, and dry, / In order to their stations leap" (9–10) in response to the "tuneful voice" of the Creator. Text modernized from Dryden's *Poetical Works*, ed. John Sergeaunt (Oxford, 1945).

37. On C major and the Mass, see Landon, *Haydn*, vol. 4, *Years of "The Creation,"* 400.

38. Christoph Martin Wieland, quoted in Gotwals, *Joseph Haydn*, 28–29.

39. Kirkendale, "New Roads to Old Ideas in Beethoven's *Missa Solemnis*," 176–78.

40. See Hollander, *Untuning of the Sky*, 146–61, 272–94.

41. John Milton, "On the Music of the Spheres," in *Prose Selections*, ed. Merritt Y. Hughes (New York, 1947), 19.

42. The quotations from Haydn, Gabriela von Baumberg, and Heinrich von Collin are from Gotwals, *Joseph Haydn*, 49, 258, and 255 respectively.

43. On natural light (*lumen naturae*, the faculty of knowledge), see René Descartes, *Meditations on First Philosophy*, no. 3, and *Principles of Philosophy*, 1, 30, in *Philosophical Works of Descartes*, trans. E. S. Haldane and G. R. T. Ross (Cambridge, 1967). "The light that lighteth . . . understanding" is from Aphorism 8 of Samuel Taylor Coleridge, *Aids to Reflection* (1825), ed. Henry Nelson Coleridge (New York, 1863), 162.

44. Sir Thomas Browne, *Religio Medici* (ca. 1635), ed. James Winny (Cambridge, 1963), 86.

45. Joseph Addison, "This Spacious Firmament on High," in *The Oxford Book of Christian Verse*, ed. Lord David Cecil (Oxford, 1940), 304.

46. Thomas Greene, "Magic and Festivity at the Renaissance Court," *Renaissance Quarterly* 40 (1987): 645.

47. For more on the topic, see my "Haydn's Chaos, Schenker's Order," 10–16.

48. Schenker, "Das es^3 in T. 9 übergipfelnd, erhebt es das e^3 des Lichtes in T. 9.," *Das Meisterwerk*, 2:168.

49. Kramer, "Haydn's Chaos, Schenker's Order," 16.

50. The first performances were held 29–30 April 1798. See Karl Geiringer, in collaboration with Irene Geiringer, *Haydn: A Creative Life in Music* (1946; 3d ed. rpt. with revisions, Berkeley, 1982), 159.

51. T. N. Des Essarts, *Dictionnaire universel de police*, cited in Michel Foucault, *Discipline and Punish: The Birth of the Prison*, trans. Alan Sheridan (New York, 1979), 213.

52. On Romantic reversals of traditional imagery, see Northrop Frye, "The Drunken Boat: The Revolutionary Element in Romanticism," in Northrop Frye, ed., *Romanticism Reconsidered* (New York, 1963), 1–15.

Chapter 4

1. Lord Byron, *Don Juan*, ed. Leslie A. Marchand (Boston, 1958), 461.

2. Roland Jordan and Emma Kafalenos, "The Double Trajectory: Ambiguity in Brahms and Henry James," *Nineteenth-Century Music* 13 (1989): 132.

3. A recent article by Joseph C. Kraus, "Tonal Plan and Narrative Plot in Tchaikovsky's Symphony No. 5 in E Minor," *Music Theory Spectrum* 13 (1991): 21–47, can be taken to epitomize this trend. Of undoubted technical interest, the essay hobbles itself hermeneutically by its admitted anxiety over "emotive descriptions" and its presupposition that "narrative structure" is correlative to the articulation/perception of the work as a "unified whole." For a survey and shrewd assessment of the nexus of music, structure, and narrative, see Fred Everett Maus, "Music as Narrative," *Indiana Theory Review* 12 (1991): 1–42. The issue containing Maus's essay takes narrative as its special topic; most of the essays therein exemplify the "structuralist" approach.

4. Jean-Jacques Nattiez, "Can One Speak of Narrativity in Music?" *Journal of the Royal Musical Association* (1990): 257, 253, 250 respectively.

5. Carolyn Abbate, *Unsung Voices: Opera and Musical Narrative in the Nineteenth Century* (Princeton, 1988), ix–xv, 3–29, 47–56; quotation, p. 53. Abbate's identification of moral distance with the past tense is open to question. For commentary see Joseph Kerman, "Representing a Relationship: Notes on a Beethoven Concerto," *Representations* 39 (1992): 91–92, and my "Song and Story," an essay-review on *Unsung Voices*, in *Nineteenth-Century Music* 15 (1992): 238.

6. Lawrence Kramer, *Music as Cultural Practice: 1800–1900* (Berkeley 1990), 176–203.

7. Abbate, *Unsung Voices*, 27: "Music makes distinctive sounds when it is speaking (singing) *in a narrative mode,* but we do not know *what* it narrates" (italics in original).

8. For a fuller discussion of the representational areas involved in narratography and their relation to music, see my *Music as Cultural Practice,* 184–89.

9. J. Hillis Miller, "Narrative," in Frank Lentriccia and Thomas Mc-Laughlin, eds., *Critical Terms for Literary Study* (Chicago, 1990), 72.

10. Kramer, *Music as Cultural Practice,* 186–89; Abbate, "Cherubino Uncovered: Reflexivity in Operatic Narration," in *Unsung Voices,* 61–118.

11. Anthony Newcomb, "Schumann and Late Eighteenth-Century Narrative Strategies," *Nineteenth-Century Music* 11 (1987): 164–74.

12. Ibid., 170, 169. For a musical treatment of *Witz* (and *Witz* in Schumann) closer to the one presented below, see John Daverio, *Nineteenth-Century Music and the German Romantic Ideology* (New York, 1993), 49–88.

13. Friedrich Schlegel, *Philosophical Fragments,* trans. Peter Firchow (Minneapolis, 1991), *Critical Fragments* nos. 9, 34, 90, *Atheneum Fragments* nos. 37, 53, *Ideas,* no. 26. For the remark on rupture, see Daverio, 243 n. 83.

14. As their language suggests, these formulations are indebted to Michel Foucault; see especially his *Discipline and Punish: The Birth of the Prison,* trans. Alan Sheridan (New York, 1977), and "The Subject and Power," part 1, *Critical Inquiry* 8 (1982): 777–85; part 2, trans. Leslie Sawyer, *Critical Inquiry* 8 (1982): 785–95.

15. J. L. Austin, *How to Do Things with Words,* ed. J. O. Urmson and Marina Sbisa (Cambridge, Mass., 1962); Miller, "Narrative," 72. Fredric Jameson's Marxist account of how narratives function ideologically, both constituting and concealing themselves as imaginary resolutions to real contradictions in specific social formations, can also be taken as a theory of what I am calling narrativity. Though meant to accommodate resistance as well as compliance to dominant ideologies, Jameson's theory is inflected by a pessimism that leads it to privilege compliance. See the essay "Magical Narratives" in Jameson's *The Political Unconscious: Narrative as a Socially Symbolic Act* (Ithaca, 1981), 103–50.

16. For the first model, see my "Dangerous Liaisons: The Literary Text in Musical Criticism," *Nineteenth-Century Music* 13 (1989): 159–67. For the second model, see *Music as Cultural Practice,* 183–203.

17. Susan McClary, *Feminine Endings: Music, Gender, and Sexuality* (Minneapolis, 1991), esp. 3–79; Teresa de Lauretis, "Desire in Narrative," *Alice Doesn't: Feminism, Semiotics, Cinema* (Bloomington, Ind., 1984), 103–57.

18. For discussion see Joseph Kerman, *The Beethoven Quartets* (New York, 1966), 362–67.

19. It is worth noting that this intervallic exchange, in which the diminished fourth replaces the perfect fourth, reverses an importantly situated earlier exchange. The development begins with four unison statements of "Es muß sein!," the first time with diminished fourth, thereafter with perfect fourth.

20. Christopher Reynolds, "The Representational Impulse in Late Beethoven, II: String Quartet in F Major, Op. 135," paper presented at a symposium on music and narrative, Stanford University and the University of California at Berkeley, May 1988. On the "sore note" (below), see both Reynolds, ibid., and Kerman, *Beethoven Quartets*, 356, 359, 366.

21. On generative intervals, see my *Music and Poetry: The Nineteenth Century and After* (Berkeley, 1984), 87–90, 229–31.

22. On the femininity of detail, see Naomi Schor, *Reading in Detail: Aesthetics and the Feminine* (New York, 1987).

23. Jacques Derrida, *Of Grammatology*, trans. Gayatri Chakravorty Spivak (Baltimore, 1976), 141–56; "Plato's Pharmacy," in *Dissemination*, trans. Barbara Johnson (Chicago, 1982).

24. My comments on this topic may be taken, respectively, to complement and parallel the semiotic-psychoanalytic discussions of Claudia Gorbman, *Unheard Melodies: Narrative Film Music* (Bloomington, Ind., 1987), esp. 1–69, and Mary Ann Doane, "The Voice in the Cinema: The Articulation of Body and Space," *Yale French Studies* 60 (1980): 33–50.

25. Georg Wilhelm Friedrich Hegel, *Aesthetic: Lectures on Fine Arts*, trans. T. M. Knox (Oxford, 1975), 959.

26. Walter Benjamin, *Illuminations*, ed. Hannah Arendt, trans. Harry Zohn (New York, 1969), 94, 100–101. "The Storyteller" was written in 1936.

27. On prosopopoeia, see Paul de Man, "Autobiography as De-facement" and "Shelley Disfigured," in *The Rhetoric of Romanticism* (New York, 1984), 67–82, 93–124, respectively, and Ned Lukacher, *Primal Scenes: Literature, Philosophy, Psychoanalysis* (Ithaca, 1986), 68–96.

28. See the caption of Example 4 for definitions of key terms and graphic symbols.

29. Maus, "Music as Narrative," 34.

30. Kramer, "Song and Story," 238. A more complex, and still more impersonal, literary parallel is the monologue, in which the voice of a character displaces the voice of the narrator, which occupies (and often highlights) an ongoing present of narration even when the monologue runs in the past tense. See Gerard Genette, *Narrative Discourse: An Essay in Method*, trans. Jane E. Lewin (Ithaca, 1980), 172–75, 216–19.

31. On this aspect of *Carnaval*, see my *Music as Cultural Practice*, 210–13, and "*Carnaval*, Cross-Dressing, and the Woman in the Mirror," in Ruth Solie, ed., *Musicology and Difference: Gender and Sexuality in Music Scholarship* (Berkeley, 1993), 305–25.

32. For a fuller discussion of this issue, see my "Song and Story," from which the remainder of this paragraph is adapted.

33. Abbate, *Unsung Voices*, 251.

Chapter 5

1. The sources for the epigraphs are: Felix Mendelssohn, letter to Rev. Albert Bauer, 4 March 1833, quoted in Peter le Huray and James Day, eds., *Music and Aesthetics in the Eighteenth and Early Nineteenth Centuries* (Cambridge, 1988), 310; Donald Francis Tovey, *Essays in Musical Analysis: Symphonies and Other Orchestral Works* (1935–39; new ed., London, 1981), 411.

2. "Image repertoire" is Roland Barthes's term for the specific content of the Lacanian imaginary, either realized for the personal subject or prescribed for the cultural subject. See, for example, Barthes's *A Lover's Discourse: Fragments*, trans. Richard Howard (New York, 1978).

3. Michael André Bernstein, "'These Children That Come at You with Knives': *Ressentiment*, Mass Culture, and the Saturnalia," *Critical Inquiry* 17 (1991): 360–61, 362–63.

4. George Bernard Shaw, *The Great Composers: Reviews and Bombardments*, ed. Louis Crompton (Berkeley, 1978), xvi.

5. On Goethe and Mendelssohn, see George R. Marek, *Gentle Genius: The Story of Felix Mendelssohn* (New York, 1972), 107–45, 170–72.

6. Bernstein, "'These Children That Come at You with Knives,'" 362.

7. August Schlegel, "Lectures on Dramatic Art and Literature," Lecture 1; Novalis (Friedrich von Hardenberg), "Teplitz Fragments" no. 455; Wilhelm von Humboldt, "On the Imagination"; in A. Leslie Willson, ed., *German Romantic Criticism* (New York, 1982), 183, 75–76, and 160 respectively. Goethe's statement is quoted in Thomas McFarland, *Romanticism and the Forms of Ruin* (Princeton, 1981), 303.

8. J. P. Eckermann, *Conversations with Goethe*, ed. Hans Kohn, trans. Gisela O'Brien (New York, 1964), 192.

9. On the naive and sentimental, see M. H. Abrams, *Natural Supernaturalism: Tradition and Innovation in Romantic Literature* (New York, 1971), 213–17, and Tilottama Rajan, *Dark Interpreter: The Discourse of Romanticism* (Ithaca, 1980), 30–41.

10. Johann Wolfgang von Goethe, "On Truth and Appearance in the Art-

work," quoted by M. H. Abrams, *The Mirror and the Lamp: Romantic Theory and the Critical Tradition* (New York, 1958), 206.

11. Abrams, *Natural Supernaturalism*, 184. Thomas McFarland links the concept of *Steigerung* to a network of late eighteenth-century ideas linking the Kantian subject-object polarity with scientific studies of material, especially magnetic, attraction and repulsion. See *Romanticism and the Forms of Ruin*, 289–341, esp. 297–313.

12. For an analysis of Schubert's song, with a brief nod at Beethoven, see my "The Schubert Lied: Romantic Form and Romantic Consciousness," in Walter Frisch, ed., *Schubert: Critical and Analytical Studies* (Lincoln, Neb., 1986), 210–15.

13. Walt Whitman, "A Passage to India," l. 220, in *Leaves of Grass*, ed. Sculley Bradley and Harold W. Blodgett (New York, 1973).

14. See, e.g., Georg Wilhelm Friedrich Hegel, *Philosophy of History*, trans. J. Sibree (New York, 1956), 438–57.

15. Tovey, *Essays in Musical Analysis: Symphonies and Other Orchestral Works*, 402.

16. Johann Wolfgang von Goethe, letter of 9 Sept. 1831, my translation from *Goethe's Briefe*, ed. Karl Robert Mandelkow, 4 vols. (Hamburg, 1967), 4:447.

17. Johann Wolfgang von Goethe, *Werke in sechs Bänden*, ed. Erich Schmidt, 6 vols. (Leipzig, 1910), 1:194.

18. Hélène Cixous, "The Laugh of the Medusa," trans. Keith Cohen and Paula Cohen, in Elaine Marks and Isabelle de Courtivron, eds., *New French Feminisms* (New York, 1981), 255. The significance of the Medusa's head as an image of castration, and its high prominence in the nineteenth century, has been a leading theme in recent cultural and literary criticism. The critical discourse originates with Freud's miniature essay "Medusa's Head" (1922), in Freud, *Sexuality and the Psychology of Love*, ed. Philip Rieff (New York, 1963), 212–13; for a small sampling of the literature, see Neil Hertz, "Medusa's Head: Male Hysteria under Political Pressure," in his *The End of the Line: Essays on Psychoanalysis and the Sublime* (New York, 1985), 161–93; Bram Djikstra, *Idols of Perversity: Fantasies of Feminine Evil in Fin-de-Siècle Culture* (New York, 1983), 309–11 and *passim;* Elaine Showalter, "The Veiled Woman," in her *Sexual Anarchy: Gender and Culture at the Fin-de-Siècle* (New York, 1990), 144–68; and, with specific reference to music, my "Culture and Musical Hermeneutics: The Salome Complex," *Cambridge Opera Journal* 2 (1990): 269–94.

19. Berlioz, for one, was sufficiently disconcerted by the sexual politics of this passage (which he nonetheless admired; see below) that he mentally rewrote it: "I would especially single out . . . the final chorus, in which the voice of the priest rises solemnly and serenely at intervals above the din of the

decoy demons and sorcerers" (Hector Berlioz, *Memoirs*, trans. and ed. David Cairns [London, 1969], 294.) To ensure the triumph of patriarchy, Berlioz conflates the central "howling round" and the concluding hymn to light.

Mendelssohn's sexual politics have so far been looked at only in relation to his opposition—eventually withdrawn—to Fanny Mendelssohn Hensel's publication of her compositions. (See Nancy B. Reich, "The Power of Class: Fanny Hensel," in R. Larry Todd, ed., *Mendelssohn and His World* [Princeton, 1991], 86–99.) This episode, however, by no means tells the whole story; Mendelssohn, after all, is the man who decided that (Queen) Victoria's secret was—her nursery. (Offered any favor he pleased, Mendelssohn chose a guided tour of the royal nursery; see the anecdote reported by Felix Moscheles in Norman Liebrecht, *The Book of Musical Anecdotes* [New York, 1985], 297.) In this context it is worth citing what Mendelssohn told Fanny in April 1834 about the genesis of his overture to *Die schöne Melusine*. He composed the overture, he explains, in response to the only thing he liked about Conradin Kreutzer's opera on the Melusine legend: the "very engaging" Melusine herself, "especially in one scene where she appeared in her fish-form and combed her hair." (Quoted in Tovey, *Essays in Musical Analysis: Symphonies and Other Orchestral Works*, 395.) The juxtaposition of woman's hair and a quasi-serpentine form (in most versions of the legend, Melusine's lower body is literally serpentine) suggests the Medusa again, and again a sublimated Medusa who is attractive rather than terrible.

20. Berlioz, *Memoirs*, 294.

21. For a survey of anti-Semitic discourse in early nineteenth-century Germany, see Leon Poliakov, *The History of Anti-Semitism*, vol. 3, *From Voltaire to Wagner*, trans. Miriam Kochan (New York, 1975), 380–429. For more on the philo-Semitic element in *The First Walpurgisnight*, see Leon Botstein, "The Aesthetics of Assimilation and Affirmation: Reconstructing the Career of Felix Mendelssohn," in *Mendelssohn and His World*, 22–23.

22. Reported in Devrient's memoirs; quoted by Jack Werner, *Mendelssohn's "Elijah"* (London, 1965), 85.

Chapter 6

1. Roland Barthes, "The Romantic Song," in *The Responsibility of Forms: Critical Essays on Music, Art, and Representation*, trans. Richard Howard (Berkeley, 1991); the quotation is collaged from pp. 290–92.

2. Carl Dahlhaus, *Nineteenth-Century Music*, trans. J. Bradford Robinson (Berkeley, 1989), 99.

3. Thus Dahlhaus: "A tiny number of works with unimpeachable claim to artistic status stand out against the vast output of nineteenth-century works which served an estimable social function but leave us under no compunc-

tion [*sic*] to include them in a history of music as art" (ibid., 102). Barthes and Dahlhaus, otherwise antipodes, join forces on this issue; Barthes's concept of the *inactuel* character of the Lied serves all but explicitly to protect the genre from the disenchantments of sociality.

4. With chapter 4 in view, it is worth pausing to observe that the music-image relationship in song is not supplemental, unlike its counterpart in film. In saying that music is the supplement of narrative, including the fragmentary or implicit narratives found in lyric poems, we identify music as a surplus signifier, a role it retains in film. In saying that music is the imaginary of the image, we identify it as a material but not external form, which is to say the imaginary form, of the image's signified. Music can be said to take over this role from the phonetic-rhythmic-stanzaic "music" of poetry, which is usually effaced in the musical setting.

5. For an overview of this development, see Constance Penley, ed., *Feminism and Film Theory* (New York, 1988), 1–24 and *passim,* together with Mary Ann Doane, "Film and the Masquerade: Theorizing the Female Spectator," in *Femmes Fatales: Feminism, Film Theory, Psychoanalsyis* (New York, 1991), 17–32; Tania Modleski, "Hitchcock, Feminism, and the Patriarchal Unconscious," in *The Women Who Knew Too Much: Hitchcock and Feminist Theory* (New York, 1989), 1–16; and Teresa de Lauretis, "Imaging" and "Desire in Narrative," in *Alice Doesn't: Feminism, Semiotics, Cinema* (Bloomington, Ind., 1984), 37–69, 103–57, respectively.

6. Christian Metz, *The Imaginary Signifier: Psychoanalysis and the Cinema,* trans. Celia Britton, Annwyl Williams, Ben Brewster, and Alfred Guzzetti (Bloomington, Ind., 1982), 49.

7. Christian Metz, "History/Discourse: A Note on Two Voyeurisms," trans. Susan Bennett, *Edinburgh '76 Magazine* 1 (1976): 21–25.

8. Situating song within the general framework of musical subject formation theorized in chapter 1, it can be said—too briefly, and only suggestively—that different types of music offer the subjects they summon different primary objects of psychical-ideological investment. With song it is the image heightened emotively and sometimes metaphorically, the latter by musical representation; with nonvocal representational music it is the movement of metaphor through the communicative economy; with nonvocal nonrepresentational music it is the interplay of structural (cultural) tropes. The categories, naturally, overlap and coexist as a matter of course; opera mixes them (up) superabundantly as a matter of principle. There is a similar variation in the locus of the listening subject's identification, but it is less easy to speak of typical positionalities outside of song, where position is almost always determined by the relationship to voice. We might speculate that instrumental music sometimes defines its subject positions in relation to im-

pelling musical processes, sometimes in relation to the vicissitudes of particular rhythmic, melodic, or instrumental "agents," and sometimes in relation to dialogues or colloquies among evocations of song, dance, and instrumental touch, the three sites of interaction between music and the social body. Although I couldn't resist this footnote, the topic is obviously too large for it—and for the chapter.

9. Guy Rosolato, "La voix: Entre corps et langage," *Revue française de psychoanalyse* 37 (1974): 38–83.

10. Kaja Silverman, *The Acoustic Mirror: The Female Voice in Psychoanalysis and Cinema* (Bloomington, Ind., 1988), 84–86.

11. Rosolato, "La voix," 81. For an exploration of recent musical evocations of the nostalgia Rosolato speaks of, see David Schwartz, "Listening Subjects: Semiotics, Psychoanalysis, and the Music of John Adams and Steve Reich," *Perspectives of New Music* 32 (Summer 1993): 24–56.

12. On Fanny Mendelssohn Hensel and publication, see Nancy B. Reich, "Fanny Hensel: The Power of Class," in R. Larry Todd, ed. *Mendelssohn and His World* (Princeton, 1991), 86–99.

13. Immanuel Kant, *On History*, ed. Lewis White Beck, trans. Lewis White Beck, Robert E. Anchor, and Emil L. Fackenheim (Indianapolis, 1963), 3.

14. Friedrich A. Kittler, *Discourse Networks: 1800/1900*, trans. Michael Metteer, with Chris Cullens (Stanford, 1990), 3–173.

15. Ibid., 148, 150, 151.

16. Ibid., 126.

17. For a detailed account, to which my discussion is strongly indebted, see Joan DeJean, "Sex and Philology: Sappho and the Rise of German Nationalism," *Representations* 27 (1989): 148–71.

18. J. J. Bachofen, *Myth, Religion, and Mother Right* (1861), quoted by DeJean, "Sex and Philology," 160.

19. John Addington Symonds, *A Problem in Greek Ethics* (1873), quoted by DeJean, "Sex and Philology," 161; as DeJean notes, "Symonds's discussion of the centrality of Greek love to the Greek 'esthetic morality' is . . . straight out of the philological tradition."

20. Kittler, *Discourse Networks*, 171–72.

21. Robert Musil, *Young Törless*, trans. Eithne Wilkins and Ernst Kaiser (New York, 1955), 127.

22. DeJean, "Sex and Philology," 152.

23. Felix Mendelssohn to Johann Wolfgang von Goethe, letter of 21/24 May 1830, text from Felix Mendelssohn, *Letters*, ed. G. Selden-Goth (New York, 1945), 69. Further references are given in text by date (day and month).

24. I take this image, not from Mendelssohn, but from Rilke, whose

poem "David Sings before Saul" (1905/06) celebrates the tradition of amatory tutelage:

> Wenn wir uns nur aneinanderhalten,
> du am Jungen, ich am Alten,
> sind wir fast wie ein Gestirn das kreist. (3, 11–13)

[If we but hold fast to each other, you to the young man, I to the old, we are almost like a wheeling constellation.]

> —Text from Rainer Maria Rilke,
> *Werke in drei Bänden,* 3 vols.
> (Frankfurt am Main, 1966), 1:245–46.

25. Kittler, *Discourse Networks,* 128.

26. Novalis, from *Pollen,* aphorism 104, trans. Alexander Gelley, in Leslie Willson, ed., *German Romantic Criticism* (New York, 1982), 67; Clemens Brentano and Dorothea Schlegel, cited by Kittler, *Discourse Networks,* 128 and 129 respectively; August Schlegel, quoted by Friedrich Schlegel, "On Incomprehensibility," trans. P. Firchow, in *German Aesthetic and Literary Criticism: The Romantic Ironists and Goethe* (Cambridge, 1984), 36.

27. Kittler, *Discourse Networks,* 148.

28. This curricular apotheosis of Goethe did not survive Niethammer's administration, at least in boys' schools. As Kittler notes, however (*Discourse Networks,* 150–56), the transfer of the new German classics to free-time reading, where they prepared the student for the German essay, only enhanced their authority.

29. Betty Gleim, quoted in Kittler, *Discourse Networks,* 147.

30. The extract gives the text as Mendelssohn set it; Geothe's original has "stets" instead of "nur" in l. 6.

31. See Susan Winnett, "Coming Unstrung: Women, Men, Narrative, and Principles of Pleasure," *Publications of the Modern Language Association of America* 105 (1990): 505–18; Teresa de Lauretis, "Desire in Narrative," in *Alice Doesn't: Feminism, Semiotics, Cinema* (Bloomington, Ind., 1984), 103–57; Luce Irigaray, "*Così Fan Tutte,*" in her *This Sex Which Is Not One,* trans. Catherine Porter with Carolyn Burke (Ithaca, 1985), 86–105; and Susan McClary, *Feminine Endings: Music, Gender, and Sexuality* (Minneapolis, 1991), 12–17, 125–27.

32. Kittler, *Discourse Networks,* 46–47.

33. For the nonspecialist: bar form, best known for its association with the German Meistersinger, consists of the formal design A A B. The A sections are known as *Stollen* (props), the B section as the *Abgesang* (aftersong).

34. Roland Barthes, *The Pleasure of the Text,* trans. Richard Miller (New York, 1975), 7.

35. For a synoptic version of the important debate about this nascency,

see John Boswell, "Revolutions, Universals, and Sexual Categories," and David Halperin, "Sex before Sexuality: Pederasty, Politics, and Power in Classical Athens," in Martin Baumal Duberman, Martha Vicinus, and George Chauncey, Jr., eds., *Hidden from History: Reclaiming the Gay and Lesbian Past* (New York, 1989), 17–37, 37–53, respectively.

36. For discussion see Constance Penley, "Introduction—The Lady Doesn't Vanish: Feminism and Film Theory," Elizabeth Cowie, "The Popular Film as Progressive Text: A Discussion of *Coma*," and Janet Bergstrom, "Enunciation and Sexual Difference," in Penley, ed., *Feminism and Film Theory*, 1–24, 104–40, and 159–85, respectively.

37. For the classical formulation of the being-having dichotomy in relation to desire, and the acknowledgment of slippages between the terms, see Sigmund Freud, "Identification," in *Group Psychology and the Analysis of the Ego*, trans. Franz Alexander (New York, 1960), 46–53. For discussion incorporating recent perspectives, see Silverman, *The Acoustic Mirror*, 149–59.

38. Quoted in DeJean, "Sex and Philology," 156.

Chapter 7

1. Jean-François Lyotard, *The Postmodern Condition: A Report on Knowledge*, trans. Geoff Bennington and Brian Massumi (Minneapolis, 1984), 81.

2. This idealizing reception is importantly exemplified by the pivotal volume *An Ives Celebration: Papers and Panels of the Charles Ives Centennial Festival-Conference*, ed. H. Wiley Hitchcock and Vivian Perlis, (Urbana, Ill., 1977); see especially Robert M. Crumden, "Charles Ives's Place in American Culture," 4–13, and William Brooks, "Ives Today," 209–21. For Ives's rivalry with Strauss and Debussy, see the composer's comments in the Epilogue to his *Essays Before a Sonata*, in *"Essays Before a Sonata" and Other Writings*, ed. Howard Boatwright (New York, 1961), 70–95.

3. Cornel West, *The American Evasion of Philosophy* (Madison, 1985), 212. West further characterizes prophetic pragmatism as an Emersonian "reconception of philosophy as a form of cultural criticism that attempts to transform linguistic, social, cultural, and political traditions for the purposes of increasing the scope of individual development and democratic operations" (p. 230). The account of the *Universe* Symphony, by Ives's secretary Christine Loring, is from Vivian Perlis, ed., *Charles Ives Remembered: An Oral History* (New York, 1974), 117.

4. For a brief (if typically contorted) account of immanent critique in relation to the arts, see Theodor W. Adorno, *Philosophy of Modern Music*

(1948), trans. Anne G. Mitchell and Wesley V. Blomster (New York, 1973), 24–28. For another discussion of a composer's oeuvre along these lines, see Alastair Williams, "Music as Immanent Critique: Stasis and Developmemt in the Music of Ligeti," in Christopher Norris, ed., *Music and the Politics of Culture* (New York, 1989), 187–225. Adorno's relevance to current musical criticism is most memorably formulated by Rose Rosengard Subotnik in her *Developing Variations* (Minneapolis, 1991).

5. Maynard Solomon, "Charles Ives: Some Questions of Veracity," *Journal of the American Musicological Society* 40 (1987): 443–70. Part of Solomon's argument rests on the claim that Ives back-dated many of his pieces; for a challenge to this claim, see Carol K. Baron, "Dating Charles Ives's Music: Facts and Fictions," *Perspectives of New Music* 28 (1990): 20–57.

6. The metaphor of technology derives from Michel Foucault, *The History of Sexuality,* vol. 1, *An Introduction,* trans. Robert Hurley (New York, 1978), 100–114.

7. Robert P. Morgan, "Spatial Form in Ives," in *An Ives Celebration,* 146.

8. Under the rubric *chronotopes,* recurrent interlocked patterns of space and time have been explored in the European novel by Mikhail Bakhtin. See the essay "Forms of Time and of the Chronotope in the Novel," in Bakhtin's *The Dialogic Imagination,* ed. Michael Holquist, trans. Michael Holquist and Caryl Emerson (Austin, 1981), 84–258. For a general consideration of musical hermeneutics, see "An Outline of Musical Hermeneutics," in my *Music as Cultural Practice, 1800–1900* (Berkeley, 1990).

9. Philip Fisher, "Democratic Social Space: Whitman, Melville, and the Promise of American Transparency," *Representations* 24 (1988): 61–62. My account of democratic social space differs from Fisher's in some respects, especially in not subsuming the play of heterogeneity under a broader category of social and psychic uniformity.

10. Walt Whitman, *Leaves of Grass,* ed. Sculley Bradley and Harold T. Blodgett (New York, 1965).

11. H. Wiley Hitchcock, *Ives,* Oxford Studies of Composers Series (New York, 1977), 62.

12. Larry Starr, *A Union of Diversities: Style in the Music of Charles Ives* (New York, 1992). My paraphrase of Starr's argument omits an important difference in emphasis. Where I see a curb placed on full heterogenity, Starr sees stylistic heterogeneity as a source of unity.

13. Fisher, "Democratic Social Space," 75–79.

14. Perlis, *Charles Ives Remembered,* 112.

15. For a summary account of the purity movement, and its even more aggressive heir, the "social hygiene" movement, see John D'Emilio and Estelle B. Freedman, *Intimate Matters: A History of Sexuality in America*

(New York, 1988), 150–56, 203–8. For an account of the power of a parallel, slightly earlier purity discourse, see T. Walter Herbert, Jr., "The Erotics of Purity: *The Marble Fawn* and the Victorian Construction of Sexuality," *Representations* 36 (1991): 114–32, esp. 121–25.

16. For this and the following paragraph, I am strongly indebted to two essays by Michael Rogin, " 'The Sword Became a Flashing Vision': D. W. Griffith's *The Birth of a Nation*," *Representations* 9 (1985): 150–95, and "The Great Mother Domesticated: Sexual Difference and Sexual Indifference in D. W. Griffith's *Intolerance*," *Critical Inquiry* 15 (1989): 510–55.

17. Rogin, " 'The Sword Became a Flashing Vision,' " 163, 174.

18. On Ives's politics, see Frank Rossiter, *Charles Ives and His America* (New York, 1975), 126–44. As we will see, Ives's sense of racial harmony generally depends on the casual presumption of white superiority. It may be indicative that as head of his insurance firm, Ives passively acquiesced in a parent-company rule against writing policies for blacks until a middle manager, on his own initiative, finessed a groundbreaking exception. For the story, offered as evidence of Ives's progressive racial attitudes, see Perlis, *Charles Ives Remembered*, 59.

19. For more on this topic, see Charles Hamm's remarks in his interview with Peter Winkler, *Review of Popular Music* 7 (1985): 8–10. My thanks to Geoffrey Block for bringing this interview to my attention.

20. The most notable exception to this rule is a poignant one: Ives's last completed composition, "In the Morning" (1929), was an arrangement of the spiritual "Give Me Jesus."

21. Charles Ives, *Memos*, ed. John Kirkpatrick (New York, 1972), 54.

22. "Spiritual," *The New Grove Dictionary of American Music*, ed. H. Wiley Hitchcock and Stanly Sadie, 4 vols. (London, 1986), 3:285.

23. Charles Ives, "The Majority," in *Essays Before a Sonata*, 163, 142, 144, 197.

24. Rossiter, *Charles Ives*, 25–37.

25. Sigmund Freud, "Analysis Terminable and Interminable" (1937), in Freud, *Therapy and Technique*, ed. Philip Rieff (New York, 1963), 270. The term *masculine protest* originates with Alfred Adler, who, unlike Freud, celebrated rather than demystified it. For further psychoanalytic inquiry along these lines, see Solomon, "Some Questions of Veracity." For a fuller account of Freud's critique of masculine pathologies, see my "Victorian Poetry/Oedipal Politics: *In Memoriam* and Other Instances," *Victorian Poetry* 29 (1991): 351–64.

26. Ives, *Memos*, 74.

27. It is striking that Hitchcock (*Ives*, 61–62) edits most of the homophobia and misogyny out of Ives's account of the Second String Quartet and

declines to mention Rollo even in passing. His focus is on formal innovation and continuity, about which he has good things to say, but his procedure ends by repeating the virilizing intentions it represses. His putatively genderless attention to structure amounts to a masculinist dismissal of that "women's issue," gender. For a corrective, see Judith Tick's full-scale investigation of Ives's misogyny, "Charles Ives and the 'Masculine' Ideal," in Ruth Solie, ed. *Musicology and Difference: Gender and Sexuality in Music Scholarship* (Berkeley, 1993), 83–106.

28. For a usefully synoptic account, though a tonally and interpretively problematical one, see Bram Dijkstra, *Idols of Perversity: Fantasies of Feminine Evil in Fin-de-Siècle Culture* (New York, 1986), 210–34.

29. Ives, *Essays Before a Sonata*, 25, 82, 83, 78.

30. On manner and substance, see ibid., 75–82; Rossiter, *Charles Ives*, 286–87; and Lawrence Kramer, *Music and Poetry: The Nineteenth Century and After* (Berkeley, 1984), 172–75. Rossiter's account and mine have complementary failings; his overstates, where mine overlooks, the gender-coding of the manner/substance duality. It is worth stressing that Ives introduces the duality as a genderless abstraction, then invokes (or discloses) its gendered character where he perceives manner to be replacing substance as a historical norm. His treatment of the duality thus forms a classical case of nineteenth-century male hysteria, the use of gender-out-of-place as an instrument of social control. On male hysteria, see Neil Hertz, "Medusa's Head: Male Hysteria under Political Pressure," in his *The End of the Line: Essays on Psychoanalysis and the Sublime* (New York, 1985), 161–93.

31. See especially Hélène Cixous, "Sorties," in Hélène Cixous and Catherine Clement, *The Newly Born Woman* (1975), trans. Betsy Wing (Minneapolis, 1986), 63–131. Cixous's account of binary opposition is in turn indebted to Jacques Derrida, whose work on the subject is effectively expounded by Jonathan Culler, *On Deconstruction: Theory and Criticism after Structuralism* (Ithaca, 1982). It should (but still doesn't) go without saying that recognizing the historical importance of binary opposition is not the same as crudely reducing Western culture to the binary principle.

32. *Pace* Larry Starr (*A Union of Diversities*, 137–38), it is not a "mistake" to hear the final cadence as V–I in F rather than as I–IV–(I) in C. The cadence can probably bear either construction; what is most important about it is its formulaic character.

The ending also incorporates a presumably unintentional irony I can't forbear pointing out. Ives paraphrases Browning in order to invoke the virile optimism popularly associated with him. But did Ives forget, or simply not know, that the lines he paraphrases are assigned by Browning to a young girl?

33. Ives, *Essays Before a Sonata*, 17.

34. For a detailed account, see my *Music and Poetry*, 184–86.

35. Rossiter, *Charles Ives*, 108. Subsequent quotations from Ives's program for the Fourth Symphony rely on the same source.

36. Ives, *Essays Before a Sonata*, 42, 39.

37. For more on the third movement of the *Concord* Sonata as a false resolution, see my *Music and Poetry*, 186–87.

38. The hierarchical effect of these figure-ground textures should not be confused with that of the melody-accompaniment textures to which Ives (as J. Peter Burkholder observes in a letter to me) is often drawn. The figure-ground textures are presented so as to claim a general and axiological supremacy for their figures. The melody-accompaniment textures claim only a local and perceptual priority for their melodies, which in Ives's heterogeneous pieces serve only as more or less fleeting elements in a kaleidoscopic display. When Ives's melody-accompaniment textures are polystylistic, moreover, they render moot the effect of perceptual hierarchy, which largely depends on stylistic uniformity. Elsewhere, textural density has the same effect. One might restate the paradox in Ives's commitment to heterogeneity by saying that this commitment is so thoroughgoing that only extraordinary means can overcome it, yet so threatening that extraordinary means *must* overcome it.

39. Ives, *Memos*, 92.

40. For brief accounts of women's "going public," see D'Emilio and Freedman, *Intimate Matters,* 188–201, and Miriam Hansen, "Adventures of Goldilocks: Spectatorship, Consumerism, and Public LIfe," *Camera Obscura* 22 (1990): 51–72. For the photo of the Ives and Myrick office, see Vivian Perlis, *Charles Ives Remembered,* 49. The photo is undated, but the firm occupied the office shown between 1914 and 1923.

41. Ives, *Memos*, 92.

42. Ibid.

43. Michael Rogin, "Blackface, White Noise: The Jewish Jazz Singer Finds His Voice," *Critical Inquiry* 18 (1992): 437, 439.

44. Hitchcock, *Ives*, 89.

45. Strictly speaking, the flute is optional, not obligatory, but Ives observes, in a note to the published score, that "Thoreau much prefers to hear the flute over Walden."

46. Ives, *Essays Before a Sonata*, 69.

47. For a more detailed account of closural effects in "Thoreau" and their relationship to the sonata as a whole, see my *Music and Poetry*, 187–91.

48. Ives, *Essays Before a Sonata*, 47.

49. Ibid., 68.

50. My thanks to David Lewin for bringing my attention to the importance of a Cartesian-Hegelian detachment in the attitude of Ives's Thoreau—and of Ives himself.

Chapter 8

1. " . . . non seulement une des meilleures oeuvres de Ravel, mais aussi une des plus belles productions de la musique française." Igor Stravinsky, *Chroniques de ma vie* (1935; rpt. Paris, 1962), 48.

2. Roland-Manuel, *Ravel*, trans. Cynthia Jolly (1938; rpt. London, 1947), 125.

3. Emile Zola, *The Ladies' Paradise*, trans. unattributed (1883; rpt. Berkeley, 1992), 352–53.

4. Edward Downes, program note for the New York Philharmonic, re-printed as jacket copy for a recording of *Daphnis and Chloe,* Columbia LP MS-6260 (1961).

5. Thorstein Veblen, *The Theory of the Leisure Class: An Economic Study of Institutions* (new ed., 1918; rpt. New York, 1934), 68–101.

6. Miriam Hansen, "The Adventures of Goldilocks: Spectatorship, Consumerism, and Public Life," *Camera Obscura* 22 (1991): 54.

7. Maurice Ravel, "Memories of a Lazy Child," rpt. in Arbie Orenstein, ed., *A Ravel Reader: Correspondence, Articles, Interviews* (New York, 1990), 395.

8. Maurice Ravel, "Contemporary Music," in Orenstein, ed., *Ravel Reader,* 46.

9. The details about Ravel's villa are drawn from Madelaine Goss, *Bolero: The Life of Maurice Ravel* (New York, 1940), 207; the quotation, from p. 210.

10. Maurice Ravel, "An Autobiographical Sketch by Maurice Ravel," in Orenstein, ed., *Ravel Reader,* 31.

11. On this cultural equation of space and time, see Johannes Fabian, *Time and the Other: How Anthropology Makes Its Object* (New York, 1983). The equation lent itself equally well to mythological narratives about a golden age and anthropological narratives about the march of progress; the contrary narrative types continually intertwined.

12. Rosalind Williams, "The Dream World of Mass Consumption," in Chandra Mukerji and Michael Schudson, eds., *Rethinking Popular Culture: Contemporary Perspectives in Cultural Studies* (Berkeley, 1991), 201–2. Williams's essay is a mine of information, on which I draw freely (and gratefully) below.

13. Marianna Torgovnick, *Gone Primitive: Savage Intellects, Modern Lives* (Chicago, 1990), 75.

14. Walter Pater, *The Renaissance: Studies in Art and Poetry,* 1893 text ed. Donald Hill (Berkeley, 1980), 99.

15. Debora L. Silverman, *Art Nouveau in Fin-de-Siècle France: Politics, Psychology, and Style* (Berkeley, 1989), 75–106.

16. It should be added explicitly that not just any wordless chorus would

have this significance, but only one like Ravel's that acts nonmelodically (so Debussy's is out), apart from verbal associations (which lets out Ives), and as a persistent textural element rather than as a climactic extra (so Ives is out again, and so is Holst).

17. The card was first reproduced and discussed by Naomi Schor, "*Cartes Postales:* Representing Paris 1900," *Critical Inquiry* 18 (1992): 195–96.

18. Williams, "Dream World," 210.

19. Ravel, "Autobiographical Sketch," 31.

20. See Arbie Orenstein, *Ravel, Man and Musician* (New York, 1975), 69–70.

21. Worth noting in this connection is Ravel's 1912 review of performances of the Brahms D-major and Franck D-minor symphonies. "The will to develop," he writes, "can only be sterile." Of Franck in particular, Ravel says that his symphony offers "melody of an elevated and serene character, bold harmonies of particular richness; but a distressing poverty of form. . . . awkwardly abus[ing] out-of-date academic formulas" (in Orenstein, ed., *Ravel Reader*, 345).

22. Zola, *Ladies' Paradise*, 93.

23. On desire and liquidity in the period, see my *Music as Cultural Practice: 1800–1900* (Berkeley, 1990), 136–46. On the sexualizing effect of consumer culture after the mid-nineteenth century, see Lawrence Birken, "Madame Bovary and the Dissolution of Bourgeois Sexuality," *Journal of the History of Sexuality* 4 (1992): 618–19.

24. Louis Haugmard, writing in 1913; quoted by Williams, "Dream World," 213–14.

25. Mention of *The Rite of Spring* (and of Gaugin, below) inevitably introduces the concept of the primitive, which overlaps but does not coincide with that of the exotic. Perhaps the two concepts are best thought of as defining a continuum. The pure exotic represents the (civilized) other as purely compliant with its appropriation; the pure primitive represents the (uncivilized) other as purely resistant. Most actual manifestations fall in between. From this perspective, *The Rite of Spring* counts as a primitivist version of *Daphnis and Chloe:* the former stressing brutal rhythm, the latter sumptuous melody, the former projecting gratification in the sacrifice of a woman, the latter in a woman's escape from sacrifice. For a discussion of the concept of the primitive, see Torgovnick, *Gone Primitive*, 3–41. For a fierce critique of the primitivism of *The Rite of Spring*, see Theodor Adorno, *Philosophy of Modern Music*, trans. Anne G. Mitchell and Wesley V. Blomster (New York, 1973), 145–60.

26. H. H. Stuckenschmidt, *Maurice Ravel: Variations on His Life and Work*, trans. Samuel R. Rosenbaum (Philadelphia, 1968), 124.

27. Ibid., 127–28.

28. Maurice Ravel, quoted by Olin Downes, "Mr. Ravel Returns," *New York Times,* 26 Feb. 1928; rpt. in Orenstein, ed., *Ravel Reader,* 459.

29. Charles Baudelaire, "Invitation to the Voyage," text from *Flowers of Evil,* bilingual edition, ed. Jackson Matthews and Marthiel Matthews (New York, 1955); translation mine.

30. The quoted phrase hails from a handbook issued by the French colonial department for the Universal Exposition of 1889 and passed on to Gauguin by a friend. For more see Wayne Anderson, *Gauguin's Paradise Lost* (New York, 1971), 134–35.

31. Paul Gauguin, "Notes on Painting," quoted in John Rewald, *Gauguin* (New York, 1938), 161.

Epilogue

1. Kofi Agawu, "Schubert's Sexuality: A Prescription for Analysis?" *Nineteenth-Century Music* 17 (1993): 81.

2. For a detailed discussion of the subject associated here with the autonomous artwork, see Terry Eagleton, *The Ideology of the Aesthetic* (Oxford, 1990), 13–30.

3. Marjorie Garber, *Vested Interests: Cross-Dressing and Cultural Anxiety* (New York, 1992), 372.

4. Jacques Derrida, *Cinders,* trans., ed., and with an introduction by Ned Lukacher (Lincoln, Neb., 1991), 27.

5. Ibid., 9, 8.

6. Ibid., 43.

7. Ibid.

8. Garber, *Vested Interests,* 369–74, 372; "mystical anagram," above, is Garber's phrase.

9. Agawu, "Schubert's Sexuality," 81.

10. Philipp Spitta, *Johann Sebastian Bach: His Work and Its Influence on the Music of Germany, 1685–1750,* trans. Clara Bell and J. A. Fuller-Maitland, 3 vols. (1889; rpt. New York, 1951), 2:55.

11. Lawrence Kramer, "The Real in Embers, the Arts Inflamed," *Modern Language Quarterly: A Journal of Literary History* 54 (1993): 290.

12. This first subject is more often said not to "be" the motto; it would be more accurate to say that the motto is a nonpresence in the subject. (This wording can, of course, be taken in more than one sense.) The subject's first half (D–A–[G]–F) alludes to the motto's D–A–F–D but leaves it hanging; the second half ignores the motto but follows it in leading to a new statement beginning on D.

13. Johann Sebastian Bach, *Der Kunst der Fuge,* ed. Hans Gal (London, 1951), 111. Spelling modernized. Although my interest is more in the Figu-

rative than the literal truth of this statement, I should add that I am not persuaded by Christoph Wolff's conjecture that Bach finished the last figure on a lost manuscript page. Wolff's evidence, in "The Last Fugue: Unfinished?" *Current Musicology* 19 (1975): 71–76, consists only of a debatable impression of the ruling on Bach's music paper and the supposition that so complex a figure must have had at least a preliminary sketch. For a more plausible account, see Hans Eggebrecht, *J. S. Bach's "The Art of Fugue": The Work and Its Interpretation*, trans. Jeffrey L. Prater (Ames, Iowa, 1993), 3–4, 25–28.

14. The German from Paul Celan, "Todesfuge," *Mohn und Gedachtnis* (Stuttgart, 1952); the French from Derrida, *Cinders*, 73; the English from Geoffrey Hill, "Two Formal Elegies: For the Jews in Europe," I, *Somewhere Is Such a Kingdom: Poems, 1952–1971* (Boston, 1975). In translation:

he cries strike your fiddles more darkly then you'll rise up as smoke in the air
What a difference between cinder and smoke: the latter apparently gets lost,
   and better still, without perceptible remainder, for it rises, it takes to the air,
   it is spirited away, sublimated. The cinder—falls, tires, lets go, more material
   since it fritters away its word; it is very divisible
your golden hair Marguerite
your ashen hair Shulamith
In clenched cinders not yielding their abused
Bodies and bonds to those whom war's chance saves
Without the law: we grasp, roughly, the song.

15. Perhaps there is good reason not to resist it. The excess over "Bachian affect" may well be Bach's own; certainly I have heard enough inexpressive jog-trot performances of this piece to think so. On the question of Bach performance in relation to issues of authority and autonomy, see Susan McClary, "The Blasphemy of Talking Politics during Bach Year," in Richard Leppert and Susan McClary, eds., *Music and Society: The Politics of Composition, Performance, and Reception* (Cambridge, 1987), 13–62.

16. Derrida, *Cinders*, 75.

Index

Compositor:	G&S, Inc.
Music setter:	Mansfield Music Graphics
Text:	11/13.5 Caledonia
Display:	Caledonia
Printer and Binder:	Thomson-Shore, Inc.